FOUR SHOTS IN OSKIE

MURDER AND INNOCENCE IN MIDDLE AMERICA

JUSTIN WINGERTER

MISSION POINT PRESS

Published by Mission Point Press
2554 Chandler Rd.
Traverse City, MI 49686
(231) 421-9513
www.MissionPointPress.com

ISBN-13: 978-1-950659-98-2

Library of Congress Control Number: 2021901716

Manufactured in the United States of America
First Edition/First Printing

For Meg

"What strange creatures brothers are!"

– Jane Austen, *Mansfield Park*

ONE

Interstate 70 slices crookedly, east to west, through Kansas, bisecting it as the Santa Fe Railway once did. North of the interstate and the eastern college town of Lawrence, the terrain toughens and the topography defies the myth of a flat state. In some parts, cell phone reception is spotty on a good day and the air is thick with the smell of farm waste.

Oskaloosa is a town of one grocery store, two gas stations, four restaurants and about eleven hundred people. Situated somewhere near the buckle of the Bible Belt, there are more than a half-dozen churches in or around town. To the extent there is any fear in Oskaloosa, it is a fear of God.

The first building that greets visitors from the south is the boxy and bland headquarters of the Jefferson County Sheriff's Department, a structure so plain it can go unnoticed. In the town's center sits the Jefferson County Courthouse, an equally bland, equally boxy building. Small shops and cafés are nestled in red brick structures around a red brick town square. Each shop faces toward the courthouse at the center, the public hub of Oskaloosa.

Life is uncomplicated here; work, church, children, hunting, farming. Most are here because their parents were and most stay long after they can leave. It is a decent town of decent people working decent jobs for decent wages. It is the middle of middle America. The locals call it Oskie.

North of town, houses thin out and fields spread wider, the most rural sector of a rural community in rural Jefferson County. Pavement concedes to dirt and gravel roads that lead to small trailers beyond thick trees. Pickup trucks kick up dust as they blitz down, leaving a trail behind them like a steel animal's tail. Deer and wild turkeys roam with little to fear when it isn't hunting season. Some folks drive, rather than walk, to their mailbox.

It was here, north of Oskaloosa, that Tom Bledsoe lived with his parents, Cathy and the senior Floyd Bledsoe, in a rickety wood paneled home with a gravel road in front and wide spans of timber behind. In a ditch on the property, the family burned its trash, along with spare wood and whatever else needed set ablaze.

It was also in this rural north that fourteen-year-old Zetta "Camille" Arfmann lived with her sister, Heidi Bledsoe, and Heidi's husband, the younger Floyd Bledsoe, Tom's brother. They lived in a trailer set back from a paved road, which school bus driver Dorothy McClung parked in front of at 4:20 p.m. on November 5, 1999.

"Have a nice weekend," McClung told Camille as she slung open the bus door. The girl had seemed her usual shy, joyous self during the drive, sitting alone toward the front of the bus in a dark blue zip-up sweater, dark t-shirt and blue jeans.

"You too," Camille replied.

McClung could hardly see the Bledsoes' trailer, covered in timber, from her vantage point. The day before, Camille's mother was waiting at the trailer for her daughter to arrive but on this day McClung saw no one.

Thirty-eight-year-old Richard Bolan had left work at Fort Leaven-worth forty-five minutes before and was behind the bus as he made his long commute home in a Subaru four-door. He watched as Camille stepped off and walked up the driveway toward the trailer. A dog trotted out to meet her but no one else was around.

Shy but friendly, the ninth-grade honor student at Oskaloosa High School smiled constantly. She was small, just five-foot-four and a hundred pounds, with long blonde hair and a small round scar over one of two brown eyes. She wanted to be a police officer, helping those who have suffered from tragedies, especially children. Her namesake was Zetta Grace McCoy, the wife of a longtime and legendary family physician in Jefferson County.

Though her home life was unsettled at times – the youngest of seven children, her parents had been divorced for nearly her entire life and she spent weekdays at the Bledsoes' but weekends with her mother in nearby Winchester – the girl rarely complained. After struggling at a school in the neighboring town, her grades had improved at Oskaloosa High.

On that unseasonably warm day in November, Camille had plans. Countryside Baptist Church, where she attended every service, was hosting a youth retreat at Sunday school teacher Jim Bolinger's farm east of Oskaloosa. Camille was known for her punctual attendance, for volunteering to help with dishes, and for her boundless faith in a higher power.

Between 4:30 and 4:45 p.m., Robin Meyer left her job at TLC Daycare in Winchester and drove her white Sunbird to the Bledsoes' trailer. Meyer had grown up with Camille and the two remained friends, hanging out at the house after Camille returned from school. When Meyer arrived about 5 p.m., all the lights were off, but the door was unlocked.

"Hello?" she asked the empty trailer and received no response.

Camille's school bag and books were on a couch, as if she had dropped them off before leaving. There was a half-eaten brownie. Her Bible and coat were by the door, a reminder to herself to grab them before the youth retreat. Meyer assumed Camille's mother had picked her up. She went home and watched TV.

***

That afternoon, twenty-five-year-old Tom Bledsoe drove south twenty-five miles to Lawrence and grabbed his check at Farmland Industries, a nitrogen fertilizer plant where he worked as a security guard. His testimony would later differ on the timing of his arrival, which was somewhere between 2 and 3 p.m., after which he went to Lunker's Bait and Tackle to look at a rifle and consider buying a boat. While at Lunker's, Tom asked the staff if he could use the store's firearm license to buy a gun but was denied. He then went to Rusty's Outdoor Equipment in Lawrence to buy rifle cartridges and nine-millimeter bullets. Behind the driver's seat of his pickup truck were a Jennings nine-millimeter and a semi-automatic twenty-two caliber.

Tom was stout, with round glasses over beady blue eyes and a round, freckled face. His hair was copper red and combed to the right. Limited intellectual abilities gave him a childlike demeanor at times. Despite being in his mid-twenties, he attended youth events at Bolinger's Countryside Baptist Church, where he was as devout an attendee as Camille.

As a child, Tom had suffered from a fungal infection that ate away at his eardrums, leaving him hard of hearing. As a result, he was quiet and had almost no social life outside of church. Bolinger, the Sunday school teacher and a close friend, would later recall that Tom didn't drink beer or socialize with women. Even at the age of twenty-five, he lived a strictly devout lifestyle. By his own admission, Tom had few friends and, aside from hunting, did little that didn't involve work, church or helping his parents.

Tom left Rusty's sometime after 3:30 p.m., called his father and drove to his parents' house at 11477 Osage Road, north of Oskaloosa.

***

At twenty-three, the younger Floyd Bledsoe possessed, like his brother, a diminutive, stout stature. He was five feet two, a hundred and thirty pounds, with a boyish face, reddish blonde hair and pale blue eyes. Some relatives called him "Little Floyd." He was a dairy farmer, working the one place he loved to be – outside – and the father of two young sons: Cody and Christian. His marriage to Heidi was failing and divorce was imminent.

Floyd was the lone employee of Richard Zule, owner of Zule Dairy near the town of McLouth, northeast of Oskaloosa, working for $271 a week. On the day Camille disappeared, he helped Zule milk 105 cows and install a sidewalk, starting at 10:15 that morning. Around 4 p.m., Zule handed Floyd the keys to his 1969 Chevy pickup and sent him to Winchester Hardware for duct tape, a trip Zule assumed would take about twenty-five or thirty minutes.

Floyd drove west down 106th Street, toward Oskaloosa, then north up the thoroughfare of Wellman Road. As he did, he passed Camille's school bus while it headed south toward his trailer. He considered stopping by the house and treating Camille to a late lunch in town, as he had the week before, but opted against it. He continued north to Winchester Hardware.

Karen Edmonds co-owned the small store with her husband but was alone when Floyd entered. He hung around for ten or fifteen minutes, talking about the sidewalk project he and Zule were working on and inquiring about customized jackets with "Zule Dairy" printed on them. He bought the duct tape and a black sweatshirt, which he would wear for several days during a nearly ceaseless search for his sister-in-law.[1]

Also in Winchester Hardware on that day was thirty-three-year-old Billie Summerville. Floyd spoke briefly with him about his pending divorce; they were prior neighbors but not exactly friends. As Floyd hopped into the

---

[1] Bizarrely, the receipts at both Winchester Hardware and Rusty's Outdoor, where Tom had stopped the same afternoon, were later determined by detectives to show the wrong time, a detail that would impact their investigation.

'69 Chevy, Summerville started up his blue Chevy truck and they headed south down Wellman Road, toward Oskaloosa, with Summerville leading. Floyd made a left to head back toward Zule Dairy and saw Summerville turn right down Fairview Road, the street that would take him past Floyd's trailer, where Camille was home alone.

Forty minutes after he left, Floyd returned to Zule's place.

"Where'd you go to get the duct tape, Kansas City?" his boss snidely asked.

***

U.S. Army Colonel William Knoebel walked through the fallen leaves in camouflage pants, a wool plaid shirt, face mask and boots. The forty-six-year-old carried a bow, arriving at his deer stand around 3:30 p.m. on that warm November afternoon in Oskaloosa. By 5:30, twilight was approaching, and his hunt was coming to an end.

"As I was sitting there, I heard a scream and words to the effect of 'Please don't hurt me,'" he recalled. "At first, I thought this was a – it could have possibly been somebody who was, you know, outside playing or something like that but there was that peculiar sound when you hear a girl or a woman scream that just was not of the ordinary – of a little fight or a tiff between individuals."

He waited a few minutes and pondered his options. Then he heard it a second time.

"The words came out again, 'Please don't hurt me, somebody help, please don't hurt me' and continued like that. At that time, it was very clear in my mind that somebody was in need of some help, so I got out of my deer stand – very quickly got out of my deer stand – and I went directly to the north, northwest, to where I believe that the screams were coming from, because they were clearly to my back."

Knoebel was in a small valley, along Fall Creek, facing south. To one side was nothing but corn fields, on the other was soybeans. Behind him, in the direction Knoebel believed he heard the screams emanate from, were houses. About a half-mile to the northeast was Zule Dairy.

In addition to his bow, Knoebel carried a twenty-two caliber pistol when he hunted. He grabbed it and began running toward the screams.

"I moved off in that direction to see if I could assist whoever was crying

5

out for help and I moved…across the creek, I moved through the woods and I moved up in the vicinity…of a home that was directly to the north and at that time two very large yard dogs.…came after me and so I immediately was faced with somewhat of a dilemma of do I shoot the dogs and continue to run where the screams were at or do I just get up in the tree here and see if I can, in fact, see out where this person was asking for help. I did that, rather than shoot the dogs, and when I got up in the tree the atmospheric conditions were still absolutely pristine, so you could hear everything and I could not see anything at that time nor hear anything more after that, after that second scream I heard while I was in the deer stand."

Knoebel never heard gunshots but for six months after his encounter with the screams he agonized over his decision to hide in the tree. He grew convinced that he should have shot the dogs and continued running toward the screams he heard that afternoon. "It was very clear to me that somebody was in distress. I mean, there was – there was no doubt about it."

Instead, he walked to a nearby house, that of retiree Gerald Dunfield, arriving at 6 p.m. He told Dunfield about the screams. The old man had not heard them.

Around that same time, another forty-six-year-old, Randy Turner, heard a dog barking at his home on nearby Wild Horse Road. Dunfield called to ask if Turner heard a girl's screams; he had not. Neither had Zule or his wife.

At 7:02 p.m., Knoebel called the Jefferson County Sheriff's Department to say he heard a woman screaming near Wild Horse Road. The screams would not be investigated until the next day.

***

Around 6:40 p.m., Jim Bolinger parked his Countryside Baptist Church van at Floyd and Heidi's trailer to pick up Camille. On any other Friday, she was waiting out front, eager for her ride to the retreat. Jennifer Snell, a church member, walked to the front door and knocked. Like Robin Meyer ninety minutes before, Snell was met with silence. A few lights were on inside, but Camille never came to the door. Like Meyer, they assumed Camille was with her mother.

Tommie Sue Arfmann, the mother of Camille and Heidi, could be peculiar. She was prone to long drives, traveling to neighboring counties for nothing more than a loaf of bread. Tommie Sue never insisted her children go to school but adamantly required them to take part in household chores, dragging them away from social events or church activities to do so.

Donald Bolinger, Jim's brother, lived on the property where the youth retreat was being held. It was he who first noticed Tom Bledsoe's arrival at the event around 6:30 p.m., just as the other guests were appearing. Tom and another man set up lights before dinner; everyone who spoke to Tom that night would later recall him acting as he was always did. To the Bolingers, nothing yet seemed out of the ordinary, though that would soon change.

Tom left the retreat about 9:30 p.m. and went home to his parents' house, a three-bedroom, one-bath, wood frame home built during the William Howard Taft administration. A covered porch wrapped around the outside. Behind it, nearly a hundred and twenty acres of wooded Bledsoe property sprawled.

Cathy Bledsoe and her husband were operating a food booth in the town of Tonganoxie, twenty miles to the southeast that night, returning home after 10 p.m. Cathy, who always checked on Tom before going to bed, found her son asleep in his bedroom.

TWO

"Do you know where Camille is?" Tommie Sue Arfmann asked her son-in-law.

Floyd Bledsoe was still at Zule Dairy when ten o'clock rolled around that night. Tommie Sue had been expecting her daughter home from the church retreat. Growing worried, she called the Bolingers at 10:15 and was told Camille never arrived at the retreat that night. Worry turned to fear.

Phone records show there were several calls from Zule Dairy to Tommie Sue's home between 11 p.m. and midnight as Floyd checked in on the search for Camille. Tommie Sue wanted to call police, but Floyd wanted to wait until he could search for Camille himself. Shortly before midnight, he finished his fourteen-hour shift and drove home.

At 11 p.m., Heidi Bledsoe left work in Lawrence and headed home as well, arriving at about 11:40 p.m. with the co-worker who drove her, Scott Harries. Before long, the home was bustling with activity. Floyd arrived a few moments after Heidi, followed by Tommie Sue, Robin Meyer and others.

"Have you seen Camille?" Floyd asked Heidi as they walked to the front door.

"Not since last night," she said. "Is she inside?"

Heidi grabbed the handle and leaned into their front door, expecting it to be locked. Instead, she stumbled through an unlocked door. The couple split up, hurrying through different ends of the trailer. Heidi went to Camille's bedroom, Floyd went toward his bedroom and they met back in the living room.

"She's not in her bedroom," Heidi said.

"Yeah, she's not this way."

Camille was not inside, though her coat and backpack were. The half-eaten brownie was still on the couch. The family dogs were there, indicating Camille had let them in. In the kitchen, Heidi found a note she had written to Camille that morning, applauding her recent honor roll report card and asking Camille to pick up her twenty dollar reward over the weekend. Heidi's realization that Camille had not written back frightened her. "I knew that it wasn't like Camille to stay out late and not let anybody know."

The girl was mature beyond her fourteen years. She did not, would not, go somewhere without letting her sister or mother know, Heidi was sure of that. Something was wrong. Something had to be done, and quick.

The makeshift search party began in the woods around the Bledsoes' trailer, where Camille liked to stroll some nights. Heidi feared an accident may have left Camille incapacitated. Yelling Camille's name and scouring the darkness with flashlights, the crew came up empty.

The search for Camille, spearheaded by Floyd, would last all night. Heidi filed a missing person report at the Jefferson County Sheriff's Department at 12:50 a.m. as Floyd hit the road, traveling for hours to three cities across three counties in search of the girl. Tommie Sue did what came easy for her: She hopped in her car and drove the countryside of northeast Kansas.

At the sheriff's department, Heidi's concerns were met with skepticism. The girl had likely gone to a party, deputies told her. When she explained that Camille did not party, the officers reluctantly agreed to file a missing person report.

Floyd conducted the overnight investigation sheriff's deputies would not. About thirty minutes after midnight, seventy-three-year-old dairy farmer James Gardner looked out his window and found Floyd talking with his neighbor to the west. Floyd made his way to Gardner's door and told him a girl was missing, had he heard anything unusual? Neighbors had heard a girl crying, he told Gardner. But James Gardner hadn't heard a thing. Floyd scribbled his own name and phone number down, ripped the page from its notebook and handed it to Gardner with instructions to call him or police if he heard anything.

Brandi Wampler, who had been babysitting Floyd and Heidi's two young children, Cody and Christian, since 12:45 p.m. that day, continued watching them until 12:45 a.m., at which time Floyd picked them up. But two hours later, around 2:45 a.m., Floyd asked Wampler to watch the children for several more hours as he drove to the town of Pomona, an hour away, to see if Camille was staying with a sister. The children remained with Wampler until 8:30 a.m.[2]

Around 2 a.m., Floyd called an uncle, Gary Bledsoe, who lived down the street from his trailer. He wanted to know if Gary had gas for the Chevy Nova, so he could keep driving. Floyd stopped by his uncle's house, told him Camille was missing, thanked him for the one can of gas Gary had and resumed his search.

"We quit looking for her around 4:00, 4:30 that morning," Heidi recalled. "[We] laid around for about two hours, trying to figure out where she could be. Some of us crashed."

At 5:40 a.m., a phone rang at Richard Zule's house, waking him up. Floyd wanted to use his ATV for the search and asked if Zule knew where he could find bloodhounds. Zule denied him use of the ATV, hung up and fell back asleep. It wouldn't be the last time the dairy farmer would urge his lone employee to relax and let police search for Camille.

A fog had crept over Oskaloosa and the search party was stretched to the limits of its energy. Several people slept. Others, led by Robin Meyer, Camille's childhood friend, began making fliers with Camille's face on them. Floyd went to a gas station in town, Casey's General Store, for donuts.

In his baby blue deputy uniform, with loosely parted and thinning hair and a thick mustache, Sergeant Robert Poppa looked every bit the part of a rural sheriff's deputy. He had been off work for several days. Before beginning his shift that Saturday morning, he stopped off at Casey's. He was unprepared for the questioning he was about to receive from an anxious young man.

"Can I ask you a question?" Floyd asked.

"Yes."

"Why aren't you guys looking for her?"

The missing person report had been disregarded to such an extent that Poppa had no idea who Floyd was talking about. Floyd quickly filled him in on the search.

---

[2] Because Wampler couldn't watch the children beyond 8:30 a.m., Floyd dropped Christian off with his mother, Cathy Bledsoe. Floyd attempted to leave Cody with his parents as well but "Cody did not want to stay there with [Floyd's] mom and dad," according to a police report. Instead, the boy stayed with his own mother, Heidi.

"Do you think she's been kidnapped?" the sergeant asked.

"Yes," Floyd told him.

Only then, seven hours after Heidi filed the missing person report and fifteen hours after Robin Meyer knocked on the Bledsoes' door, did the Jefferson County Sheriff's Department become involved in the search for Camille.

Poppa followed Floyd back to his trailer and learned more about the girl's disappearance. When he stopped by headquarters to pick up a K-9 unit, he was told by Deputy Heather Kyle that a girl's screams had been reported the night before near Wild Horse Road. Like the missing person report, Poppa was hearing this for the first time.

He led the bloodhound to Camille's pillow case and nightshirt at the trailer, then to the wooded area where Knoebel heard screams in an attempt to pick up the girl's scent. He carried a photo of Camille in his shirt pocket. He was accompanied by his boss.

Round and gregarious, with a well-groomed, gray mustache and matching gray hair, fifty-six-year-old Roy Dunnaway had been a police officer for thirty years and Jefferson County sheriff for sixteen, coinciding with stints as a city councilman. His strong viewpoints would shape his department's investigation into Camille's disappearance.

Poppa and Dunnaway spent the day combing the area where the colonel had heard the screams, along with several other patches of Oskaloosa, to no avail. They were joined by one of the more colorful people in the county, a large forty-four-year-old Texan with a bushy handlebar mustache named Wayne Buford. He had attended high school in Germany, flew his first airplane at age sixteen, raced motorcycles in Europe, constructed a darkroom as a teenager and taught search operations to the Kosovo Army before landing in rural Kansas as a police officer. Upon hearing of the search for Camille over a police scanner, he and his bloodhound Barney offered their services.

After grabbing the scent in Camille's bedroom and being given a one-word command – "Find" – Barney led them to Camille's locker, number 102, at Oskaloosa High, which offered no further clues to her whereabouts. Poppa had hoped Camille left a note explaining where she was, but no note was found amid her Bible study books. The area around Floyd's place of employment, Zule Dairy, turned up nothing. So, too, did the wooded area where Knoebel had heard screams. As Buford wrote in a report, "Barney showed no interest in the area that would lead me to believe that the screaming was related."

"I believed that she was possibly a runaway," Dunnaway would later recall. "We had information that we'd received that she wanted to leave and it's not an uncommon thing, unfortunately, that we do have a lot of young girls and young men both that run away from home. I had no reason to think that somebody had kidnapped her or taken her."

Floyd, meanwhile, was still hard at work searching for Camille. With a photograph of the girl in his hand, he and Scott Harries, the coworker of Heidi's who had driven her home the night before, began stopping traffic on Fairview Road in front of the trailer, asking drivers and passengers if they had seen Camille. That, too, was fruitless.

"I was thinking along the lines that somebody had came and gotten her," Heidi recalled, "because it wasn't like Camille to stay out that late and not let anybody know where she was. I did have that thought going through my mind."

Before he and Dunnaway had begun their search, Poppa called Detective Randy Carreno away from his training to interview Camille's family at Floyd and Heidi's trailer. They recounted their sleepless search for the girl and repeated their firm belief that she would not have left willingly. Carreno asked Floyd if he believed the girl had been kidnapped. He did believe that; several in the search party did. Carreno asked if Floyd had a suspect in mind, someone capable of hurting Camille.

Yes, he did.

***

A few miles away, Tom Bledsoe began his day the way he began most Saturdays, by drinking coffee with his parents. He watched the morning news but heard no mention of a missing girl. As the three drank their coffee, they received a phone call from Floyd telling of Camille's disappearance.

The elder Floyd was a battle-hardened, gruff man with balding light blond hair and equally blond facial scruff. He was partial to t-shirts and jeans, along with a white cowboy hat. He asked his youngest son if Camille could have run off with a boyfriend. When asked later why he didn't participate in the search, he would say it was none of his business. That day, Heidi ran into Floyd Sr. at a relative's home and asked if he had seen Camille.

"I heard she was running away with her boyfriend," the elder Floyd remarked before rambling about Camille's plans to move to Lawrence. The comment confused Heidi, who didn't believe Camille had a boyfriend. Could her husband's father really know something she didn't about her sister? When she pressed for the boyfriend's name, he said he didn't know it.

At 8:20 a.m. that morning, forty-eight-year-old Dan Courtney drove north on Osage Road near Floyd Sr.'s house. He noticed a shiny black truck in the brome field, matching descriptions of Tom's truck. There was one man inside, though he couldn't tell who it was or what he was doing.

Back in town, there was a freshman basketball tournament at Oskaloosa High School and Annette McNary was keeping score when Floyd Jr. approached. "He had a flier that had a girl's picture on it and he brought it to the scorekeeper's table and asked me if I had seen that girl," McNary recalled.

"I was busy. He came at one point and asked me if I'd seen the girl and I informed him that I was busy right then, at that moment. I didn't know what had happened and I asked him if he could come back and he did. He came back a little bit later when there was either a timeout or halftime, possibly even after the game, I don't recall. But he came back, and he said, 'This is important. This girl is missing, have you seen her?'"

McNary had not seen Camille. Other students at the school had not seen Camille. No one, it seems, had seen Camille. It was another dead end in a series of dead ends in the search for his sister-in-law. But still, Floyd distributed fliers that morning with Detective Carreno, just as he had with Scott Harries, stopping cars as they passed through rural Jefferson County.

"Oh, I bet Randy Carreno really enjoys talking to him," Tommie Sue quipped as she looked on. "Floyd hasn't changed clothes or even taken a shower."

In Oskaloosa's Sunset Trailer Park, where he had formerly lived, Floyd interrogated a teenager, David Slifer, quizzing him on his whereabouts the night before. David said he had not seen Camille since the Bledsoes moved out of the trailer park. "If I find the person who did it, I will do the same to them," Floyd told him.

Heidi, Tommie Sue and other members of the ever-changing search party continued to cruise the countryside and small towns, hanging up fliers wherever they could. Their mood grew sullen and rumors of an abduction circulated wider. Camille's female relatives often broke into tears. No one had slept more than a few hours.

Tom went about his Saturday, working on a lawnmower and helping his parents unload a trailer before leaving for work sometime after noon. At 2 p.m., he went to the farm of Louis Gamble to drop off some food Gamble had purchased from the Bledsoe family's small catering operation. There Tom ran into Rod Lacy, who cut wood for Gamble in exchange for permission to hunt on the elderly man's land.

Before long, the topic of Camille's disappearance arose. Tom repeatedly tried to tell Lacy that the girl had been abducted but, unable to pronounce "abducted" after several tries, said, "someone took Camille." Billie Summerville had likely been involved, Tom told him.

***

The Bledsoe brothers, to put it plainly, did not like each other. Aside from a short stature, they had little in common. Jim Bolinger, the Sunday school teacher, only half-jokingly called the two Cain and Abel. Tom hated Floyd because his younger brother teased him, and the two had not spoken in the month before Camille's disappearance.

Despite this hatred, Floyd did not believe Tom was responsible for Camille's disappearance. He had another young man in mind. The man from the hardware store. The same man Tom was blaming.

Summerville, known by Detective Carreno to be a liar, thief and womanizer, lived near Camille in Sunset Trailer Park before Floyd and Heidi moved to their second trailer to get away from him. It was Carreno who investigated a May 1999 complaint about Summerville filed by Camille.

Summerville had asked Camille to take showers and sleep with him, to put on a white T-shirt and no bra so he could spray her with water, Camille wrote to Carreno six months before her disappearance. The thirty-three-year-old Summerville would allegedly walk around in a towel for her to see and compliment her body. According to Camille, he had told her brother that 14-year-old girls are not too young to have sex with.

Six months later, in the overnight hours of November 6, 1999, Floyd suspected Camille was with Summerville. Gil Crouse, a Lawrence police officer, was working security at a Conoco gas station in northeast Lawrence when Floyd, refilling his tank and exhausted from a fruitless night of searching for the girl, noticed Crouse's police radio and approached.

Floyd said he was looking for a missing teenage girl and was on his way to Coyote's, a Lawrence bar, to search for her, fearful that she was with a man by the name of Summerville. As Crouse recalled, "He made a statement: If he catches them together, he's going to kill him."

Crouse tried to talk Floyd down, advising him to call police if he found Summerville rather than take matters into his own hands. He described the young man as "extremely tired" and "a little bit overly excited about a runaway teenager." Crouse, like Jefferson County police, had seen his fair share of Friday night runaways and assumed Camille was just one more.

Following up on Floyd's hunch, Carreno interviewed Summerville later that morning at a café the Summervilles owned, Downtown Café on the courthouse square. It was an orange brick building squeezed beside the Bank of Oskaloosa and sharing space with a realtor's office. Later renamed Rose's Café and the Wind Wagon, at its dozen tables sat a clientele that skewed toward the middle age and elderly. Its menu was a simple Midwestern one: eggs, bacon, burgers and a few less popular items, such as salads.

Seeing Summerville's right arm marked with four long scratches, Carreno grabbed a camera and snapped photos. Summerville said he suffered them at a job site and became offended when asked if Camille scratched him. He told the detective he was a lot of things, but not a man who would hurt someone like that. He had been off probation for just five days and was avoiding trouble. Despite his low opinion of the man, Carreno left with a belief that Summerville had nothing to do with Camille's disappearance.

Summerville's alibi for November 5, 1999, seemingly ruled him out. He was working with his father on a barn west of Oskaloosa from 7 a.m. until he saw Floyd at Winchester Hardware and again after. His father later corroborated this under oath: "I had him all day, 'til dark. After dark I don't know what he did but up 'til then I could account for him." According to Knoebel, the Army colonel and bow hunter, dusk came at about 5:45 or 5:50 p.m. that night, more than an hour beyond the time Camille was taken.

After interviewing Summerville, Carreno returned to Floyd's trailer. He found Floyd in the middle of Fairview Road, stopping vehicles and showing drivers a photo of Camille. Had they seen her? The only answer he heard was no.

Carreno went about questioning the young man; about his marriage, his friendship with Camille, his workday. He asked if Floyd had returned home that fateful Friday after the trip to Winchester Hardware. Floyd told him no.

A middle-aged neighbor, Jim Penry, pulled up in a hurry. He had seen a stalled truck near a county shop and a woman walking away from it toward an open field. As Carreno rushed to his patrol car, Floyd asked if he could tag along. They found the stalled truck but no one in the area and no shoeprints indicating anyone had walked away from it. The detective and Floyd drove together to another dead end. A woman claiming to have seen Camille the night before in a Grand Am or Grand Prix couldn't be sure it was the girl.

Shortly after noon on that Saturday, Dale and Danielle Hawk were at their house on Wild Horse Road when a green Chevy Nova stopped in front and Floyd stepped out. He asked the couple if they had noticed any strange cars in the neighborhood the night before. They had not. Floyd asked if he could search their property and they allowed it. He told them, "I hope I find her alive or I'm going to have to hurt someone."

He and Carreno spent the rest of that Saturday afternoon together. At 4:20 p.m. they stopped by Summerville's trailer court and met up with Dunnaway and Poppa as those two searched with Barney the bloodhound. Floyd kept asking strangers if they had seen Camille, holding up a now-weathered photo of her. He asked Carreno if he thought Camille was okay. As time dragged on, Floyd was becoming convinced she wasn't.

THREE

Built in the early 1980s and as white as pure driven snow on a Kansas prairie, Countryside Baptist Church is a rectangular building with a rectangular parking lot surrounded by rectangular farm fields northeast of Oskaloosa. The church was without a pastor at the time of Camille's disappearance, making Sunday school teacher Jim Bolinger its de facto clergy.

For Camille, who had attended since she was six years old, the church was a source of stability at a time when she was shifting between schools and homes. She never missed a service and grew close to the Bolingers. To friends she confided her desire to live with them after Floyd and Heidi divorced. It was not an absurd proposition. The Bolingers had taken in a fourteen-year-old girl after her mother expelled her, caring for the girl until she was twenty, even seeing her off to the University of Kansas. Prior to offering Camille shelter, they had offered the same to Heidi, though she had declined.

"Her home life wasn't what it could have been. But her mother wouldn't let her live with us," said Rose Bolinger, Jim's wife.

For Tom, the church was a rare source of camaraderie. Jim Bolinger was his best friend and one of the few people he spoke to consistently. Like Camille, Tom never missed a service, stopping in for Sunday morning and Sunday night worship, Wednesday night prayer meetings and Friday night youth events. He collected the offerings at each service. Vacations from work were spent at church camps. Despite his age, the twenty-five-year-old still attended the children's Sunday school class. Tom preferred it, so Bolinger allowed him to stay.

The church was without a pastor because Reverend Michael Wagoneer had left months before amid philosophical differences. The church was growing fundamentalist, he would later tell police. Adherence to Scripture was paramount. The Bible was to be read literally; every event in it had occurred as the Bible said, without error. After more than three years as its pastor, Wagoneer left a congregation continuing along a fundamentalist path. By some accounts, he was forced out by the Bolingers.

Wagoneer had known both Tom and Camille during his time as pastor. Camille, he said, was extremely shy and sweet, bashful to a fault. He worried about her shaky home life but never feared she was at risk for substance abuse or teenage pregnancy. Tom, he said, was faithful and intellectually challenged. The two had hunted together and Tom had visited the pastor's house, where he flirted with Wagoneer's fifteen-year-old niece at a time when Tom was in his twenties.

On matters of sex, the church was strict. Masturbation and pornography were adamantly condemned. Males and females were separated on most occasions, even when they were young adults. At Sunday school, the boys sat at one end of the table, the girls at the other. At Friday night church camps, the sexes could play kickball together if supervised but otherwise could not socialize until they turned twenty.

The church also did not condone alcohol use. When later asked if Tom drank beer, Bolinger said, "[I] just don't believe he'd do it" because Tom "cared about the Lord."

The Bolingers believed strongly in Tom and would be his strongest character witnesses in the months ahead, reiterating that he was a good and God-fearing man. When an Oskaloosa High School psychologist heard rumors that Tom had attempted to molest boys on a church fishing trip, Jim Bolinger dismissed them outright, saying he didn't believe the claim could be true.

By the time Sunday service began at Countryside Baptist Church on November 7, 1999, Camille had been missing for forty-one hours. Bolinger asked his gathering to pray for the missing member of their congregation. Tom sat in the crowd. Cheryl Bryant, a forty-two-year-old friend, sat in front of him and thought he was quieter than usual. With Tom it could be difficult to tell though.

As Tom was walking out of Sunday school that morning, Bolinger mentioned Camille. "I, in jest, actually asked him if he knew where Camille was, and I don't know if he answered me, but I told him that this is what makes old people have gray hair and might even put a little gray in his red hair. I remember those words," Bolinger recalled.

Giving no indication he heard the interim pastor's question, Tom kept walking.

***

Across town, sixty-year-old Dick Stevens pulled his blue Dodge Dakota pickup into a parking space at Casey's General Store to buy Merit 100 cigarettes for his wife. Before he could, Little Floyd Bledsoe walked up and began talking.

Floyd wanted a well on his property filled as quickly as possible and knew Stevens was in that line of work. He couldn't get to it today, Stephens told him. There was a water leak out west in Ozawkie to fix first.

Floyd turned the conversation to Camille. He wanted to know if Stevens had seen her or a newer-model Trans Am she might be in. As Stephens would later tell police, Floyd didn't believe detectives were working hard enough to solve her disappearance.

***

After morning church, Tom helped his parents unload some machinery before going to an evening service at Countryside Baptist. Again, Bolinger presided and again he asked his congregation to pray for Camille. The pastor also noticed something unusual about Tom: he was uptight. "Tom and Floyd, I go way back with them. I know 'em. I know 'em well. I knew something was the matter with him because I just know Tom."

After the evening service, Bolinger was talking with a few people, including Tom, when he made another off-hand remark about Camille. "He made a comment that if he knew where Camille was he'd go get her, bring her home, and he said, 'Right, Tom?' Using me as an example," Tom later recalled.

It was all he could take. Either fearful those around him knew his secret or overcome with remorse for what he had done, Tom drove to the Jefferson County Sheriff's Department intent on turning himself in to police for the murder of Camille. After parking his truck at headquarters, he sat inside and dialed Bolinger's number on his cell phone. When the pastor didn't answer, he left a voicemail message at 8:55 p.m.:

"Hi, Jim. This is Tom. I wanted you to be the first to know. I know I lied to you. I know where Camille is. When you get this message, I'm going to turn myself in to the police. I wish I never did it. I hurt the church, I hurt God. Most of all, I let everyone down. All I can say is I'm sorry. I'll pay for the rest of my life for what I've done. All I can ask is for the church to remain strong. Please forgive me. As a favor, please remember my mom and dad. Help them when they go through, help with the pain I'm about to – thank you, Jim. Sorry. Goodbye."

Next, Tom called his parents' house and spoke to them both.

"He said he knew – knew something about her body," Floyd Sr. recalled later, "and he was going to go, he was going to go into the sheriff's office and tell them. I told him I didn't want to hear nothing else about it. I said just wait there, I'll get a lawyer, then you and your lawyer can go in and do whatever, because I didn't know whether he just found it or what."

As he waited for a lawyer to arrive, Tom called Bolinger's number again, getting the answering machine for a second time at 9:01 p.m. His voice was quivering.

"Hi, Jim. Me again, Tom. Please help me and my dad. Please help my mom and dad through this. Right now, they're disappointed. I know that the church will be, too. All I can ask, forgive me for what I have done, and I will pay for the rest of my life. I wanted to tell you in front of the church, but I didn't have enough guts. I'm sorry. I don't know what went through my mind. Right now, you're probably pretty shocked. I wish I could turn the clock back, but I can't. I made my choice. I wish I didn't. I'm sorry. Bye."

Bolinger knew instantly it was Tom, speaking in an uptight monotone, the only time he had heard his friend get emotional. He listened to the messages, struggling to understand. After replaying them several times, he did not believe Tom was a killer. He believed Tom had lied to him – he did, after all, know where Camille was – and felt guilty for doing so.

Bolinger called the home phone of a longtime friend, Captain Orin Turner at the sheriff's department. Turner could hear the stress in his voice as he asked the captain if a girl was missing. Turner, who had been on limited duty that weekend, did not. Bolinger explained that a girl was missing, and a member of his congregation may know where she is. Turner told him to preserve the answering machine tape and to call the sheriff's office.

Bolinger called and told Deputy Heather Kyle he had received two messages on his answering machine he believed she should hear. Kyle and another deputy drove to his house and recorded the messages onto a micro-cassette tape, consoling the deeply upset Bolinger as they did.

Tom, meanwhile, met his mother and father at the sheriff's office. He hugged his mother, said he loved her and was sorry for what he had done. She knew immediately what he was saying: Tom had killed Camille. Cathy told Tom she loved him as well. The three of them drove to the home of Jim Swoyer, a former county attorney who had been practicing law for nearly 50 years. There they met Tom's lawyer, Mike Hayes, whom Swoyer had invited over.

To say Mike Hayes was the most influential attorney in Oskaloosa is an understatement. He was, of course, but his reach went even beyond that. By 1999, at age fifty-two, he had already been the lead prosecutor in Jefferson County, held the same position in neighboring Jackson County, and been appointed Oskaloosa's city attorney. His electoral rise to the Jefferson County attorney post occurred just eighteen months after he graduated from law school. He would return to that position in the 2000s.[3]

Lean and fit, Hayes had been a cross-country captain at the University of Kansas known for tenacity and boundless effort; he ran a cross-country meet on a broken foot. In conversations, he casually mixed in sports metaphors about sticking to a game plan or running a good race.

As a prosecutor, Hayes had worked alongside detectives and deputies from the Jefferson County Sheriff's Department, including Dunnaway, the longtime sheriff. If it had been the previous decade, Hayes would be standing ready to prosecute whoever killed Camille. But it was 1999 and Hayes was a defense attorney for hire. After receiving a call from Tom Bledsoe's parents asking him to help their son, he was on the other side of the courtroom.

Dunnaway had just returned home from a day of searching for Camille when he received a call from the sheriff's department. "I was told that the information we received was that Tom Bledsoe knew where Camille was at and that he was sorry that he hadn't told people sooner. I broke the speed limit coming to Oskaloosa. It was very important. You're a father and so it's

---

[3] Jefferson County has a habit of electing young and relatively inexperienced county attorneys; one of Hayes' successors was elected at twenty-seven.

23

very important that you find her…Just before I got to the office I received a call that Mike Hayes wanted to talk to me at the office."

"Are you looking for a young girl?" Hayes asked Dunnaway when he arrived at headquarters.

"Yes."

"We know where she is. She's not alive."

In a conference room at the Jefferson County Law Enforcement Center, Hayes, with Tom by his side, told the sheriff, his deputies and Kansas Bureau of Investigation detectives that Camille had been fatally shot in the back of the head. Her body had then been dragged to a trash dump and buried under a foot of dirt. Tom was willing to take them to the body.

Sergeant Poppa found out soon after. He had just wrapped up his day with the K-9 unit and laid down to sleep when he received a call from Dunnaway around 10:30 that night. Camille had been murdered, the sheriff said. Tom's confession was a shock to law enforcement officers who had been told they were searching for yet another runaway teenager.

"We had gained information that she may have had a boyfriend and we even had information that she may have been in a car with this boyfriend," Dunnaway recalled. "We went looking for the boy, he wasn't home. I can't remember his name, lived in the trailer court down here. They told me what kind of car he drove. At that time…we were looking at the car."

Murders in Oskaloosa could be a once-in-a-decade occurrence. It was not unheard of for detectives to spend a half-dozen years on the force without taking on a homicide case there.

And yet, it was the second in less than a month. In October, three men had robbed and shot to death Clarence Rinke, a fifty-five-year-old gun collector involved in a massive marijuana selling scheme. Two murders in four weeks was an anomaly around Oskaloosa. As Undersheriff Jeff Herrig would tell reporters the next day, "We've had too many around here lately."

The sheriff's office was not well-equipped to handle homicides, so outside help from the Kansas Bureau of Investigation was almost always utilized. Because the sheriff's office didn't have a database for its files, they were instead kept in disorganized banker's boxes and searched by hand. Some boxes were ordered by case numbers, others by suspect names, others by booking numbers and still others by date. For a twenty-four-year span between 1960 and 1984, offense reports are missing.

At the Bledsoe property, Poppa joined Tom, Dunnaway, Hayes, Carreno, Detective Troy Frost, County Attorney Jim Vanderbilt and KBI senior special agent Jim Woods, a thirty-seven-year law enforcement veteran who would head the KBI's side of the case. As Carreno photographed the scene, others searched inside the four-and-a-half-foot-deep, 225-feet-long ditch northwest of the house. The clock passed 1 a.m. Sitting in a car, Tom looked on, saying nothing.

Poppa: "It was dark. There was a long, like a ravine, a ditch where they dump all their trash. Lot of plywood, clothes, bags of trash. I could tell that the edge of the bank had fresh marks on it like shovel marks when you dig and…there was fresh dirt. Mostly, you couldn't tell a lot 'til we really started removing the trash and plywood.

"We removed the trash and plywood and underneath the trash and plywood was kind of like a lump of fresh…dirt that had been tossed on an object. Myself and Troy Frost started slowly moving the dirt away. We first discovered there was somebody under there [when] we saw her foot."

Frost: "There was part of her shoe that was kind of sticking out over here on the side, so me and Sergeant Poppa…with our hands, gently followed her body until we got her mostly uncovered, except for the dirt on top of her. We really didn't want to mess with that too much."

Vanderbilt: "She was lying on her back with her arms folded across her chest and legs slightly crossed. Her upper torso was slightly elevated and her head was tilted forward, appearing to be resting on her chest…she was wearing jeans, socks and shoes. Her face was bloody and caked with dirt."

Fifty-five hours after her best friend, Robin Meyer, noticed she was missing, setting off a multi-day search, it was over. Camille was dead. Her chin was on her chest, her left leg was bent under her right, her right arm slung across her waist. Her dark t-shirt and bra had been pulled up over her chest. Her black tennis shoes were still tied. Seven dollars and a school ID card were inside her pockets. Among the garbage around her: a pornographic film and Countryside Baptist t-shirt.

Tom turned over the murder weapon, his Jennings nine-millimeter semi-automatic, to Hayes who, in turn, gave it to Poppa in a white plastic bag at 1:44 a.m. It had been wiped clean and contained no fingerprints. Floyd Sr. then offered up some of his son's other guns and ammunition.

The officers did not enter the house or Tom's black Mazda pickup truck.

Bullets and shell casings would not be discovered until a week later. Woods, the KBI agent in charge, declined to seal off the crime scene, leaving it open to tampering by the Bledsoe family and guests in the days after Camille's body was found. When shell casings were found the next week, it was by accident. Reports of blood on Tom's truck were not investigated until several days later.

Hayes walked over to Dunnaway and asked if his client could go to bed or if he was going to jail. Dunnaway said Tom was going to jail.

Bullets and shell casings later found underneath Camille were inspected by a forensic scientist, T.L. Price, who determined they were fired from Tom's nine-millimeter. The bullet in the girl's head was too damaged to link to Tom's gun but was determined to be a Winchester silvertip, hollow-point bullet, one of the many styles of ammunition Tom's father turned over to police. Tom had bought nine-millimeter bullets at Rusty's Outdoor on the same afternoon he killed Camille.

At the law enforcement center, Tom was interrogated by KBI special agent George Johnson as Dunnaway and Frost looked on. "At the very beginning he said, 'I killed her,'" the sheriff recalled. Frost would later say he couldn't remember exactly what Tom told Johnson but it was either "I shot her" or "I killed her." Tom went on, confessing to killing Camille in his pickup truck. Either no police reports were written during Tom's interrogation and confession or those reports were later destroyed.

The nearest forensic pathologist was Erik Mitchell, the coroner for Shawnee County in the capital city of Topeka, thirty miles to the southwest. He was called to the Bledsoes' house around 3 a.m. to diagnose the dead and arrived an hour later. He spoke with detectives at the scene, snapped some photographs and placed the body into a bag.

Every body tells a story. Camille's was in rigor mortis, indicating her death had not occurred within the past dozen hours. The body was transported to the Shawnee County Morgue in Topeka, where Mitchell and Frost went to work examining it.

Two gunshots had entered the chest, traveled through the heart and exited, Mitchell found. A third shot to the chest went through her left breast, exited out the other side, and then through her left forearm. A fourth shot was to the back of the head.

Camille suffered five gunshot wounds from four bullets. The most likely explanation, according to Mitchell, is that Camille was shot first in the back of the head and then shot three more times as she lay dying or already dead.

There were cuts along Camille's back, indications she had been killed elsewhere and dragged to the brome field. This hypothesis did not explain her chest being exposed, however. That likely occurred before she was dragged, according to Mitchell.

Small cuts and discoloration on Camille's knuckles may indicate the girl fought her attacker, though Mitchell's examination was inconclusive in that regard. Also inconclusive were the results of a sexual assault kit; he couldn't say whether Camille had been raped.

Tom was booked into the Jefferson County Jail at 3:10 a.m. wearing a flannel shirt, blue jeans and boots, along with a University of Kansas hat. He had one dollar in his pocket and was listed as suicidal.

Heidi was at Robin Meyer's house that morning when she got a call from police, urging her to meet them at the trailer. *This is it*, she thought. *They found her.* Heidi and Robin picked up Tommie Sue and drove to Heidi and Floyd's trailer with hope in their hearts.

When they arrived, Camille was not there. Poppa and a priest were the only guests. Heidi fell to her knees next to Floyd as her husband delivered the news: "Camille's dead." The women burst into tears. Tommie Sue said Camille had been reading about death in the Bible just a week before and asked her mother, "What's it like to die?"

When Floyd spoke again, his next words were even more shocking than the last.

"Tom killed her."

"Tom? Your brother Tom?" Heidi asked.

Sure, Heidi had her concerns about the in-laws. Her husband's parents drank heavily and their mood fluctuated accordingly. Camille didn't visit unless Heidi and the younger Floyd were there as well. She told Robin that the elder Floyd frightened her.

And yes, Tom made Camille and Heidi uncomfortable. He was known to have a crush on Heidi and once left a pornographic magazine lying around when alone with her and Camille. There were rumors within the family that Tom, a virgin, wanted the fourteen-year-old Camille to be his first.

On the other hand, the Bledsoes had welcomed Camille to family meals, invited her along on trips and bought her gifts. Camille helped them sell burgers from their food truck, the B&C Chuckwagon, at county fairs. Tom had even given Camille a ride home, a clear and rare violation of church rules, a few days before she went missing.

At 6:50 a.m. that Monday, Floyd called his boss to tell him what had happened. "They found her, she's dead. She was found in the back of my mom and dad's place. My brother may have killed her. He had better stay in jail or I'll butcher him." Richard Zule asked if she had been raped; Floyd said he didn't know but had heard Camille was still clothed. As he began to cry, he hung up, only to call back and say he would try to milk the cows later. He never arrived at Zule Dairy.

By the time the sun rose over Oskaloosa on November 8, 1999, the disappearance of Camille Arfmann had been solved. Her body had been found, her confessed killer was in jail and his murder weapon was in an evidence room. A call to the Bureau of Alcohol, Tobacco and Firearms had confirmed it was Tom's. It should have been an open and shut case.

It also should have been a singular tragedy: the heinous and untimely death of a sweet young girl at the hands of a perverse murderer and habitual liar. Instead, what happened in the week following Tom's arrest turned Camille's death into a dual tragedy, one that would hang over the town like a thick, dark nimbostratus for sixteen years.

FOUR

The Bledsoes had been in Oskaloosa for generations. Floyd's grandparents, Ida and Ray Bledsoe, opened a grocery store just northwest of the courthouse square in 1959 and expanded to two more stores. The couple amassed land north of Oskaloosa, where later generations of Bledsoes would settle.

Ida and Ray had three sons: Lloyd first, then Floyd and then Gary. Floyd joined the National Guard in 1966, as America's involvement in Vietnam increased. Believing he could shield his oldest brother, who he considered unfit for war, from being drafted, Floyd volunteered. Within a couple years, he was in the A Shau Valley, not far from the Laotian border, carrying 100-pound packs on week-long patrols and eating a water buffalo when rations were scarce, he wrote in letters home.

Gary and Floyd wrote to each other routinely. In May of 1969, word reached Oskaloosa that there had been a protracted battle in the valley, what would later be called the Battle of Hamburger Hill. No one heard from Floyd for a month after. Dark thoughts seeped in about his whereabouts.

He had been wounded in the leg but was alive. He would not talk about the war much over the following decades, alluding to it only on occasion. He gave Gary a souvenir: the shell casing from an AK-47. The bullet he kept for himself. Only later did Gary learn the mark on his leg was not a scratch, as Floyd had said, but a bullet wound. His brother had kept the bullet that sliced through. Years later, when Gary showed his brother an AR-15, Floyd warned him that the tip of the gun was faulty; it would break if slammed onto someone's head.

The war had an effect on Floyd. His drinking intensified and car crashes followed. There was a divorce, then a second marriage, to Cathy. His temper grew shorter and feuds with his brothers were common.

Five months before Camille went missing, Ida Bledsoe died at a Topeka hospital at the age of seventy-eight. The ensuing estate battle lasted for years and bitterly divided her three sons. Gary and Floyd argued over construction of a fence, a matter that went to court. Before long, the brothers' divisions bordered on absurdity. When their mother's savings was split three ways, a single penny remained. A bank gave Gary the penny, much to the chagrin of Lloyd, who hated that his youngest brother had received one cent more. At the time of Camille's disappearance, Gary had not spoken to his brother Floyd for months. They would not speak for decades after.

One day, Gary's wife told him that a man was on the couple's front porch and wanted to speak with him. As Gary tells it, he opened his door to find a drunken man irate, threatening to beat him to death for what he did to the man's wife. As the man explained, his wife was undergoing psychiatry and their marriage was struggling due to molestation she had suffered as a child. Gary, knowing the man must be confused, asked, "Who are you talking about?" His response: Floyd Bledsoe Sr. After calmly explaining that his name was Gary and Floyd was his brother, he volunteered Floyd's address and gave the man directions to his house a few miles down the road. The drunken man stormed off, even more angry and confused than when he arrived.

Floyd Sr.'s wife, Cathy, had two other children before the couple met, Cindy and Richard. After Tom and Floyd were born, the six of them lived for several years in a cramped trailer before moving into the house on Osage; Richard nearing adulthood, Cindy a teenager and the Bledsoe boys still children. Life inside the home was, in Cindy's recollection, a miserable experience full of abuse. "I would not wish it on anybody."

The Bledsoe parents were insistent on chores being completed, punishing an unclean dish with a crack of the belt. When Tom set toilet paper on fire, Cindy was beaten. When Floyd cut his arm, Cindy was beaten. If a child left a cabinet door open, his or her head would be placed inside of it and slammed. The resulting bruises were such a deep shade of black and blue that the children occasionally stayed home from school, Cindy recalls. During a particularly heinous fight between Richard and Floyd Sr., Cindy feared her stepfather would actually kill her brother.

Cindy says she largely raised young Floyd, changing his diapers as her mother did next to nothing. Each morning, she would prepare Floyd for school, prepare herself for school and pack her stepfather a lunch. Sometimes, if her parents were in the living room and wanted a drink from the neighboring kitchen, they would order Cindy down from her upstairs bedroom to pour them a cup of coffee or fetch them a beer.

Beer flowed fast in the house but Cindy didn't mind it. Her stepfather, a longtime Kansas Department of Transportation engineer after the war and before his retirement in 1996, was mellower when he was drunk and meanest when he wasn't. She learned to have a beer ready when he arrived home from work and to deliver many more as he needed them. Her mother took to keeping pace with his drinking and Cindy's role as a guardian to Tom and Floyd increased as she neared adulthood.

Little Floyd had a protector, at times, in his grandmother. Ida Bledsoe doted over the child and became worried about his home life. She would find an excuse to babysit him, bringing him over to her home, where he could play uninterrupted and without fear.

The household was only hard on three of the four children. Tom was placed on a pedestal, Cindy says, and could do no wrong in his parents' eyes. He, in fact, did little, right or wrong. Quiet and insular, he was largely excused from the unending chores completed by the other children. He was also largely shielded from the abuse endured by others.

By the time Cindy heard of the murder, she was thirty-four years old and living in Missouri. She was surprised, at first, by Tom's arrest. "What, Tom? Murder?" Then she considered his blazing temper, a dangerous hand-me-down from his father. She had considered her stepfather capable of murder and Tom less so. Still, it wasn't impossible to imagine.

When Gary heard that Camille had been killed, her body found on his brother's property, a thought entered his head and refused to leave: my God, he killed her. Floyd Sr. killed her. A fatal gunshot to the head seemed like the modus operandi of a combat veteran and longtime gun enthusiast, he thought. He also thought of the angry drunk at his door, of the accusations of molestation that had hovered for decades. Tom, Gary thought, was reliant on his parents and would do what they said in a moment of crisis, even take the blame for murder. He had always been their baby, their favorite child, the one they doted over. Now, his uncle believed, Tom was taking the fall for his father's crimes.

Gary's son, Gary Bledsoe Jr., was a military reservist at the time. He received a call that Monday morning from Michelle Scott, a friend. "One of your cousins is in jail." He assumed it was one of his uncle Lloyd's sons.

When she said Camille's body had been found and Tom had been arrested, he nearly dropped the phone. He called his boss and told him he wouldn't be coming into work. There had been a murder in the family, he said.

***

Camille's murder had an effect on Oskaloosa, the kind of effect that can only come from a heinous crime in a small town. An effect so common it has become cliché.

Two days after Camille's body was found, *Topeka Capital-Journal* reporter Lou Ann Thomas, who lived just outside Oskaloosa, wrote that the town "is a place where drivers stop for jaywalkers and people take casseroles to those who are ill or who have suffered a loss. This is a place where concerned friends put coffee cans with crude slots cut in the plastic tops near cash registers for donations to help families in need.

"The killing of a 14-year-old girl shouldn't happen anywhere, but especially not here."

It was a cliché, sure, but it was also what many in Oskaloosa believed. There was a reason they chose not to live in nearby cities, where they assumed crime occurred rampantly. And for those who lived north of Oskaloosa, like the Bledsoes, even residing in a town of eleven hundred people was too much. They lived where they lived for a reason and many believed unabashedly that it was the best place to live.

Take Jo Miller, for example. When the elderly woman first heard of Camille's death, she ran to her garage door, closing it as quickly as she could. She then walked the length of her home, locking every lock, securing herself inside. "It gave me an eerie feeling that I wasn't safe anymore," she told Thomas.

Miller's grandchildren lived near Tom and the Bledsoe parents, near where Tom had left Camille's body. They rode their bicycles along the street in front. Would that continue? Should it? Miller feared the answer was a resounding no.

Steve Kruse, an employee at the town's hardware store, Harvey's True Value: "It's just a bad deal all around…there's nothing that can make up for that little girl being gone."

Mike Moore, an eighteen-year-old auto mechanic and lifelong resident: "I never would've imagined anybody would've been killed in this town. It's made a lot of people around town feel like it's not safe…like the kids are a bunch of degenerates."

In the minds of many around town, something had changed. The town had lost its innocence. As resident Lynn Luck put it, "You think something like this would never happen in a small town but it did. We're not immune to these things anymore."

Crimes against children inevitably make people think of their own. Are they safe? Millie Ellerman, the local postmaster, became afraid for her grandchildren. "I don't want to let them out of my sight for even a second," she told Thomas. "Isn't that a terrible way to live? This is a horrible thing that has happened."

"What's happening to our children?" she asked, not expecting an answer and not receiving one.[4]

***

Around the courthouse square, Camille's murder was the talk of every office. Production slowed as employees whispered. Debbie Scrivner, an insurance agent on the square, recalled those confusing days: "No one can concentrate on work. It's the main topic of conversation. You can actually feel the sadness around town."

"It's not fair that she died this way," Peggy Craig said. "She was young. It isn't fair. It isn't right." Craig was a counselor at Oskaloosa High. On that Monday morning, it was her job to console students who had come to know the shy girl who was now dead. Teachers had told students about the murder during first-hour classes. They shared memories of Camille's friendliness. No one could recall a mean word escaping her lips.

"I've been here nineteen years and nobody's ever been murdered," Craig told a reporter that morning. "We've had kids killed in car accidents."

Someone at the Jefferson County North school district, where Camille had previously attended classes, called Oskaloosa High principal Patrick

---

[4] The town's sense of an innocence lost would be felt further three months later when a fifteen-year-old boy, Joshua Stark, put a nine-millimeter pistol to thirteen-year-old Cody Back's head and pulled the trigger as the two smoked pot and drank beer in a bedroom at 3 a.m. Stark later pleaded guilty to unintentional second-degree murder and was sentenced to six and a half years in a youth detention facility.

McKernan to ask that the school's American flag be flown at half-staff to honor the deceased. So it was.

"Everybody said she was a shy, quiet student, but very friendly," superintendent Bob Overstreet said. "She always had a smile on her face."

Katie Parker, a junior at Oskaloosa High, was Camille's partner in the school's physical education class. When she went to P.E. that day and read Camille's name next to her own, she broke down. The quiet freshman girl she had only just begun to know was dead.

Among the girls who had known Camille – and those who did not – rumors emerged from thin air. One girl, Brittany, told people that her friend Megan had spoken to Camille and Camille had said she was being sexually abused. After Megan told police that wasn't true, Brittany admitted she had invented the rumor, though not before several hours of detective time spread over three weeks was wasted.

Tommie Sue Arfmann had not slept since Friday, despite suggestions from sheriff's deputies and detectives that she rest. She told the officers there were memories of Camille everywhere she looked, making rest impossible. After Camille left teeth marks in a door frame as a toddler, Tommie Sue had refused to let anyone repair it. That morning, still sleepless, she sat on the steps of the Bledsoes' trailer and thought about her youngest child.

"She thought God would see her through," she said. "She wanted to be a police officer. She wanted to help with kids who had been in car wrecks and give them teddy bears."

Tommie Sue and other family members were frustrated that police had not established a hotline during the search for Camille and that news outlets were not alerted earlier in the weekend. The *Topeka Capital-Journal*, the largest newspaper in the area, did not publish a story about the disappearance until November 8, a brief article of fewer than two-hundred words. The second-largest, the *Lawrence Journal-World*, did not report on Camille's disappearance until her body was found. Its headline: "Girl's death leaves family, children with questions."

"It would have been nice to have something like that," Dunnaway told the newspaper when asked about the hotline, but rightly acknowledged "it wouldn't have helped us any in this case." Floyd, strung out from sleepless nights, lashed out at a *Journal-World* reporter for the paper's failure to cover the disappearance, saying, "It seems like you always jump in after the kill has been made."

Public interest in the case was so intense around Oskaloosa that Captain Orin Turner had to send a memo to Jefferson County Sheriff's Department employees reminding them they were not authorized to share any information outside of the office, except with the KBI. "As always, details of any active investigation being conducted by the sheriff's department are to remain confidential," it said.

Jim Bolinger spoke to youth group members that day, recalling Camille's religiosity and generosity. "She was faithful. She was a good girl. She was quiet, she didn't talk. She always seemed to have a smile. She was an excellent worker. She was always willing to help wash dishes or clean up."

Jim Woods, the KBI agent, visited Shane Gatewood, a twenty-seven-year-old district manager for Silverhawk Security, which staffed security guards at Farmland Industries. Gatewood said Tom had worked there for about two years and was among his most dependable employees, always arriving early and always willing to work overtime or exchange shifts. He was well-liked, Gatewood told the detective, and his arrest had shocked coworkers. Gatewood learned of the arrest that Monday morning when Tom's father called to say Tom had "gotten himself in a jam" and wouldn't be returning to work. Floyd Sr. asked Gatewood to mail Tom's last check to him.

There had been a criminal background check when Tom started in early 1998; it came back clean because Tom was not yet a criminal. When he was given a pay raise that July, his supervisor wrote, "Tom is a complete blessing for me…no matter if it's two months or twenty minutes, Tom is always ready and willing to cover an open shift." He received another raise that October, four weeks before killing Camille, due to his spotless disciplinary record at Farmland.

The only unusual behavior he showed that previous weekend was on Saturday, the day after the murder. He usually loitered an extra thirty minutes after his shift to talk with graveyard shifter Susan Oxandale but hadn't that night.

Before the detective left, Gatewood asked for a list of visitation days at the Jefferson County Jail. Tom's coworkers had plans to stop by.

Tom received a lot of visitors in the three days after his arrest. His attorney, Mike Hayes, visited nine times and his parents visited on several occasions. Michael Wagoneer, his former pastor, visited three times. His half-sister, Cindy, would leave her visit with a shiver down her spine. He stared and smiled at her as she entered. When she asked a question, he continued to stare and smile. When she asked another question, his demeanor did not change. During the twenty-minute visit, he didn't say a word. "That was really eerie," she recalled.

Rose Bolinger, meanwhile, was babysitting Floyd and Heidi's eldest son, Cody, and several other children that Monday afternoon. Cody was just two years old when his uncle was arrested for killing his aunt, who he called Millie or Aunt Mimi.

Irritably excited, Cody walked over to Rose and started ranting. He told her that Tom had shot his Aunt Millie, "boom, boom, boom, boom, and dumped her in the water." Tom then put Cody's blanket around Camille, Cody said, before placing her in a dump truck "that goes beep, beep, beep." Tom closed Camille's eyes and kissed her cheeks, according to Cody. There was red stuff on her legs; her shoes and shirt were wet.

"The first time that Cody talked to me it was hard to understand him," Bolinger recalled, "because he was excited and there was some other boys there that was talking to him also and that's the reason that the truck came into it, because the other kids was thinking when Cody said 'dump' that he meant truck."

Frightened by what she had heard, Bolinger retold the story to Orin Turner at the sheriff's department. Rose was asked if she believed Cody had been given those details second-hand. "No. He had seen it. It was real to him."

That night, Rose saw Heidi at church and pulled her aside. She believed Heidi needed to hear her son speak. They took him downstairs, away from any commotion.

"Cody, what happened to Aunt Camille?" Rose asked.

"Uncle Tom shot Aunt Mimi. Bang, bang, bang, bang."

Camille had been shot, fell to the ground and shook, Cody told his wide-eyed audience of two. He said Tom put the girl in a dump truck, though Heidi and Rose assumed he meant he had put her in a dump, which was true.

"How do you know?" Heidi asked her son.

"I watched it through the window," Cody said.

"What window?"

"A car window. They put her in a van."

"Was it Mama and Papa's van?" Heidi asked, referring to her husband's parents.

"No. Mama and Papa were gone. They came back later," Cody said.

Heidi and Rose took him outside and pointed to one of the church vans but that wasn't it either, Cody told them.

Heidi, like Rose, was a believer. Both became convinced then that young Cody Bledsoe had seen his paternal uncle kill his maternal aunt. His gory story, graphic and detailed, led them to believe Cody was the sole eyewitness to the murder of Camille.

"He was saying things no two-year-old would know," Heidi recalled. "He walked us through the whole thing in full detail and all anyone knew at that time was that Tom shot her."

In reality, Cody was at the home of a babysitter, Brandi Wampler, when Camille was killed. He did not see Camille's murder but almost certainly overheard details in the days that followed her disappearance, interwove those with his own vivid two-year-old imagination and told a disturbingly graphic story to his mother and anyone else who would listen.

The imagined stories of a two-year-old boy do not meet evidentiary requirements in a murder case and are typically not deemed worthy of serious cogitation in a court of law. But the Arfmann case was far from ordinary.

***

The next day, November 9, a student at Oskaloosa High School walked into the office of school psychologist Claudine Boldridge around 9 a.m. to discuss Camille. A second girl followed her in. The two told Boldridge that a friend of theirs at Countryside Baptist Church knew Tom had molested young boys during a church fishing trip. A third student stopped by a short time later with another story from Countryside Baptist: Cody Bledsoe had reenacted Tom's murder of Camille at the church, saying, "bang, bang" and "bam, bam," just as he had with Heidi and Rose Bolinger. Boldridge typed up a report about the students' claims and sent it to Detective Carreno.

At 3 p.m., Tom was led into the Jefferson County Courthouse, a homely, two-story building of orange brick in downtown Oskaloosa. It has one large courtroom, a drab chamber surrounded on three sides by cinderblocks painted white, and a second, smaller room, where Tom's hearing took place.

As he scooted along in shackles and orange jail-issue clothes, security was tight around him. Court officials had heard rumors of what they called "vigilantes" plotting to attack him. None appeared.

Tom was formally charged with first-degree murder but was not required to enter a plea yet. Jim Vanderbilt, the thirty-seven-year-old county attorney, asked that he not be given a bond due to the heinousness of his crime. "We need to protect the public from it happening again," he told Jefferson County District Magistrate Judge Dennis Reiling. The judge agreed and ordered Tom held without bond, raising his voice to ensure the defendant could hear him. His next hearing was scheduled for the morning of December 20. It would never take place.

Among the family members in attendance was the elder Floyd Bledsoe, who sat with his head bowed, a hand pressing against his mouth. After the hearing ended, he asked if family members could have a few moments alone with Tom. A jail official declined and Tom was led away to a squad car.

That same day, Jefferson County Undersheriff Jeff Herrig told a reporter that Tom had not confessed to killing Camille, which was untrue. Sheriff Dunnaway, who heard Tom's confession, told a reporter, "He has not confessed to us."

"We have a lot of work to do," Herrig told the *Journal-World*, calling the investigation ongoing. "We'll let the attorneys work out the legal aspects." Despite the mound of evidence piled high against Tom, Herrig and his boss, Sheriff Dunnaway, had strong doubts about Tom's guilt. Dunnaway was Herrig's mentor; the two had worked together for 17 years, since conducting lake patrols in 1982.

To Dunnaway, it didn't add up that a quiet, ardent churchgoer without a criminal history would commit murder. He replayed repeatedly Tom's confessional voicemail messages to Bolinger. "I listened to that tape over and over and he never did say he had killed her."

Then there were the screams Knoebel, the Army colonel, had heard while hunting. On the day Tom was arrested, Dunnaway told the *Journal-World*, "we don't believe [Camille] was out there" near Wild Horse Road, where the screams were heard. But now the sheriff wasn't so sure. Maybe Camille had been killed there and driven several miles to the brome field where she was shoddily buried.

"We were still looking at that area out there to see if there was anything, because we was concerned about the screaming, that I may have another person out there also," Dunnaway said. "I was looking at a map and on that map I seen Zules' property, Zule Dairy, and at that point I had not realized that Zule's dairy was right [at] the area where the screaming was heard and I knew that Floyd worked at Zule's dairy. I felt there was…more to the story than I could put together."

As he pondered the case in his mind, Dunnaway returned often to a short exchange he had with Floyd over the weekend, before Camille's body was found.

"She's dead, isn't she? Do you know if she's dead?" Floyd asked.

"I don't think she is, Floyd," Dunnaway told him.

Dunnaway considered Floyd's discussion of death to be off-putting at a time when his office was working at an unhurried pace to find a teenage girl it believed had ran off with her boyfriend. "I think most people put them thoughts out of their mind and still have hope that she was going to be found. I had hopes that she would be found…be all right. This to me is unusual."

The Bolingers, steadfast defenders of the more outwardly devout brother, Tom, encouraged further investigation of Floyd. Rose Bolinger told police that Camille was scared of her brother-in-law. She, like Dunnaway, thought Floyd was putting on a show, working overtime in the search for Camille to mask his own role in her disappearance.

Rose's brother-in-law, Charles Bolinger, called Captain Orin Turner one day at the sheriff's department to say he couldn't imagine Tom killing someone. The Bledsoe brother was a devout churchgoer, he said, and always helped Charles, who has multiple sclerosis, walk to and from Countryside Baptist. Sure, Tom had seemed unusually tense that Sunday, but he was his usual self that Friday, the day of the disappearance.

Jim Bolinger called Turner, a longtime friend, at home one night. "He said he had been giving the case a lot of thought and he thinks something isn't right about the case," Turner wrote in his notes. "He said he doesn't think Thomas Bledsoe killed Zetta Camille Arfmann. James Bolinger said he thinks Thomas Bledsoe is covering for someone or taking the total blame for something he had very little to do with."

The police captain and the de facto pastor gossiped freely about the case. Bolinger said Floyd was eagerly awaiting his polygraph test. "He wants to be in the spotlight, he wants all the attention focused on him…this is just the nature of Floyd." The rumor, like many that fly around a small town after a tragedy, was not true.

They speculated about the fourteen-year-old victim's promiscuity. According to Turner's notes, "Bolinger said the latest rumor he heard was that Camille was pregnant. I told him we have heard the same rumors at the sheriff's office but we are waiting for the coroner's report before we would know anything and if I did know I couldn't tell him." That rumor, like the last, was far from true. Not only was Camille not pregnant, she was believed to be celibate and had urged other girls to swear off sex until marriage.

They gossiped about Camille's family, speculating that her mother likely chose the cheapest casket possible and pocketed money from the state's Crime Victims Compensation Board. Bolinger told Turner, a detective investigating the crime, that he should interview more of Bolinger's family members, all of whom would vouch for Tom's character. Soon after, police interviewed those that Bolinger recommended.

Turner visited the Bolingers to formally interview his friends about Camille and the Bledsoes. Rose Bolinger told him the girl was afraid to be at home alone with Floyd in the evenings, a claim disputed by Heidi Bledsoe and Camille's friends. Rose said Heidi, whose youngest sister had been murdered the week before, was acting "bitchy and aloof." Like her husband, she hurled rumors about the Bledsoes, many of which made their way into police reports and, eventually, a court of law. She claimed Camille was in a black car the day she disappeared; there is no evidence that's true.

The night before, there had been a memorial service for Camille at Countryside Baptist. As it began, attendees spoke of Camille's sweetness, her altruism. It proved too overwhelming for Heidi, who collapsed into tears and ran outside. Her husband followed, as did Rose Bolinger and Gary Bledsoe Jr., Floyd's cousin. Floyd, too, became overwhelmed, slamming his fists on his thighs. "If only I had been there five minutes earlier," he said.

The statement confused the others. Floyd had said he did not return to the trailer that afternoon. For Rose, it was further evidence of his role in Camille's death. "I didn't have no sympathy for him because it was fake.

It was a show. If someone is grieving, they go off into a corner. They don't pound their legs and put on a show."

Floyd had slept too little and worried too much. He had become convinced that police and parishioners were blaming him for Camille's death; he was at least half right. There was pain and devastation and sadness in his voice, along with confusion at what his brother had done. He and Gary Jr. never stepped back into the church.

***

When Floyd walked into the Jefferson County Sheriff's Department on November 9, the day after Tom was arrested, he was hoping to solidify the murder case against his brother. He had seen a spot of blood on Tom's truck, he told a KBI special agent.

Instead, Floyd was interrogated for the first time, beginning at 8 p.m. and lasting until after midnight. Unlike Tom, Floyd did not have an attorney, due, in part, to his parents' preferential treatment of his older brother. They had long considered him ungrateful and had no plans to help him now. After convincing Floyd to waive his Miranda rights, Detective Carreno asked about Floyd's whereabouts on November 5, the day Camille went missing. Floyd recalled his entire day: waking up at 7 a.m., getting Camille on the bus by 7:30, going to the doctor's office, depositing a check, work at the dairy and a trip to the hardware store.

As Floyd passed Mike Hayes in the hallway at the law enforcement center, Tom's attorney told him, "I'm taking my client off the hot seat and putting you on it," according to Floyd. (Hayes, through his lawyer, has denied saying this.) Just a day after his brother had confessed to the crime, handed over the murder weapon and taken police to the body, the investigation was turning toward Floyd.

***

Carreno, with Sergeant Poppa in tow, followed up his interrogation of Floyd with a search of Floyd and Heidi's trailer and the wooded slice of land it sat on. When he found burnt blue jean fragments, the detective quizzed Floyd about them. They were old and covered in dirt, Floyd said, and he had no use for them, so he burned them.

"I've never known you to wear a decent or clean pair of jeans," Carreno told him.

It was clear to Floyd then, if not before, that he was being investigated for a crime his brother had committed. He lashed out at Carreno, quivering and crying. "You've got to believe me!" Carreno pushed him further, calling Floyd a liar. The fragments would be sent to a KBI lab and tested for blood, Carreno said. "I had nothing to do with Camille's death!" Floyd pleaded.

Inside the trailer, the detective spoke to Heidi. The twenty-year-old led Carreno to a carpet stain in Camille's bedroom, which both believed could be blood. As he did with the jeans, Carreno arranged for KBI testing.

Heidi pulled Poppa aside, out of earshot of the others. She wanted to know if it was safe to have Floyd around their children at a time when he was being questioned about a murder. Poppa wrote in his notes: "I advised her, if we had evidence that Floyd had committed the murder or was involved, we would not put her or their children in danger. We would tell her. She seemed OK with that."

Floyd made his case yet again as Carreno was leaving, telling the detective he was innocent. Carreno challenged Floyd to a lie-detector test and Floyd accepted. He knew his brother was attempting to frame him and he wanted to set the record straight. It was scheduled for the afternoon of November 12, the same day Tom was undergoing a lie-detector test – and the day of Camille's visitation.

Carreno, the lead detective on the case, had suspected Floyd from early on and Floyd knew it. At 10 p.m. that past Sunday, the night Tom confessed, Floyd drove to Zule Dairy to tell Richard Zule he was scared. Unaware that Tom was, at that moment, preparing to lead police to the girl's body, Floyd believed Carreno was attempting to pin the disappearance of Camille on him, a belief exacerbated by paranoia after days of nearly no sleep. It was evident he was exhausted and he looked like hell. Zule told him to go home and get some sleep; he followed the first order if not the second.

"You don't think I did it, do you?" Floyd asked his wife after the detectives left. No, she didn't think he did it. But she wasn't sure. Her sister had been murdered, her brother-in-law arrested and her husband interrogated. It had been the strangest week of her life and Heidi Bledsoe was sure about very little.

***

Floyd could feel the pressure he was under. His cousin Gary had told him to clear his mind but it was no use. His uncle Gary had told him the same thing. Still, the polygraph test dragged on. KBI agent George Johnson's questions were seemingly endless.

"Do you know for sure who shot Zetta Arfmann between November 5 and November 8, 1999?"

"No."

"Did you shoot Zetta Arfmann between November 5 and November 8, 1999?"

"No."

"Were you physically present with Zetta Arfmann at the time she was shot?"

"No."

"Did you take part in transporting Zetta Arfmann at the time she was shot?"

"No."

"Was the gun used to shoot Zetta Arfmann in your possession when she received any of those gunshot wounds?"

"No."

Other questions were interspersed, so-called control questions. At the bottom of his report, Agent Johnson wrote: "It is the opinion of this examiner that Floyd Bledsoe was being deceptive when answering the relevant questions." Floyd was asked if he would like to confess to murder. He refused; there was nothing to confess to.

Floyd was found to be withholding information, not telling the whole truth. There had been a control question that tripped him up: Do you have any knowledge of Camille's death? Well, he thought, *of course I have knowledge of it. Everyone in town knows about it.* But he knew if he answered "yes," police would consider it an admission of guilt and pin the murder on him. So, after much hesitation, he said "no." That wasn't entirely true and the test registered it as a lie.

A few hours before, Johnson had administered the same test to Tom with similar questions and similar answers.

"Do you know for sure who shot Zetta Arfmann between November 5 and November 8, 1999?"

"No."

"Did you shoot Zetta Arfmann between November 5 and November 8, 1999?"

"No."

"Were you physically present with Zetta Arfmann at that time she was shot?"

"No."

"Was the gun used to shoot Zetta Arfmann in your possession when she was shot, between November 5 and November 8, 1999?"

"No."

Tom was found to have flatly lied when he responded "no" to the second question, the most important question of all: "Did you shoot Zetta Arfmann between November 5 and November 8, 1999?" And yet, Johnson wrote in his summary: "It is the opinion of this examiner that Thomas Bledsoe was being truthful when answering the relevant questions."

Sheriff Dunnaway told a reporter that Tom passed his lie-detector test "with flying colors. We kept pushing him closer and closer to the truth, and his answers appeared to be consistent with the truth." Johnson passed along that same message to Vanderbilt, the prosecutor.

Sheriff's deputies told John Kurth, Floyd's attorney, something else entirely, that both brothers narrowly failed the tests, which are not admissible in Kansas courts. Kurth said detectives decided to analyze the results diametrically. "They said, 'Tom, you're close, so we're going to say you pass' and they said, 'Floyd, you're close, so we're going to say you fail.'"

Floyd never went to Camille's visitation that night. Instead, he was arrested at 3 a.m. and held on suspicion of first-degree murder. Dunnaway told a reporter the arrest was based on "information the investigation has brought out." Etched into Floyd's mind for the rest of his life is a time – 1:30 p.m. on November 12, 1999 – the last time he saw his young children. This is what he had told them: "I'll be back. I've just got to go talk to some people. I'll be right back to see you."

At first, Floyd was told he was being questioned, not arrested. Detectives asked about Tom and the brome field where Camille's body was found, not if Floyd had killed the girl. He realized he was being detained when he asked to use the restroom and was taken to a locked cell. When Heidi stopped by the law enforcement center in search of her husband, she noticed his car in the parking lot with the windows down but she was told he wasn't there.

Detective Kirk Vernon with the sheriff's office was tasked with making the arrest. He was a young, relatively green detective with just a few years of experience on the force. He had followed up on several leads during the investigation but remained on the periphery. Still, he knew there was not probable cause to arrest Floyd.

"Typically, when I filled out an arrest report," he recalled sixteen years later as he held the report in front of him, "there's a place at the bottom of the page for the officer's signature where I signed my name. On this one… my name is on there but it's signed differently."

At the bottom of the arrest report for Floyd Bledsoe is a signature: "Arresting Officer Roy Dunnaway by Kirk Vernon." In an audacious move, the young detective had refused to arrest Floyd, leaving the task to his boss, Sheriff Dunnaway.

"I had concerns at that point in time that we had reached a level of probable cause concerning Floyd," Vernon said.

Tom, who had been arrested just three days before, was released on a $2,500 bond. With a simple signature on a dotted line, Camille's killer walked free. A few days later, the first-degree murder charge against him was formally dropped.

"I know it seems like a yo-yo to you guys," Dunnaway told reporters on the day one brother was arrested and another released. "It seems like a yo-yo to us."

Tommie Sue, Camille's mother, was livid. She called police, demanding to know why Tom was walking the streets the day before his victim was to be buried. Dale Arfmann Jr., Camille's brother, drove to the law enforcement center and asked to speak to an officer about the decision. Captain Orin Turner told him the decision was made by the county attorney, not by law enforcement, and "there must have been a very good reason to release Thomas Bledsoe coupled with an agreement with Thomas Bledsoe's attorney." Dale replayed November 5 and November 6 to Turner, telling the captain that someone was always with Floyd; he was never alone.

Dunnaway told reporters that Tom did not know exactly where in the brome field Camille's body was, an indication he was not the killer. Pressed to explain his hunch about Tom's innocence, Dunnaway returned to religiosity. "Church is Tom's life. We found that out from talking to people and from talking to him." Vanderbilt, the county attorney, said he and law enforcement officers had "become uneasy" with the idea that Tom killed Camille.

***

A hundred and fifty people stood around the black casket with silver handles. Pocket-size photos of Camille's classmates were scattered around the coffin next to her body, alongside a teddy bear. A black leather-bound Bible was between her hands.

It was a Saturday, November 13, one week after she went missing and four days after she was found dead in a ditch. The air was still unseasonably warm, as it had been the week before.

"Brief as her life was, she fulfilled divine purposes," Rev. Jim Masqua, an associate pastor at McLouth Church of the Nazarene, told the gathered mourners.

The burial was out of place both figuratively – someone so young, so healthy, being buried by her parents – as well as literally. It was not held at Countryside Baptist, the place where Camille spent more time than almost anywhere, because the church was without an official pastor. An earlier service was held at the church that morning.

"She set the example Jesus would want us to follow," Jim Bolinger had said then.

At the burial service, Masqua spoke directly to the children who had become friends with Camille – and, in some cases, Tom – through Countryside Baptist's youth group.

"You see, this isn't a funeral, this is graduation day. We pass from death unto life. Hallelujah."

"Hallelujah" was the response from the crowd.

FIVE

Floyd Bledsoe went to jail and Tom Bledsoe went free because Tom told a story. It was an impossible story, wholly unbacked by physical evidence, corroborating testimony or common sense. It was, even to the untrained eye, complete fiction. Yet, for reasons that are still confounding twenty-one years later, it was believed by the most powerful people in Oskaloosa.

Within a day of sitting in jail, Tom was tired of it. Like any human in a cage, he wanted out. So, like countless other criminals before him, he recanted his confession. The real murderer, he said, was his brother. The man he had hated since childhood killed Camille, Tom told police.

The fiction he told went like this: On the afternoon of Saturday, November 6, the day after Camille went missing, Tom was driving along rural Osage Road on the northern edge of Oskaloosa when he spotted Floyd's green Chevy Nova up ahead. He stuck his arm out to flag Floyd down and the two cars stopped. Sitting in their vehicles with the engines running and the windows down, the brothers talked.

Tom asked if Camille had been found and was told no. He recommended printing fliers and Floyd informed him that had been done already. When Tom told Floyd that the police were searching for Camille, Floyd got nervous.

Overwhelmed by emotion, Floyd put his forehead on his arm. Tom asked what was wrong and Floyd, shrugging his shoulders, mumbled that Camille is dead.

"I asked him, 'What?' And I don't know if he, or if I heard. He was mumbling and I don't know what he was saying at first – I don't know if he said 'I' or 'we' but I heard 'accidentally shot her' and I asked him, 'What?' And he said, 'she's dead, accidentally shot her,'" Tom would later claim.

Tom, in his story, next asked Floyd if he had raped Camille. Floyd gave a rambling, incoherent answer that included a description of Camille's breasts.

Tom: "What did you shoot her with?"

Floyd: "Your pistol."

"Why?"

"I shot her two or three times, once in the back of the head, twice in the chest."

"Why? Where is she?"

"In the trash dump behind the house, underneath some plywood and trash and dirt."

At this point in the story, Tom said Floyd told him to take the blame for Camille's murder. If Tom refused to take the blame, Floyd would expose Tom's history of sexual perversions.

It was a history that ran contradictory to the strict teachings of Countryside Baptist Church. Though Tom was a virgin and mostly avoided contact with women, as the church suggested men do until they are twenty years old, he had watched pornography and masturbated. Tom had also attempted to have sex with a dog as a child. By some accounts, his repeated rape of the family dog resulted in its untimely death.

At work that day, Tom smelled his gun. As his story goes, he was surprised to find the burnt, smoky smell of used gunpowder. It had recently been fired.

So that night, after work, Tom went to the makeshift grave of Camille on his parents' property. He stared down at the plywood and trash that covered the dead girl, her chest still exposed. In his story, this was done to discover whether Floyd was telling the truth. In reality, he knew who was under the plywood in that brome field.

The only corroborated elements of Tom's outrageous tale are his perversions. The rest was pure fiction and not particularly intelligent fiction at that. Take, for example, Tom's description of the conversation. It occurred between two vehicles, both of which were running. Tom struggled to hear people in quiet rooms. The notion that he would be capable of hearing Floyd mumble into his forearm between running vehicles should have been preposterous to anyone who had met Tom.

Then there is Floyd's alibi. Floyd was handing out fliers with Detective Carreno along a different road from 9 a.m. to 12:17 p.m. and again from 1:48 p.m. to 5 p.m., according to the detective. Around 12:30 p.m., Floyd knocked on the front door of Danielle and Dale Hawk. As the Hawks later told the Kansas Bureau of Investigation, Floyd asked if they had seen any unusual cars along their stretch of Wild Horse Road, about ten miles from where Tom says he met Floyd. A few minutes later, a man by the name of James Gardner saw Floyd talk to his neighbor. Floyd then walked over to Gardner, told him a girl was missing, and asked for permission to search an old trailer on Gardner's property. Gardner also lived about ten miles from where Tom claimed to have met Floyd. There was little to no time for Floyd and Tom to have spoken that afternoon.

Further straining the credibility of Tom's story is Floyd's supposed choice in a confidant. Why, if he were to confess to murder, would he confess to the brother he so disliked? The two had not spoken for months before Camille's disappearance. In fact, Floyd didn't know Tom owned the nine-millimeter he had purchased just two weeks before at a gun show in Lawrence. Not even Tom's parents knew that. Floyd could not have known where his brother kept a gun he was unaware existed.

In the span of a few days, Tom Bledsoe had told two wildly disparate stories. The first, his confession, was a selfless act. It was a plausible story backed strongly by evidence: his gun was the murder weapon, he knew where Camille's body was, his alibi was lacking for the ninety minutes in which she went missing. It was a rare bit of honesty from him.

The second story he told was a wholly selfish act. He had a taste of imprisonment and cared little for it. Facing life in prison, he opted to blame someone else. This story, pointed at Floyd, was unbacked by evidence. Worse yet, it ran contrary to what detectives already knew about the case. Floyd could not have left Zule Dairy, raped and killed Camille, bought the supplies he needed from the hardware store, and returned to Zule Dairy in the time span he was gone. He could not have grabbed a gun he didn't know existed from a truck that was, according to Tom, not near the crime scene, and somehow returned it. He could not have told Tom all of this at a time when he was elsewhere, fruitlessly and tirelessly searching for his missing sister-in-law.

It is unsurprising that Tom, a murderer, would add perjurer to his criminal résumé. It is unsurprising that he would blame Floyd, the brother whom he hated. Considering his limited intellectual abilities, it is unsurprising that the tale he spun out of whole cloth was impossible – an almost comically bad attempt at passing the blame.

What is surprising – baffling, in fact – is that Sheriff Dunaway and Jim Vanderbilt, the county attorney, believed him. They believed a story that ran contrary to evidence, their investigation and common sense. They believed Camille's killer when he said someone else committed the crime.

***

"You have the right to remain silent," Floyd said, reading aloud from the statement of rights before him. He wrote his initials, FSB, neatly to the left.

"Anything you say can and will be used against you in a court of law," he said before again scribbling his initials.

"You have the right to talk with a lawyer and have him or her present with you while you are being questioned." Though no lawyer was present, he wrote his initials.

"If you cannot afford to hire a lawyer, one will be appointed to represent you by the court before questioning, if you wish." He didn't wish. Again, he wrote "FSB."

"You can decide at any time to exercise these rights and not answer any questions or make any statements." This time, along with his initials, he signed his full name to signify he understood his constitutional rights and was waiving them. Below that, Sergeant Robert Poppa signed and dated the sheet. It was 12:46 p.m. on November 13, 1999.

Poppa's handwritten notes from the forty-nine-minute interview span seven short pages. The sergeant began with Floyd's alibi for the time of Camille's disappearance. What time did you arrive at the hardware store? 4:15 p.m., Floyd told him. What time did you arrive back at the dairy farm? Between 4:35 and 4:50 p.m., he told him, detailing his exact route back, road for road. Did you see Billie Summerville? Yes, Floyd said, replaying their brief conversation.

Poppa asked Floyd if he had ever fired a handgun. Yes, Tom's twenty-two caliber when he was a child. He asked Floyd if he had seen blood in the bed of Tom's pickup. It was, after all, Floyd's reason for visiting the law enforcement center, to tell the police about further evidence. He told the sergeant he saw a quarter-sized spot that Monday afternoon, not long after Tom's arrest.

Then the questions turned to Camille, according to Poppa's notes.

I said to Floyd, if during the testing of the rape kit your pubic hairs show up on Camille what will that mean? He said that I had to be with her.

50

I asked Floyd if he had ever purchased a handgun and he said no. I asked Floyd more than once if he killed Camille and he said no. I said, 'Who did?' He said he did not know.

***

The next day, November 14, 1999, nearly a week after Camille's body was discovered, the Jefferson County Sheriff's Department conducted its first full search of the brome field where the body was found. They bagged the bullets that killed her, a cigarette butt, a black Countryside Baptist Church t-shirt, pieces of a black belt and dirt samples. Shell casings from three of the four bullets were found when a detective unknowingly sat on them. Tom's bedroom was searched for the first time, turning up a box of nine-millimeter bullets that matched the shell casings.

Searches of Floyd's trailer and his Chevy Nova were also conducted with help from the Lawrence Police Department. A forensic investigator, Detective Dan Ward, sprayed luminol, which emits a blue glow when mixed with blood. There was no glow in the trailer, however, and red stains in the Nova were found to have come from a baby bottle of juice. There was no evidence a gun had been fired in the car or trailer. The search was a bust.

In their request for a search warrant, Jefferson County detectives made their first attempt at explaining how Floyd might have killed Camille. Their theory imagined Floyd leaving the Winchester hardware store immediately after purchasing items at 4:20 p.m., ignoring evidence he stayed to talk with Karen Edmonds. He then, according to the theory, drove to his trailer before returning to Zule Dairy. The affidavit for a search warrant doesn't state that he killed Camille then, only that she disappeared and that there is a stain in Floyd's trailer that could be blood.

"After Floyd returns home at approximately 12:00 a.m. on November 6, 1999, he had opportunity to put the body in his 1974 green Chevrolet four-door," detectives wrote in the affidavit.

On November 15, Floyd was formally charged with first-degree murder. In a four-page affidavit, rife with spelling errors and typos, Vanderbilt laid out the preliminary case against the defendant. He never mentioned Tom's confession or that it was Tom who told police where they would find Camille's body.

Instead, the affidavit centered around November 12, the day Tom told his fictitious tale. It included the sentence, "Tom passed a polygraph indicating he was not present when Camille was shot or buried." It included no mention of the question Tom was found to be lying about – whether he shot and killed Camille Arfmann – or the inadmissibility of polygraph tests in Kansas courts.

Tom's fiction was the only piece of evidence against his brother. The affidavit referenced two supposed pieces of physical evidence: that spot on the carpet in Camille's bedroom believed to be blood and a spot on Camille's bed believed to be semen. Both spots would later be ruled irrelevant.

Vanderbilt, in his affidavit, never bothered to accurately explain how Floyd could have traveled so far and committed the crime he was accused of, then dumped the body, in the brief span of time he was gone from the dairy. In lieu of an explanation, the affidavit misquoted Richard Zule's quip when Floyd returned: "What did you do, go to Kansas City to get the tape?"

On the same day that affidavit was filed, Sergeant Robert Poppa and a colleague, Captain Mark Roberts, visited Zule at home. Zule told them he didn't think it was possible for Floyd to have committed the crime since he drove Zule's '69 Chevy to the hardware store and returned it spotless.

Elsewhere on that mid-November day, Sheriff Dunnaway pulled up to the home of Floyd Sr. with Mike Hayes, Tom's attorney, around 5:35 p.m. The elder Floyd opened the front gate at Hayes' recommendation. Dunnaway told Floyd Sr. what he had come for: Tom's ammunition clip for the Jennings nine-millimeter and the bullets Tom purchased the day of the murder. The father handed them over without complaint.

***

Even before his arrest, Floyd had a troubled marriage rapidly careening toward divorce. He and Heidi had met at the Old Settlers Reunion, a beloved summer festival on the courthouse square in Oskaloosa, in 1995 when Heidi was sixteen years old and Floyd was nineteen. By the next summer, Heidi was pregnant. To get married, they needed her mother's permission because Heidi was only seventeen.

Floyd's parents liked their new daughter-in-law but Heidi's mother, Tommie Sue, wasn't so sure about her son-in-law. She agreed to sign the marriage license in exchange for a used car from Floyd. When the car broke down, Tommie Sue reportedly attempted to revoke her signature but it was too late. (Tommie Sue has denied this arrangement occurred.)

There was no formal ceremony. In fact, Heidi didn't even know she was getting married. On what would become their wedding day, Floyd said they were visiting relatives in town. As he began driving, he told her they were going to the county courthouse to get married. He asked her not to object; it would embarrass him. "Let's just go through with it," is not the most romantic phrase but it was Floyd's phrase on that day, July 15, 1996. Their belated wedding announcement in the *Oskaloosa Independent* was a mere thirty-seven words long and misspelled Heidi's maiden name.

They had bounced around in search of a town to work and raise their children in. For a couple of months, it was Centropolis, an hour south, where Floyd milked cows. Heidi wanted to move closer to her family so they did, first to Sunset Trailer Park in Oskaloosa, then to a rented house in neighboring Winchester, then to the piece of property Floyd had inherited and dropped a trailer on north of Oskaloosa.

"Oskaloosa was great," Floyd recalled many years later. "It was, you know, a nice, quiet town. Your average small community. Everybody knew everybody, very peaceful."

Still, infidelity led to arguments which led to separations. Around the time of her untimely death, Camille was debating who to live with next. But Heidi Bledsoe, once unsure about her husband's guilt, was now adamant about his innocence.

"I just know Floyd didn't do it," she told reporters at the Jefferson County Courthouse after his arrest. "No. That's not the kind of person Floyd is. There were no problems between Floyd and my sister."

In the days after Floyd was arrested and charged, Heidi was interrogated and accused, by detectives, of helping her husband murder her sister. The emotional rollercoaster she had been on since Camille's disappearance careened further downward. She cried constantly.

Floyd's first appearance before a judge on November 15 was a mirror image of his brother's hearing, without the threats of vigilante violence. He wore a bulletproof vest, just in case, and scooted along in an orange jumpsuit. Cuffs were around his hands and feet and a chain around his waist connected the two sets of cuffs. As he waited, he asked Sergeant Poppa a question.

"Are you still looking into the case?"

"Yes."

"Good. Please keep looking."

The week before, Vanderbilt had told District Magistrate Judge Dennis Reiling that Tom Bledsoe must be held without bond to protect the public from such a heinous criminal. Then, in an agreement between Vanderbilt and Mike Hayes, Tom's attorney, Tom was released, free to roam among the public that Vanderbilt once sought to protect from the threat Tom posed.

Vanderbilt stood before the same judge at Floyd's hearing and demanded the defendant be held indefinitely. "Based on the circumstances standing around Camille's death, the method she was killed and the disposal of the body, the facts say this crime could be committed again. We believe it is necessary to hold him without bond."

John Kurth, of Atchison, had been appointed to represent Floyd. Unlike his brother, Floyd would not be represented by the highly influential Hayes. There would be no private defense investigator combing evidence and conducting interviews in search of exculpatory evidence. The prosecution would have the full weight of the Jefferson County Sheriff's Department, along with KBI agents, at its disposal; the defense would have only Kurth and his law partner. Gary Bledsoe Sr. was livid to hear Floyd's parents had taken out a $60,000 loan for Tom's defense but refused to give Floyd twenty dollars to spend at a jail commissary.

The case had drawn considerable media attention in the week since Camille's body was found, and the brothers' bizarre legal saga was the talk of the courthouse square. At Floyd's first appearance, four television crews, two newspaper reporters and two newspaper photographers were on hand, an unusually large contingent for a routine hearing in rural Jefferson County. Vanderbilt's poorly-written affidavit was sealed, making it unavailable to the press and public, shielding it from the inevitable questions it raised about the razor-thin evidence.

Sheriff Dunnaway and his deputies, meanwhile, continued to investigate the murder, along with KBI agents who had taken to working twelve to eighteen hours each day on the case. "It'll be awhile before we're done," Dunnaway told the mass of journalists. "The way you do this is you look at everybody." When a reporter asked Dunnaway if Tom remained a suspect, the sheriff said, "He may be, he may not be."

Police reports from that time show Tom was not investigated but other men were. On November 17 and 18, detectives seized several items from Gary Bledsoe Jr., including a Glock nine-millimeter handgun, two clips and a sidekick holster.

Also on November 18, Billie Summerville was interrogated by Carreno about his whereabouts on the weekend on November 5. He said he had no idea what happened to Camille, that he had been working at the time of her disappearance. Yes, he had passed the trailer that afternoon, soon after Camille walked off the bus. No, he had not spotted anything unusual. He said he didn't kill Camille, didn't know who did and wasn't present when she was killed. When the detective bluffed, telling Summerville he was spotted driving with Camille on the afternoon of November 5, Summerville didn't take the bait. He maintained that he did not see the girl that day.

Tom's friends, meanwhile, were thrilled to hear of his release. They had spent days confused about how that timid, nearly-deaf Christian man could be charged with murder. Turns out, it was all just a crazy mistake. "I never heard him say a bad word," said Cathy Reid, whose fifteen-year-old child had been saddened to hear of Tom's arrest. "He was always speaking with respect around me as a lady."

Several days after Floyd's hearing, the *Lawrence Journal-World* quoted Reid and other acquaintances expressing their joy at Tom's freedom. "I would trust Tom with my child," said Kathy Reusch, the parent of an 8-year-old. "Yes, I would trust my children with him," added another parent. "My daughter knows Tom. She knows he's a very good man. She's 15 years old. She was very sad to hear what happened to him."

One person who knew Tom called him "a sweet and honest person who wouldn't hurt a fly." Another called the twenty-five-year-old "a good kid" and "very sincere Christian." An acquaintance said, "Tom's life was his church and his belief in God."

On the Sunday after he was released, Tom Bledsoe was back at Countryside Baptist Church for worship. With tears in their eyes, congregants welcomed him wholeheartedly. Jim Bolinger, whom Tom had called to confess his murder to just seven days before, was there with open arms for his friend. When Tom left Bolinger those confessions on his answering machine, he predicted the church would be disappointed. He was wrong.

In the *Journal-World* article, an unidentified acquaintance was quoted as calling Tom "easily intimidated." It was an apt description, due in large part to Tom's intellectual limitations and poor senses. In the eyes of Vanderbilt, it was also evidence of Tom's innocence and, in turn, Floyd's guilt.

Not everyone was at ease with Tom's release. James White, a former coworker and occasional hunting buddy, had made plans weeks earlier to shoot deer with the elder Bledsoe brother. When Tom called to ask if he was still interested, White ignored it, unsure if he wanted to be around the former murder suspect with a gun.

Meanwhile, young Cody Bledsoe's story had changed. The two-year-old boy had heard the adults around him talking about his father's arrest. It had an effect. "Daddy shot Camille. Daddy put her in a grave," Cody told his mother soon after his father's arrest.

Standing alongside Heidi at Camille's gravesite, the young boy looked down at the dirt and told the deceased, "Aunt Mimi, I didn't shoot you. It wasn't me."

SIX

A preliminary hearing in the *State of Kansas v. Floyd Scott Bledsoe* took place on November 29, 1999. For Floyd and his attorney, John Kurth, it would provide a sample of the evidence prosecutors harnessed. For County Attorney Jim Vanderbilt, it was an opportunity to test the viability of his witnesses.

Colonel William Knoebel, the bow hunter who had heard screams the night Camille went missing, was in Korea and could not testify. Kurth and Vanderbilt agreed to enter his testimony into the record.

The county attorney began his opening statement not with November 5, the day Camille disappeared and was killed, but on November 6, the day Tom alleged he spoke to his brother on the side of Osage Road. Vanderbilt told Tom's tall tale and made clear to Judge Dennis Reiling, who had officiated at Floyd's wedding, that it was the premier piece of evidence against Floyd.

"Probable cause lies in Thomas Bledsoe's statement and in the stipulation that a woman was heard screaming at the Zule Dairy where Floyd was working, screaming 'please don't hurt me, somebody help me' and that the body was found on the Bledsoe family trash dump and that he admitted to Tom what had happened," Vanderbilt said.

In fact, Knoebel heard the screams about a half-mile away from Zule Dairy, not at the dairy or in the direction of the dairy, and Floyd had no connection to the Bledsoe family trash dump. He did not visit his parents often. Tom, on the other hand, lived on the property.

Kurth began his opening statement by reminding the court that Tom, not Floyd, was originally charged in the case. He explained the events of November 5 and his client's alibi for the time at which Camille disappeared. The window of time was too narrow for him to have committed a crime, disposed of a body, purchased duct tape, chatted with the owner of Winchester Hardware and returned to the dairy.

"It doesn't add up, judge. It just doesn't add up," Kurth said. "Now, we know he was [at Winchester Hardware] at 4:30 p.m. We know he got back at approximately 5:00 p.m."

Kurth's remarks then took a detour. He described how Floyd and Heidi had a disagreement with Billie Summerville, the man Floyd first believed had kidnapped Camille, after Summerville made sexual comments to Camille. Though Summerville's alibi was seemingly solid, Kurth assumed Tom was physically incapable of kidnapping, assaulting and murdering Camille on his own, and mentally incapable of getting away with it. The assumption among many in Oskaloosa, including some investigators, was that multiple men were involved.

Returning to the topic of Tom, Kurth again reminded Reiling of the voicemail messages on Bolinger's phone, that his story changed only after spending time in jail, that it was Tom who owned the murder weapon and knew where the body was. "Judge, there will be no evidence that this lady was captured or taken against her will by my client. It simply could not have happened the way they propose it, time wise. He didn't kill her. He didn't have the gun."

The first witness to testify for the prosecution was Tom. Vanderbilt turned his microphone up to its highest setting so his star witness would hear him. As he did during the opening statement, Vanderbilt began his timeline on November 6, asking Tom about his itinerary for that day. Tom told of his supposed roadside meeting with Floyd, his brother's supposed confessions, and how he went to the burial site to see if his brother was telling the truth.

He described his itinerary for the next day, November 7, including his confessions to Bolinger, his decision to turn himself in, and his later recantation. He did it all, he said, with Floyd's two young sons, Cody and Christian, in mind.

"I was thinking about Floyd and his two boys."

"What were you thinking about Floyd and his two boys?" Vanderbilt asked.

"That I wanted them to grow up to have a father and a good family and go to church and stuff."

"You were willing to do that for your brother?"

"Yes."

"While you were in jail you changed your mind?"

"Yes."

"Why?"

"Because I realized that if I didn't do that he could turn on them like he did Camille."

When asked if he loved his brother, Tom said he did. But they did not get along, he admitted, because Floyd would tease and embarrass him.

Jerry Kuckelman, a defense attorney who was assisting Kurth, handled the cross-examination of Tom. He began on November 5, taking Tom through his actions that day. After returning "straight home" from Lawrence, around the time Camille was stepping off her school bus, and before attending the church gathering after 6 p.m., there was an almost 90-minute gap in Tom's alibi that he never accounted for, saying only that he showered and got ready. Kuckelman did not press him on this.

Vanderbilt noticed the gap in Tom's testimony. After Kuckelman finished, he asked his witness more questions about his route home that day. This time, rather than saying he went straight home, Tom described a scenic journey, visiting an acquaintance and taking time to look around his favorite hunting spot, even stopping to honk, a way of measuring how thick the woods were with venison. This description, Tom's second in as many hours, shrunk his alibi gap considerably.

When Tom said he took the blame for Camille's murder to avoid the leak of humiliating details about his past, Kuckelman pounced. What could be so humiliating that you would falsely accuse yourself of murder? Tom said he looked at dirty magazines. Was that all? Tom said he looked at dirty movies. Was that all? Tom said he played with himself. Was that all? Tom said he tried to have sex with a dog.

"Sitting in that jail caused you to change your story, didn't it?" Kuckelman asked Tom as his cross examination came to a close. Tom agreed.

"Decided to let Floyd take the blame, didn't you?"

"That I'd tell the truth."

"Decided to let him take the blame, didn't you?"

"That I'd tell the truth."

"Tom, the truth is that on November 5th you actually went over to Camille's house, didn't you?"

"No.

"You didn't see Camille at all that day?"

"No."

"Had you been looking at the dirty magazines that day, Tom?"

"No."

"You went to Camille's house with the intention of raping her didn't you, Tom?"

"No."

"You actually took your nine-millimeter and shot Camille, didn't you?"

"No."

When Vanderbilt returned to the lectern, he had Tom explain his lack of a social life. He very seldom went anywhere in the evenings, Tom said, and socialized with few outside church. He had never been on a date.

In an unusual line of questioning, Vanderbilt then informed Tom that he showed no emotion on the stand, even as he described humiliating details and discussed the senseless murder of a fourteen-year-old girl.

"Why haven't you showed any emotions about the death of Camille Arfmann?"

"Because I hide it."

"How do you feel about the death of Camille?"

"It's a sad thing for a girl her age."

"How'd you feel about her?"

"I liked her."

"How did you feel about Camille?"

"She's a friend."

The next to testify for the prosecution was Detective Carreno. He blandly recalled how he had heard of Camille's disappearance from Poppa and was told of Colonel Knoebel's interrupted hunting trip. In his questioning, Vanderbilt again described the screams Knoebel heard as being near Zule Dairy. He asked Carreno, "What do you know about the Zule Dairy, detective?" to which Carreno replied, "That's the place of employment for Floyd Bledsoe. That was the place in which Floyd Bledsoe had been working that evening."

Carreno walked the court through grainy crime scene photographs from the brome field where Camille was found, photos that would later be described by those who saw them as "horrible," "terrible" and "worthless." Kurth began his cross-examination by going through Dr. Erik Mitchell's autopsy report and asking Carreno if the rape kit came back negative. Vanderbilt came out of his seat.

"Judge, I'm going to object. I believe the officer is attempting to testify beyond his personal knowledge." But Reiling let the testimony continue and Carreno said he didn't know what a test of the rape kit showed.

Rather than keep the conversation on his client or Tom, Kurth steered it to Summerville. He asked Carreno whether he had investigated Summerville's lewd remarks to Camille (he had) and whether charges were filed (not to his knowledge). When Kurth asked if Summerville had made improper sexual advances toward Camille, Vanderbilt again stood in objection, doubting the relevance.

"I think it's relevant. We're talking about Billie Summerville," Kurth said. When Vanderbilt asked why Summerville is relevant, Kurth awkwardly replied, "Well, we want to know why he isn't" and Reiling allowed the question. Carreno explained his investigation into Summerville's alleged advances and Summerville's disagreements with Floyd.

Returning to Tom and the night he led detectives to Camille's body, Kurth asked, "Is it true that Tom confessed to the crime?"

"Not to my knowledge, no."

"Not at all? He didn't say he killed her?"

"Did he come out and tell me that he did? No, he did not."

With the next witness came a bombshell. Detective Troy Frost with the Jefferson County Sheriff's Department revealed he had interviewed Floyd at the law enforcement center late in the evening of November 12 and into the early morning hours of November 13. It was the day Floyd had taken – and supposedly failed – a polygraph.

"He said that he had went to the hardware store, got some tape, gray tape and a sweatshirt and we were talking about that and I think, you know, we just….we talked about the hardware store and when he left and when he got there and then he told me that he had turned to go toward the trailer. He got to the trailer, but he didn't go in, he just turned around and went to work, back to work," Frost said.

The theory that Floyd returned to the trailer that afternoon was uncorroborated and defied the possibilities of time. A dozen days after Camille's disappearance, KBI Senior Special Agent Terry Morgan drove the route from Winchester Hardware to the trailer and from the trailer to Zule Dairy.

Even when speeding at fifty-miles-per-hour down a gravel road – far faster than Floyd could go in a thirty-year-old truck with bad brakes – Morgan's drive took twenty-four minutes, longer than Floyd's drive on November 5. And that was assuming he spent only three minutes at the trailer, nowhere near the amount of time necessary to commit rape, murder and disposal of a body at a house miles away. Morgan would testify for only a few minutes during the trial. He was never asked about that drive.

What Floyd most likely told Frost is that he occasionally went back to the trailer during breaks from work but did not on November 5, 1999. Kurth, who heard a recording of the interrogation, said Floyd was told by Frost that he returned to the trailer. Floyd's response, repeatedly, was "No, I didn't go by the house. I said I thought about going by the house."

If Floyd's recollection of the interrogation is correct, there's a good explanation for why Frost misunderstood what he said: the detective was sound asleep. Frost left the interrogation room a short time later, returned, and asked Floyd if he had heard correctly. No, the suspect told him. "Oh, I must have been mistaken," Frost replied.

Whether true or not, Frost's testimony was more than the judge needed to bind Floyd over for trial. Here was a detective placing the defendant at the scene of the kidnapping around the time the victim was taken. Kurth was aghast. "You're interviewing a guy at one o'clock in the morning?"

"No," Frost said, "I had went in to ask him if he wanted a drink or to go to the bathroom or anything and he didn't so I stayed in there and started talking to him."

"So, you just happened to go in and…ask him if he wanted to go to the bathroom and, by the way, 'here's your Miranda warning, you want to start talking?'"

"No, that – that was already done. I didn't –"

"When did you Mirandize him?"

"Well, I didn't."

"You never – did you ever re-Mirandize him the night of the 12th, early morning of the 13th?"

"No sir, I didn't."

"You just started talking to him?"

"Yeah, I started – you know."

The detective was the third officer to interrogate Floyd that night. He argued, fumblingly, that Floyd was not actually in custody when he was questioned. He was in a lockdown facility; an interrogation room that opens only from the outside. By the time he was charged with murder, Floyd had been interrogated for twenty hours.

The first two witnesses for the defense were Jefferson County Sheriff's Department employees: Sergeant Poppa and Deputy Heather Kyle. Poppa recalled Barney the bloodhound's fruitless search – which included the colonel's hunting area near Wild Horse Road – and Floyd's efforts to find Camille. Kyle, who had recorded and transcribed Tom's answering machine messages to Jim Bolinger, read them aloud in the courtroom.

Robin Meyer testified next, explaining how she came to be the first person to notice Camille's disappearance and recalling the search for her best friend. Richard Zule took the stand after her to explain his '69 Chevy pickup with the two-wheel drive and Floyd's use of it on November 5.

Zule told the court, as he had previously told police, that Floyd left his dairy around 4 p.m. and returned around 4:50 p.m. The drive to Winchester Hardware takes about fifteen minutes in one direction or thirty minutes roundtrip, Zule said, meaning Floyd arrived back about twenty minutes later than necessary. After the wisecrack about Kansas City, Zule chalked the delay up to Floyd's conversation with Karen Edmonds and the sluggishness of his '69 Chevy. "It's an old truck. It don't run real good and the brakes aren't too good on it."

During cross examination, Vanderbilt homed in on Floyd's late night milking cows. Did Zule know if Floyd was really working? Yes, because Zule's wife was there bottle-feeding calves. Should Floyd have been work-ing so late? Yes, it can take up to four hours to milk the cows in the evening. Thanks to his boss, Floyd's alibi for that fateful Friday night was airtight.

The defense's next witness was an odd choice: Tom's best friend. Jim Bolinger explained the prayers for Camille he led at Countryside Baptist on the Sunday after she disappeared and the answering machine messages he heard that night. On cross examination, Vanderbilt had him explain Tom's near-perfect church attendance and Floyd's less-than-perfect attendance.

"How would you describe Tom as far as the way he presented himself in church?" Vanderbilt asked, to which Bolinger responded with one word: "Trustworthy."

"Do you believe that Tom told you the truth on those messages he left on your answering machine?"

"Yes, sir."

"What's that?'

"Yes, sir."

"You believe he shot Camille Arfmann?"

"No, sir."

"What did you believe?"

"I believed that Tom was under conviction after he left church Sunday night, that he'd lied to me and – and Tom didn't like to do those kind of things and he called me to tell me that he'd lied to me and that he knew where Camille's body is."

Karen Edmonds followed with some snippy testimony about why the timestamp on her Winchester Hardware receipts was incorrect, telling Vanderbilt, "Computers don't do a thing for me and I don't do anything with them." In fact, the fifty-eight-year-old Edmonds wasn't even aware the cash register had a clock in it until the clock became relevant in a murder case. Vanderbilt's quest for the simplest of details repeatedly hit a wall named Karen Edmonds.

"The register receipt said it was 5:20 when the purchase was made. It damn sure wasn't 5:20 was it?" Vanderbilt asked.

"I have no way of knowing that."

"There's no correlation between the time the register says and any other time and any other place is there? It's just randomly setting there?"

"As far as I know, yes."

"You don't even know if it ever changes. Every one of your register receipts could say 5:20."

"As far as I know they could."

"I have nothing further."

In his closing remarks, Vanderbilt reminded Judge Reiling of the low legal bar he needed to clear in order to send the case to trial. He recapped Tom's testimony, calling him a "fairly emotionless, monotoned, quiet, slow-talking young man" who didn't miss a beat while testifying and had self-lessly taken the rap so his young nephews could grow up with a father, then turned his brother in to save the lives of those same nephews.

"Is it more than a coincidence that where Floyd Bledsoe worked there was a girl screaming, 'Somebody help me, please don't hurt me?'" Vanderbilt asked, before answering himself: It was not a coincidence. Floyd had told Frost he returned to the trailer and had told Tom he killed his sister-in-law, Vanderbilt said to the judge.

"Again, in a moment of weakness, Floyd Bledsoe told his brother what happened and God only knows why. As you can see from these photographs, if he wouldn't have told his brother what happened, we still wouldn't know where Camille was."

Kurth was given the next word before Reiling made his decision. He began with theatrical flair. "You need to go home and hug your kids and then you need to pray that someone doesn't confess to a murder in Jefferson County and then a week later change their mind and maybe accuse you and you're sitting here in Floyd Bledsoe's place."

Kurth recapped the crucial four o'clock hour of November 5 and his client's alibi for nearly all of it. He noted the state's failure to offer evidence of how Floyd could have gone to his brother's truck, stolen a gun he didn't know existed, used it to commit murder and sexual assault, buried a body, and returned to Zule Dairy in the '69 Chevy during the allotted time.

Tom had sat in jail, found he didn't care for it, and decided to invent a story, Kurth alleged. "Is looking at magazines and movies and the thing with a dog enough to take the rap for a murder case? That doesn't make sense either, judge. It just doesn't make sense and that's in the light most favorable to the state." It was impossible for Tom to have seen Floyd that November 6 afternoon, Kurth said. "The only way Tom was able to talk about [the murder], he either did it or he knows somebody else who did it.

"I pray to God they find something or someone that did it, but this isn't it, judge, and like I said early on, it's going to take some courage but you've got to tell law enforcement, 'Nice try, but go back to work, you've got a lot to do.' That's what we're asking you to do."

Taking the floor again, Vanderbilt made a bold admission about Camille's disappearance, telling Reiling, "The only thing we know for sure is that she wasn't at that home. Had she been abducted? Who knows. You've been presented no witnesses to tell you where she was after that."

Despite this admitted lack of evidence from the prosecutor, Reiling bound Floyd over for trial on aggravated kidnapping as well as first-degree murder and aggravated indecent liberties with a child. Floyd's bond was set at an insurmountable half-million dollars. The trial, it was decided, would be heard by Judge Gary Nafziger.

The front-page headline in the next day's *Lawrence Journal-World* summed up the preliminary hearing succinctly: "Case pits brother vs. brother." Tom's testimony was the only testimony mentioned in the article. Its first two paragraphs explained the oddity:

OSKALOOSA – Two weeks ago, Tom Bledsoe was in the Jefferson County jail, accused of murdering 14-year-old Camille Arfmann.

But Monday, testifying in a Jefferson County courtroom, Bledsoe was the strongest witness summoned by prosecutors against his younger brother, Floyd Scott Bledsoe.

Three days later, a short memo was sent on Jefferson County Sheriff's Department letterhead. It read:

TO: KBI LAB – EFFECTIVE EXAMINERS
FROM: JEFFERSON COUNTY SHERIFF DUNNAWAY
JEFFERSON COUNTY ATTORNEY VANDERBILT
KBI SSA WOODS – CASE AGENT
REF: KBI CASE #0912-227867

Please disregard two prior memo's [sic] from SSA J. Woods and all prior requested exams on all E.C.R.'s in this case.
Refer to the attached pages for requested exam's [sic] on item's [sic] currently at the KBI lab.
Any questions please contact the above persons.
A jury is tentatively set for mid February 2000.

SSA J. Woods was Senior Special Agent Jim Woods, the KBI's lead detective on the Arfmann case. ECRs are evidence custody receipts, forms on which items for DNA testing are listed. Next to each of their names, Dunnaway, Vanderbilt and Woods scribbled their signatures. They were telling the KBI's lab examiners to immediately stop testing evidence for DNA.

Even as they claimed to be investigating the crime, the area's most powerful prosecutor and law enforcement officers were ordering the KBI not to. Just a week before, Dunnaway had told the *Oskaloosa Independent*, "The lab reports are crucial and we are still waiting for those." What that DNA would have shown, were it fully tested, would be the source of speculation for sixteen years.

***

On Christmas Eve 1999, Floyd talked to his two sons from the county jail. When he returned to his cell, the anguish was overwhelming. He began yelling out for a higher power, for God wherever he may be. After forty minutes, he plopped down on the small, hard bed. From there he could see the night sky through a small window. One star appeared in the distance. To Floyd, it was God. He was saying that the end would come. How far away that end was – how far that star was from his window – he did not know. But one day, this would all be over.

***

Eleven days before the trial, an *Oskaloosa Independent* headline read, "Judge rules Bledsoe knew Miranda rights." Judge Nafziger, who would preside over the trial, denied a motion by Kurth to suppress the testimony of Frost, who had not read Floyd his Miranda rights. In a separate motion, Nafziger ruled Vanderbilt would not be allowed to introduce the polygraph results of either brother.

With the trial approaching and his case razor thin, Vanderbilt offered Floyd a remarkable plea deal for someone accused of first-degree murder: just five years in prison. Floyd rejected it the Friday before the trial was to begin. He would not plead guilty to a crime he did not commit.

"I'm pretty sure it was a situation where Vanderbilt thought, 'If he did it, this will make him take the deal,'" Floyd recalled. It was an attempt by Vanderbilt, Floyd believed, to save face. Rather than go to trial with only circumstantial evidence, a plea agreement would eliminate the risk of acquittal. But Kurth knew Floyd wouldn't accept it.

"I was like, 'No,' immediately," Floyd remembers. "I said, 'I didn't do the crime, I'm not doing the time' and Kurth said, 'I don't blame you. I had to bring it into you. This is what they offered. You need to sign here.' That was the end."

Floyd was confident as the trial neared and for good reason. The prosecution had no evidence linking him to the crime and only one witness who would: his brother, a serial liar and the actual murderer. "I just figured the facts would speak on their own," Floyd later recalled. Kurth told Floyd the trial would be "a cakewalk."

Three days before the trial was scheduled to begin, it looked like there might be a delay. Vanderbilt introduced a list of thirty-two additional witnesses, catching Kurth off guard. He did not have time to vet the witnesses, Kurth told the court. The judge offered to delay the start of the trial to grant Kurth more time to prepare. Kurth told Floyd, "I don't believe there's anything that they'll be able to testify to that will harm you," but pledged to delay the trial if Floyd wanted him to. Floyd asked his attorney if he was ready. Kurth said he was "as ready as I'll ever be." There would be no delay.

Vanderbilt, meanwhile, had a problem. He wanted the words of Cody Bledsoe, who had just turned three years old, to be heard by the jury but knew a child so young wasn't competent to stand trial. "Based on what I observed, I didn't believe that I could successfully set the boy down on a stand and ask him questions and get him to respond." He told Kurth that he couldn't draw any information out of the boy and that "it would be fairly difficult for me to get him to say that…it was Tom or Floyd." Kurth, in a move that would later be heavily scrutinized, forged an agreement with the prosecutor: someone else would testify about Cody's words, Vanderbilt would not object on hearsay grounds to the boy's *Tom did it* statement and Kurth would not object on hearsay grounds to the *Daddy did it* statement.

It was a major coup for Vanderbilt, a verbal agreement from the defense ensuring he would be able to admit otherwise inadmissible hearsay testimony: a two-year-old's words.

"At the time, it seemed like a good idea," Kurth recalled nearly two decades later. "Floyd thought it was a good idea but he's not the attorney… it's hard to tell looking back at it twenty-twenty. I probably would not do it now."

SEVEN

April 24, 2000, was a Monday. In Washington D.C., seven children were shot outside the National Zoo by a teenager, Antoine Jones. In Florida, impassioned debates took place over the legal status of a Cuban boy, Elian Gonzalez. Al Gore and George W. Bush campaigned for president. The biographical film "Erin Brockovich" topped the box office. "Maria, Maria" from Santana was the most popular song in America.

And in Oskaloosa, Kansas, the murder trial of Floyd Scott Bledsoe began.

Buzz returned to the courthouse square. Reporters from Lawrence and Topeka made the trip. The one full-sized courtroom was reserved. The defendant entered in a light blue shirt, dark tie and jeans, a bulletproof vest noticeable underneath.

The first step was choosing an impartial jury, no easy task in a town so small for a crime so talked-about. Ninety-six people, a larger than usual jury pool, were to be considered. Vanderbilt and Kurth needed to find a dozen suitable selections among them.

Vanderbilt began by asking if anyone had heard of Camille's murder. Every member of the jury pool raised their hand. Undeterred, he asked a more specific question: "Is there anybody here that has heard of what happened that wasn't in the newspaper or a news telecast?"

One man, Donald Daugherty, raised his hand. Daugherty was a former teacher of Floyd's and felt he could not be impartial. He was removed. Another was the sister of Jefferson County Captain Orin Turner and had discussed the case with him. She was removed.

A neighbor of Floyd's believed she could be impartial but Vanderbilt asked to remove her anyway. Judge Nafziger denied the motion and she was allowed to stay. Leta Noll, who knew Floyd as a frequent customer at a nearby diner, said she could not be fair and impartial and was allowed to leave. James Hasty, who knew Floyd through his father, was also dropped.

The matter became further muddled when Vanderbilt reeled off his long list of potential witnesses and asked if anyone knew them. Hands shot up across the jury box.

"If we turn everyone loose here that knew somebody that was on that witness list, we wouldn't have anybody left," Nafziger quipped, "but just because you know a witness doesn't mean that you can't be a juror in this case."

A friend of the Arfmanns was let go. So, too, were a coworker of Heidi Bledsoe and a distant relative of Floyd. Nine people in all were allowed to leave. But a friend of Sheriff Dunnaway was allowed to stay, as was an acquaintance of the Zules.

Kurth began his jury selection by telling potential jurors, "This is a murder case, there is no getting around it. It's heavy stuff." He later added, "You're deciding the life of a person."

What followed was an abbreviated version of his opening statement. Kurth explained that his client was not the first person arrested for the murder of Camille, Floyd's brother was. That charge was dismissed, he said, and now Tom would be testifying against Floyd. He called it "a tough case" and compared it to that of Susan Smith, a South Carolina woman who drowned her two children in 1995 and blamed a nameless African-American man.

"Remember how she went on TV in front of everybody, asking where her children were and what happened and it was emotional, just like this one will be, and you wanted to believe her because you couldn't believe that somebody would do that to her own children," Kurth said. "Ladies and gentlemen, I'm going to tell you that's the same kind of situation we have here. Don't decide this case until you've heard it all, because you're definitely going to hear two sides."

It was a strange comparison for a defense attorney to make since Susan Smith was undeniably guilty of the crimes she had been convicted of. Floyd, on the other hand, was not. Sitting at the defense table, he was shocked his attorney would compare the two. Floyd had also been televised seeking the public's help in finding Camille before her body was discovered. Now his attorney was comparing that honest plea for help to the murderous lies of Susan Smith. Kurth would later say he was comparing Tom's lies to those of Smith, though few, if any, in the courtroom heard it that way.

Having spent most of his time discussing the case, Kurth made no motions to remove a potential juror. He questioned two jurors at random, felt confident they were impartial, and sat down. Soon after, the dozen jurors

– eight men and four women – and one alternate, a man, were announced. They ranged in ages from fifties to twenties, the youngest just twenty-four. There was a teacher, a UPS driver, a farmer among them.

The jurors were not sequestered. After each day of the trial, they would be free to go back to their homes and families. Despite the presence of a television news camera in the courtroom, Judge Nafziger made clear the jurors were not to watch or read media coverage of the trial or discuss it with anyone outside the courtroom.

After a short break, the trial began with opening statements.

With his round glasses on a round babyface, slick dark hair parted back and to the right, Vanderbilt looked far too green to prosecute a murder case, even a small-town one. He began with a brief recitation of the facts surrounding Camille's disappearance and then delved into the evidence against Tom, not Floyd.

"Tom Bledsoe is responsible for alerting the law enforcement officers to where she was buried. Thomas Bledsoe told the law enforcement officers that he shot her. Thomas Bledsoe is not the defendant here. Floyd Scott Bledsoe, his brother, is the defendant here. Thomas Bledsoe provided us his gun, said that it was the one that was used. [We] got KBI lab evidence indicating yes, it was Thomas's gun that was used," Vanderbilt told the court.

"Tom is going to testify in this trial and he's going to explain what *really* happened. His testimony and the circumstantial evidence – evidence that doesn't directly show somebody watched Floyd Scott Bledsoe shoot Camille, helped shoot Camille, helped facilitate Camille's murder – circumstantial evidence is going to show that the defendant did it."

There were three pieces of circumstantial evidence: Floyd allegedly told two members of the sheriff's department that he returned to his trailer around the time of Camille's disappearance, Colonel William Knoebel heard a woman scream and two-year-old Cody Bledsoe, after his father's arrest, said his daddy did it.

As Vanderbilt correctly noted, a rape kit test came back negative. There was no evidence that Camille had been raped. What he failed to mention is that his office had declined to further test DNA evidence collected at the scene.

"I want to be upfront with everything," Vanderbilt told jurors. "Alls we have is circumstantial evidence that Camille was murdered, that she was kept, she was harmed, and that for some reason whoever killed her had her breasts exposed. Thomas Bledsoe and the circumstantial evidence, putting Floyd where she was abducted, where she was heard screaming, and when the shots were fired in her body, shows that Floyd Bledsoe was involved with her murder and at the end of this presentation of the evidence I'm going to ask that you find him guilty of it."

With broad shoulders and thinning hair, Kurth towered over his small client. He took the floor with a folksy penchant for the phrase "ladies and gentlemen" and great eagerness, overloaded with information he was yearning to blurt out. The prosecution had no hard evidence, a few circumstantial details with more holes than a colander, and their star witness had confessed to the crime. Kurth had a case he could clearly win.

The defense attorney explained how Camille had come to live with Floyd and Heidi, how her grades and spirits had improved in Oskaloosa, and how Billie Summerville's unsettling remarks compelled them to move to the trailer on Fairview Road.

Skipping ahead to the day in question, November 5, Kurth explained his client's alibi for the critical 40-minute span between 4:20 p.m. and 5 p.m., the time Camille went missing.

"What the State is asking you to believe in this case, ladies and gentlemen, is that my client had time from 4:35 until 4:50 to come down from Winchester Hardware, go to his place, grab her and do something with her, and then go back to Zule Dairy in time just like he never went anywhere else. [The] timeline is accurate for going straight from Winchester Hardware to Zule Dairy, period."

Kurth detailed the search efforts for Camille and his client's relentless participation in them, drawing a contrast between the behavior of Floyd and Tom.

"Now, on Friday, the 5th, Tom Bledsoe decides to go to Lawrence. Well, you say, John, big deal. What's so big deal about that?...Guess what Tom buys, ladies and gentlemen? Nine-millimeter shells. Fifty-round box of nine-millimeter shells...Tom Bledsoe, not Floyd Bledsoe, he bought the rounds that killed Camille. It was his gun that killed Camille, period. Tom Bledsoe killed Camille, ladies and gentlemen."

He preemptively cut down Tom's testimony – testimony none of the jurors had heard yet – by mocking Tom's ever-changing story of meeting Floyd on the side of Osage Road and how a nearly deaf man could hear his brother between running vehicles.

"The evidence is going to show, ladies and gentlemen, that at no time could my client have been doing what he was doing to have committed this crime. Time and the facts do not measure up. How many people in prison, once they get into prison or in jail, say, 'I didn't do it, somebody else did?' How many people believe them? Unfortunately, in this case, somebody did because Tom Bledsoe was arrested for the murder of Camille Arfmann first and then the charges were dismissed and then my client was arrested based solely on his testimony, solely on his statement. Ladies and gentlemen, that scares me to death. Because if I couldn't have accounted for my time on the 5th and the 6th when Tom says he was speaking to Floyd, he could have said my name just as easily. I could be sitting in Floyd's place."

As they walked to their vehicles or downtown restaurants during the court's lunch break that day, some jurors were in a daze. Several hours before, they had arrived at the courthouse for an annoying formality – jury duty. Most didn't expect they would be needed. Now they were to decide a case that had been the talk of the town and they couldn't say a word to anyone about it.

When they returned to their seats in the drab courthouse, its cinderblock walls painted white and its lime green benches well worn, Rose Bolinger took the stand. The Sunday school teacher's wife was a witness for the prosecution and convinced of Floyd's guilt.

Bolinger told the court that she and Camille were "very close" friends and she was a confidant of the deceased. When Vanderbilt asked about Camille's relationship with Floyd, Bolinger said Camille had told her in the weeks before she died that she was afraid of Floyd. Floyd's horseplay led Camille to believe he was flirting with her, Bolinger said. "She didn't like to be alone with him at night."

Kurth, cross-examining Bolinger, attacked the prosecution's first piece of circumstantial evidence: the words of two-year-old Cody Bledsoe. He read from a police report Bolinger had filed after Tom's arrest. It made clear Cody first accused his uncle Tom of the crime.

"Rose said Cody told her that Tom shot her, boom, boom, boom, boom, and dumped her in the water," Kurth read aloud. "Tom put his – Cody's – blanket around Camille and also put Camille's blanket around her. Tom put her in a dump truck that goes beep, beep, beep. Tom closed Camille's eyes and he kissed her cheeks. There was red stuff on her legs. Shoes were wet and her shirt was wet."

Bolinger told the court she believed Cody was referring to a dump, not a dump truck, a reference to the brome field where Camille was found. She stressed, as she had stressed to officers before, that she believed Cody witnessed the murder of his aunt. "He had seen it, it was real to him." When Vanderbilt asked if Cody was at the scene of the crime, Bolinger, without any evidence to support her claim, said, "Yes."

"When we would question him, if we said the wrong thing he would say, 'No, no, no.' I mean, he didn't let us feed him words. He knew," she said.

Claudine Boldridge, the school psychologist, testified next. Though she was called as a witness for the prosecution, her testimony included no mention of Floyd. Instead, Boldridge described how students had approached her the day after Camille's body was found to describe allegations of sexual assault against Tom and how, thirty minutes later, a girl told Boldridge she had watched Cody act out the murder of his aunt Millie at the hands of his uncle Tom. "I asked the girl, was this something that Cody was saying took place or was he mimicking this? She said he was just talking about what he had seen."

Floyd's estranged wife, Heidi, was up next. She began by introducing herself as Heidi Arfmann-Bledsoe. Then Vanderbilt had her describe an innocuous encounter between Camille and Floyd on November 3, 1999, two days before her disappearance.

"I was in the kitchen doing dishes and I seen the bus pull up. Floyd was behind them in the green car. Camille got off the bus, started walking up to the house. Floyd then pulled in the driveway. He kind of followed her in."

That was it. That was the entire story. The anecdote had no connection to the events of Camille's disappearance two days later and yet, it had an effect. A juror, asked years later about the case, recalled the testimony vividly with one exception: he recalled Floyd following Camille into the trailer on November 5, the day of the murder, not November 3.

Heidi described the days-long search for her sister and Floyd's tireless efforts. She rebutted Rose Bolinger's claim about Camille fearing Floyd, telling the court she had never heard that accusation before and had no reason to believe it was true. Floyd, she said, treated Camille "like a sister."

Heidi, like Bolinger, described young Cody's imitations of Camille's

74

death, including his insistence that Tom had killed her. Vanderbilt asked Heidi if her son has since changed his story. Yes, Heidi said, Cody now says his daddy did it. The change came, unsurprisingly, after Floyd was arrested for the crime. As the adults around him changed their story, so too did Cody.

Ed Benton was one of those in the room listening closely. In fact, he was one of the twelve most important people in the room: a juror. He was awestruck by Cody's claims that his father had killed Camille. Benton made up his mind right then, on the first day of testimony, that the defendant was guilty. "That boy seen something and that was all we had to go on."

Benton was, like the Bledsoes, a rural man. He had raised three sons, all of whom knew the sound of gunfire from a young age. Sure, Cody was a two-year-old at the time and sure, his story had changed. But Benton was convinced that Cody had watched Floyd kill Camille.

Sergeant Poppa was the next witness for the prosecution. He described his interrogation of Floyd on November 13 and the defendant's repeated insistence that he was not involved in the murder of Camille. The reason he was called as a witness for the prosecution is because he asked Floyd whether he sought a relationship with Camille.

"I asked Floyd is he ever had an affair with Camille and he said, 'Never.' I asked Floyd if he ever thought of having an affair with Camille and he said he did eight to nine months ago. I said what kind of an affair? Floyd said, 'Like the one he has with Heidi, his wife.' I said, 'You mean like a sexual relationship, with children and all?' And he said yes."

During Kurth's cross-examination Poppa was asked whether Floyd actually said yes to the second question, about his thoughts of an affair. Poppa corrected himself. Floyd originally answered no before pausing. "Well, maybe about eight or nine months ago I thought about it once." Maybe if Camille was an adult and he wasn't married, it could happen, Floyd thought.

During much of the hour that Poppa was on the stand, crime scene photos were passed around the jury box. Some showed Camille's lifeless body, her chest exposed. Andrea Albright, a newspaper reporter in the gallery, described the jurors' faces as "stoic."

After brief testimony by Robin Meyer about her comings and goings on November 5, the first day of the trial came to a close. Judge Nafziger reiterated his stern admonition to jurors about not discussing the case, promised coffee and donuts for them in the morning and adjourned until 9 a.m. the next day.

One of the few people sitting on the defense side that day was Gary Bledsoe Sr., Floyd's uncle. Back in the 1970s and '80s, he had been a Jefferson County deputy for six years, an undersheriff for four years and an interim sheriff for a few months. He had worked under Dunnaway briefly, known him for years, and left the sheriff's department in 1983 with high opinions of the place. They had worked the twice-a-decade murder cases the sheriff's department had grown accustomed to, usually involving domestic disputes in trailer parks and always requiring KBI assistance. He had sat in the same witness chair he was now staring at, carrying on about evidence and police procedure. But now he could only watch as his nephew, who he considered to be an innocent scapegoat for his brother's crimes, endured a murder trial. As the first day of testimony ended, a thought crossed his mind: *That's it?*

"The case would have been thrown out and we would have been the laughing stock of the county when I was a deputy." Gary Bledsoe would not watch another day of the trial.

The first day of testimony dominated the front page of the *Lawrence Journal-World*. Next to the bold-typed headline "Trial starts in murder of girl, 14" was a photo of Floyd, his eyes wide with concern, as he listened to testimony. The lead photo showed Sergeant Poppa holding a gun – Tom's gun – as he testified. Heidi Bledsoe, her mouth open and her hands motioning, spoke in a lower photo.

Below a second headline – "Prosecution begins making case against Floyd Bledsoe" – was a bullet point: "The defendant's 3-year-old son may have been the only witness to the killing." The lede contained Rose Bolinger's claim that Camille didn't like being alone with Floyd. Heidi's rebuttal of that claim was not mentioned.

The article quoted at length from Kurth's opening statements informing jurors of Tom's ties to the crime. It also detailed Cody Bledsoe's storytelling; how the boy, now three years old, told anyone who would listen that his uncle Tom killed his aunt Mimi and how that story changed after his father's arrest.

In Topeka, the *Capital-Journal* began its article with the same information under the front page headline "Toddler may have witnessed slaying." Its third paragraph: "In the first day of testimony Monday, several witnesses told the eight-man, four-woman jury that Floyd Bledsoe's older son, Cody, began relating details of a shooting two days after his 'Aunt Mimi' disappeared."

Just off Oskaloosa's courthouse square sits a shabby, cramped green cinderblock building. It looks like a storefront that has lost its retail appeal; it had been a snack shop when it opened in 1953. There are only a few small rooms inside. Its occupants keep a pot of coffee warm in case someone wants to drop in and tell them a story.

The *Oskaloosa Independent* was printed then and is printed now on Thursday. Each edition includes its tagline: "Six Months Older Than The State Of Kansas." It was founded in 1860, a half-year before Kansas became a state.

Jolie Kearns, a cub reporter covering the Bledsoe trial for the *Independent*, was a graduate student in architecture from neighboring Valley Falls who took the job as a break from school. Her bachelor's degree from the University of Kansas was in architectural studies. The *Independent* would not print for several more days, allowing her a broader perspective over a strange trial than the daily reporters.

***

When court reconvened the next morning, Dorothy McClung was placed on the witness stand. The bus driver explained, with the aid of a diagram, the route she took on the day Camille disappeared, the time she dropped the girl off (4:20 p.m.), and the thick timber that prevented her from seeing whether anyone was waiting for Camille.

"There was always a lot of stuff around the house, no particular vehicle that I ever noticed, and since she was a high schooler I wasn't concerned about who was meeting her, you know," McClung testified.

"I know the day before there was a vehicle there in the driveway that met her, it was her mother, because I asked Camille when she got off the bus. I said, 'Who is that?' She said, 'It's my mom.' So I thought, okay, but that's the only time."

Next up was Detective Troy Frost, who had interviewed Floyd in the late evening of November 12 and early morning of November 13 without Mirandizing him. Frost reiterated his claim that he had no interest in interrogating Floyd, that the two were "basically just kind of BSing."

"At one point during the investigation," Vanderbilt asked, "did he indicate to you whether or not he had gone to the trailer that day?"

"At one point, yes."

"What did he say?"

"He said he had went to the – he said as he was leaving the hardware store there's a turnoff to go by the trailer. He went toward the trailer, pulled in the drive, backed out and left."

Frost told the court that his interrogation of Floyd was videotaped. The videotape, however, did not pick up Floyd's alleged admission. A microphone mounted inside a smoke detector was the only audio device in the room. Frost called the room's acoustics "terrible," the video quality equally "terrible" and the audio entirely unidentifiable.

Frost's interrogation began at 9:28 p.m. and lasted until 1 a.m., three and a half hours. The questioning contained some bizarre moments, such as when Frost held Floyd's hand to comfort him and when the detective told Floyd to tell Camille's spirit that he loved her. "Tell Camille you love her. Tell her. Say it."

So Floyd said it. He said he loved his sister-in-law. To the prosecution, it was evidence that Floyd sexually desired the fourteen-year-old.

On cross-examination, Kurth, who had attempted to listen to the videotaped interrogation of his client, cut through Frost's testimony. On several occasions, Floyd stated adamantly that he did not go to the trailer, Kurth noted. Frost admitted his mistake at one point during his conversation with Floyd, telling the defendant, "Oh, I thought I heard you say that. I must have misunderstood you."

By the time his cross-examination of Frost neared the end, Kurth had diminished everything Frost testified to about his conversation with Floyd. Still, he wasn't done. Wasn't Frost around when Tom was arrested and interrogated by the Kansas Bureau of Investigation, Kurth asked. Hadn't he heard Tom tell a KBI agent he killed Camille?

"Yes, sir," Frost responded.

"[Tom] said, 'I did it, I killed her.' Is that correct?" Kurth asked him.

"Yes."

All Vanderbilt could do in response was ask meekly whether Tom had said, "I killed her" or "I shot her." Frost didn't know the answer but Kurth's point was well-taken. Jurors had been reminded of who confessed to killing Camille and it wasn't the man at the defendant's table.

William Knoebel, the deer-hunting Army colonel, had traveled from Vermont, where he was now a professor of military science at Norwich University, to testify about the screams he heard that warm night in November. Alternating between military time and standard time, he meticulously detailed what he heard, where the property was, when nautical twilight occurred that evening, atmospheric conditions, the cardinal direction he was facing at every turn and anything else he could recall.

It was the most articulate testimony of the trial. Knoebel was an intelligent, knowledgeable expert on terrain, sights and sounds, and one who was disturbed by what he heard that night. As Sheriff Dunnaway later put it, if Knoebel told him the color green is actually red, Dunnaway would believe it is red.

"It was very clear to me that somebody was in distress. I mean, there was no doubt about it," Knoebel told the court. Vanderbilt tied the screams Knoebel heard to Zule Dairy, where Floyd worked that night, by noting their relative proximity. Kurth pointed out that Knoebel had not heard any gunshots or seen anyone in distress that evening.

Scott Harries, a longtime friend of Floyd and a coworker of Heidi, was the next witness for the prosecution, though he could just as easily have been a witness for the defense. He described the long search for Camille and Floyd's tirelessness. He testified that Floyd is not a violent person and was deeply concerned about Camille's well-being the night she disappeared. Harries was among the men who stopped traffic with Floyd as they questioned passersby, holding fliers with the girl's photo on it.

When Richard Zule walked to the witness stand, Vanderbilt's intent was clear: to home in on the time Floyd was out of his sight. Zule said Floyd left around 4 p.m. and returned at 4:50 p.m.

"How long should it have taken him to go to the hardware store?" Vanderbilt asked Zule, to which he replied, "Probably twenty-five, thirty minutes." In other words, it took him longer than Zule had expected, Vanderbilt said.

On cross-examination, Kurth refreshed Zule's memory. Had Floyd explained why it took slightly longer than expected? Zule recalled his conversation with Floyd after he returned, how Floyd had told him about his talk with Billie Summerville, his chat with Karen Edmonds, his selection of a sweatshirt. "So that kind of fit, right?" Kurth asked. Zule agreed; the timeline made sense.

Zule heard no screaming that night, he told the court. When Floyd returned from the hardware store with his truck, he saw no blood, no dead bodies, nothing out of the ordinary.

After a short break, jurors returned to their seats to hear testimony from Captain Orin Turner, the close friend of the Bolingers who oversaw investigations at the Jefferson County Sheriff's Department. Turner had a story to tell the court.

According to Turner, Floyd walked into the law enforcement center on the morning of November 8, soon after Tom had led officers to Camille's body. Tom was in jail and Floyd, according to Turner, wanted to know how the investigation was going. After being told no officers were available to talk to, Floyd began incriminating himself, Turner claimed.

Floyd allegedly told Turner that he had narrowly missed the moment Camille stepped off the bus, arriving at the trailer five minutes late. If he had arrived at the trailer sooner, she would still be alive, Floyd said.

"You went to the trailer?" Turner asked, according to his account.

"Yes, and she was nowhere to be found," Floyd responded.

"Be sure and tell the officers that when they interview you," Turner said.

If true, it was a bold admission by Floyd: he had been at the trailer immediately after Camille was dropped off. It certainly was enough reason for detectives to interview Floyd about what he saw. And yet, Turner, by his own admission, did nothing with this information. Only after Floyd had been arrested, charged and sent to trial did Turner tell anyone about the supposed conversation.

It was the second time that day jurors had been told by a Jefferson County investigator that Floyd admitted going to his trailer around the time Camille disappeared. In both instances, no credible recording of the conversation occurred. In both instances, Floyd allegedly whispered his secret to a single officer outside earshot of anyone who could corroborate the account.

On cross-examination, Turner failed to recall even basic details about the conversation he allegedly had with Floyd. Reading from Turner's police report, Kurth said Floyd told the captain he saw the school bus while driving to the hardware store.

"Now, he never mentioned any hardware store to me," Turner interjected. His police report, which was supposed to be a recitation of his conversation with Floyd, was actually a paraphrase of other details Turner had been told by detectives, Turner said. The police report claimed Floyd talked to Billie Summerville at the hardware store but Turner said Floyd never told him that. He was disputing his own written words as Kurth read them aloud.

The next witness was Billie Summerville, a man Kurth was still suggesting could have killed Camille. He walked through his alibi for November 5; how he, his father and another man had constructed a barn roof on Paradise Point at Lake Perry, about ten miles northwest of Oskaloosa. Billie and Charlie Summerville had arrived around 7 a.m., worked through lunch and drove into Oskaloosa around three o'clock that afternoon. Around 4 p.m. or 4:15 they went to Winchester Hardware for parts, where they saw Floyd. They stayed ten minutes before an early dinner at the Downtown Café, an eatery Billie's mother owned. Returning to Paradise Point, they worked until the sun set over the lake, its orange orb sinking into the horizon.

"You knew Camille Arfmann?" Vanderbilt asked.

"Yes."

"Did you have anything to do with her disappearance?"

"No, no."

Summerville learned of Camille's death when his mother called to say police had found her. "That's good," he recalled saying. "No, it's not; she's dead," his mother said. Summerville mistakenly told the court this conversation took place the next day, November 6, which was two days prior to when officers found the body. The comment was likely the result of confusion on the part of Summerville; he stammered through much of his testimony.

During cross-examination, Kurth didn't ask about Camille's previous allegations against Summerville. He instead asked if Summerville had passed Floyd's house on the way back from the hardware store. Summerville said he had.

"You didn't see anything?" Kurth asked.

"No."

Charlie Summerville testified after that, verifying his son's alibi for that day: the 7 a.m. start time, the 3 p.m. drive, the 4 p.m. stop at the hardware store for foot-long bolts, and finishing at dawn. Kurth asked just one question of the elder Summerville: "Were you aware that Zetta Camille Arfmann – the young girl that got killed – were you aware that she had made a complaint against your son Billie Summerville in May of 1999 when they lived at (Sunset) Trailer Court?"

"No, sir. No, sir," Charlie Summerville responded.

One of only two officers from outside Jefferson County to testify was Gil Crouse, the Lawrence patrolman who was working off-duty security at a Conoco gas station in the early morning hours of November 6. Sometime between 2 a.m. and 3 a.m., Floyd came into Lawrence looking for Camille and ran into Crouse.

"He said that he was out looking for a teenage girl who had been missing, asked me if I had seen a certain vehicle, if I saw it to get ahold of somebody, and that he was going to go look for them at a bar there in town," Crouse testified.

"He told me that he thought she might be with an individual by the name of Summerville and that he was going to go to Coyote's and look for them. He made a statement: if he catches them together, he's going to kill him."

Crouse suggested Floyd file a runaway report; Floyd told the officer he already had. "He looked extremely tired, basically like someone that had been awake for a long time, and seemed to me a little bit overly excited about a runaway teenager, but that's from my standpoint.

"At that point, I advised him that if he went to Coyote's and found them there the best thing to do would be call the police department and let us come out and handle it because he was obviously very upset and I was trying to avoid problems out there."

Dale Arfmann Jr., a brother of Camille and brother-in-law of Floyd, testified next, primarily about the long search for Camille that began late in the evening of November 5. Vanderbilt asked several times about Floyd's whereabouts while others searched. Each time, Arfmann explained Floyd's own search efforts.

The nineteenth witness for the prosecution was the one so many people had been waiting to hear from, the one at the center of it all. Journalists scooted closer to the edges of their seats. Jurors prepared for hours of testimony. The attorneys reached for their notes, knowing the outcome of the trial could hinge on the words of the next witness.

And Vanderbilt said, "The State calls Thomas Edward Bledsoe."

EIGHT

At the attorneys' lectern, the microphone was adjusted to its loudest setting. Tom was told that if he still did not hear a question he should let the court know, rather than rely on lip-reading, as he tended to do. He wore blue jeans and a plaid collared shirt, his copper red hair parted to the right.

The two brothers – Tom and Floyd, Cain and Abel – were in the same room for the first time in five months. They were the only two people in the room who knew with absolute certainty that Floyd was innocent. The killer was on the witness stand.

By a mix of poor hearing and low intelligence, Tom was confused from the start. Yes, he was a security guard at Farmland Industries in Lawrence, he said. Fifteen seconds later, when asked if he was a security guard, he said no. Then he corrected himself – yes, he was a security guard at Farmland and still is.

Vanderbilt's questions coasted him through his alibi for November 5, 1999. There was the trip to Farmland to pick up his paycheck, the stop by Lunker's Bait and Tackle to look at rifles. Then on to Rusty's Outdoor in Lawrence to buy ammunition for his Jennings nine-millimeter, the same gun that would be used to kill Camille, though he did not add that, of course.

His testimony described a long and scenic drive home that included a stopover at his favorite hunting spot to scan for deer, turning a thirty-five-minute drive into one that lasted well over an hour. If true, the alibi would have placed Tom far west of where Camille stepped off her school bus around the time that she did.

No one corroborated Tom's alibi during the trial and no one has since. During the two-and-a-half-hour window between when he left Rusty's after 3:30 p.m. and when he arrived at the church retreat at 6 p.m., no one could verify where he was or what he was doing.

Attempts to prove Tom was not in Oskaloosa were debunked before the jury. A receipt from Rusty's, which had been provided to police by Tom's attorney, Mike Hayes, showed he bought the bullets at 4:30 p.m. However, an investigation found the cash register's clock was 45 minutes fast, meaning Tom left the store around 3:45, giving him enough time to get to Oskaloosa soon after Camille was dropped off at 4:20.

Tom claimed under oath that he called his father from the Rusty's parking lot in Lawrence around 4:25 p.m. and his phone records did display a call to his parents' phone number at that time. However, the phone records show the number coming from the Topeka service area – which includes Oskaloosa – not the Lawrence service area. The Topeka service area showed up another time in Tom's phone records: when he called Jim Bolinger from the Jefferson County police station parking lot to confess. His phone call to his father didn't occur in Lawrence, it occurred in Oskaloosa.

At Vanderbilt's insistence, Tom told jurors every dishonest detail of how he met Floyd on the side of Osage Road the next day and heard Floyd's confession.

"I asked him, 'What's wrong?' and he said, 'She's dead,'" Tom said.

"Why is she dead? I asked him if he raped her or sexually abused her…he said, 'Yes, no, I don't know.' He recalled her shirt being above her breast…I asked him, 'What'd you shoot her with?' And he said my pistol."

Floyd, in the story, told Tom to take the blame for Camille's murder or else he would expose Tom's perverse past. "I was shocked, confused, angry," Tom told the court.

He said, as he had before, that he smelled his pistol during a work break, noticing "a burnt, smoky smell" and checked the brome field after work. There he saw shovel marks and plywood out of place. "I thought about calling the police, telling them what to do, or just keeping my mouth shut for now…I had a lot of questions running through my mind."

Returning to truth-telling, at least temporarily, Tom described his humdrum Saturday night and Sunday: how Jim Bolinger had asked him and others to pray for Camille during the morning service, how he and his father had moved machinery during the day and how he returned to Countryside Baptist that night for the evening service.

"Was two or three of us gathered around," Tom said, recalling a conversation after church. "[Jim] was talking and he made a comment that if he knew where Camille was he'd go get her, bring her home, and he said, 'Right, Tom?' Using me as an example."

From there, Tom drove to the Jefferson County Law Enforcement Center to turn himself in. From the parking lot, he called Bolinger and left the answering machine messages. In the courtroom, it was Vanderbilt, the prosecutor, who would require Tom to read transcripts of those messages aloud. He did so dutifully.

He recalled, also, his conversation with his father. Tom said he told Floyd Bledsoe Sr. "that I knew where Camille was and that she was dead." When asked if he told his father he had killed Camille, Tom said he couldn't remember.

"Tom, did you kill Camille Arfmann?" Vanderbilt asked.

"No, sir."

"Why did you leave those notes, those messages on Jim Bolinger's answering machine?"

"Because I didn't want people to know about my past."

Vanderbilt asked why jurors should believe Tom after hearing him read aloud his confessional messages. He paused for more than fifteen seconds before saying, "I have no reason to hurt Camille or anything."

"At one point during an interview, did you tell Senior Special Agent George Johnson with the Kansas Bureau of Investigation that you did it, that you shot Camille?"

"Yes, sir."

"Did you tell him the truth?"

"No."

. . .

"You eventually told the Sheriff's Department what actually happened. Is that correct?"

"Yes, sir."

Vanderbilt led his star witness through some tough terrain. He consistently referred to Tom's tall tale about the roadside meeting as "the truth," asking Tom how long after his arrest it took to tell *the truth*. In some moments, Tom had a hard time following the path the prosecutor was laying for him.

"It wasn't until awhile after [your arrest] that anybody gave you the opportunity to do that?" Vanderbilt said after another reference to "telling the truth." "Do you remember?"

"What do you mean?" Tom asked.

"Did you speak to somebody after that about it?"

Tom, catching on, said, "No one gave me a chance."

Vanderbilt had the unenviable task of portraying a man who had confessed to killing a fourteen-year-old child as a credible and somewhat sympathetic witness. He did so by homing in on Tom's explanation for why he turned himself in: to help his nephews.

"I thought about, because Floyd had family and I didn't, I wanted his kids to grow up to have a father in the home, someone to care for them, and I didn't want the family to split up," Tom testified.

Why, then, did Tom eventually agree to talk about the roadside meeting with his brother, Vanderbilt asked. Tom answered as the prosecutor hoped he would: "Because I realized that if I didn't say anything, those two boys may be subjected to what Camille had been through."

As the court took its afternoon break, Vanderbilt had done what he could to give jurors a lustered opinion of his star witness. Sure, Tom had gotten mixed up, he was suggesting to them, but he wasn't a killer. In fact, he knew who the real killer was and wanted to protect innocent children from him.

***

When the jury box was full again after the break, Vanderbilt delved into Tom's personal life and the extent of his acquaintance with Camille. They both attended church anytime the church doors were open, Tom said. Did they participate in activities together? "She went her way, I went mine." Did they associate outside church? "Very seldom" and only when she visited with Floyd or Heidi.

"When you're not at church and you're not at work, you appear to be helping your family. Is that an accurate statement?" Vanderbilt asked. Tom agreed it was.

Tom said Camille always smiled when she saw him, the way she smiled when she saw everyone. She treated him with respect and he did the same in return. They had never argued or fought. She was pretty, yes sir, but no, he had not tried to date her.

With that, Vanderbilt's testimony was over. John Kurth stood for what everyone expected to be a cutting cross-examination. It was.

Kurth began by highlighting a contradiction in Tom's testimony, albeit a comparatively minor one. Tom had previously said he met Floyd on the side of Osage Road between 1:00 p.m. and 1:30 p.m. on November 6. During the trial, however, he said it was sometime between 11 a.m. and 1 p.m. Tom claimed ignorance of the time, saying he wasn't paying attention to it, and ignorance of his previous statements, saying he couldn't recall them.

The nine-millimeter that was used to kill Camille was purchased two or three weeks prior, Tom testified, and no one knew he owned it. He hated his brother, Tom said, because Floyd teased him. The two had not spoken in at least a month before Camille's murder.

Kurth questioned how Tom, who was struggling to hear words spoken into a microphone in the courtroom, could have heard his brother's mumbled confession on the side of the road. Tom held firm, repeating his claim that he heard Floyd say he killed Camille.

"Your story, [you] made up your story," Kurth said, "because you sat in that jail for a week and you didn't like it, did you? Didn't like sitting in jail for a week, did you?"

"No, sir," Tom said.

"So, you decided you're going to tell on your brother…decided you're going to make up a story on your brother –"

"No, sir."

"– so you can get out? And that worked, didn't it? You got out?"

Vanderbilt objected to the questions because they were compound, giving Tom a brief reprieve from Kurth's interrogation.

The defense attorney turned to Tom's inaction after the supposed roadside meeting. Why was Tom scared of Floyd when it was Tom who had a gun behind his seat? How could Tom go on with his day and let Floyd drive away after hearing what he had supposedly heard?

"Why didn't you just pull out the gun and say, 'Let's go to the sheriff's office, we're going to take a little walk?'" Kurth asked. Tom said he didn't consider that option at the time.

Tom had told conflicting stories about the night of Saturday, November 6, 1999. On three occasions he told Detective Carreno that he went to the brome field to find out if Camille truly was there, moved plywood around and saw the skin of the deceased. In his testimony, however, he said he moved only a single piece of plywood and never saw Camille's body. Under oath, Tom admitted he had lied to the detective to make his story sound more credible.

"Are you telling the truth to the jury now or are you lying to them?" Kurth asked. Tom said he was telling the truth now.

Kurth noted another contradiction from Tom. During a preliminary hearing, he testified he had not watched a pornographic film in five years. During the investigation, he told Carreno he rented porn a couple months before the murder, even naming the adult store he had borrowed it from and the Lawrence store where he made a copy. An X-rated film was found in the heap of trash that Camille was buried under.

"So, which is the truth? Had it been five years or just a couple months before?" Kurth asked. Tom said it had been three or four months before. He had lied under oath at the preliminary hearing. Though his porn habits were of little interest to the case, Kurth was showing jurors that the prosecution's star witness was a liar, possibly a habitual one.

Returning to the tall tale of the roadside meeting, Kurth again said Tom was like most inmates; he didn't like jail and did what he could to get out. He called Tom's claims of protecting Floyd's sons "not really true," noting Tom had considered picking up one of the boys, Cody, from Floyd's trailer but not the infant son, Christian.

"Does that make any sense to you, if you're scared…for both boys? Doesn't really, does it?" Kurth asked. Tom said, "I wasn't thinking."

Backing up to the morning of November 6, when Tom and his parents learned of Camille's disappearance, Kurth asked why Tom had not helped find the girl. Like his father, he claimed it was none of their business.

Catching Tom in another lie, Kurth asked about a shovel he had found along a fencepost near the brome field and trash dump. Tom, in his attempts to implicate Floyd, had told Carreno there was fresh dirt on the shovel the night of November 6. Now he backtracked, admitted under oath that was a lie, saying he never checked to see if there was dirt on the shovel.

Tom had also told Carreno he loved Camille, was infatuated with her, wanted Camille to be the first girl he slept with. In a burst of questions, Kurth asked about this but Tom didn't know what the word "infatuated" meant, couldn't remember telling Carreno that and denied saying he wanted to sleep with Camille.

"Every time you talked to Detective Carreno was a lie?"

"No, sir."

"The only time we're hearing the truth is today, is that your testimony?"

"No, I told Carreno the truth."

"Which time? You gave three statements. I'd like to hear which one was the truth."

"All the ones except with the lies that I told him was a lie."

"That doesn't narrow it down much, does it, Tom?"

Had Tom also lied when he told George Johnson, the KBI agent, that he killed Camille? Yes, Tom said, that too was a lie. Kurth was again making it clear to jurors that Tom routinely lied. Tom's only defense was to say he had lied previously, sure, but he was telling the truth now. With that, Kurth ended his cross-examination and Vanderbilt stood again.

The prosecutor wanted to talk about the receipt that was forty-five minutes fast – the receipt that showed Tom leaving Lawrence around 3:35 on the day Camille disappeared, putting him in Oskaloosa just as Camille stepped off the bus. "That's not possible, is it?" Vanderbilt asked.

Unfortunately for the prosecutor, it was and Tom's testimony proved so. He had picked up his check from work around 2 p.m., stayed about fifteen or twenty minutes, went to Lunker's and stayed about the same length of time, and then to Rusty's. All three stops were in Lawrence and none of them took more than twenty minutes, according to Tom's testimony. It was not only plausible that Tom left Rusty's at 3:35 p.m. and returned to Oskaloosa by 4:20, it was true.

Kurth had a few more questions about the gun Tom kept in his truck, the gun used to kill Camille. The questions reiterated that no one knew the gun was there, least of all Floyd. Tom said, "I don't know" a few times and Kurth ended his cross-examination. Tom's testimony, which had lasted three hours – much of the afternoon – was over.

Before the court adjourned for the day, a Floyd Bledsoe took the stand, though not the one on trial. Fifty-five-year-old Floyd Laverne Bledsoe, Tom and Floyd's father, donned faded black jeans and a blue t-shirt. Crossing his legs, he rested his white cowboy hat on his left knee in the witness box.

Yes, he knew Camille but no, she didn't visit his house often, he said. Floyd Sr. explained his whereabouts on November 5, how he and his wife had served food in Tonganoxie, twenty miles to the southeast, between 4 p.m. and 10 p.m. When they returned, Tom was sound asleep, he said.

The next morning, the younger Floyd called to say Camille was missing. "He wanted to know if we had seen or heard from her." Floyd Sr., like Tom, considered it to be none of their business, he testified. "I asked him if she maybe could have run off with her boyfriend."

That afternoon and evening, they babysat Christian, their youngest grandchild. Heidi and Floyd's oldest son, Cody, felt uncomfortable and asked to remain with his mother instead. The next night, Tom called him from the police station parking lot to confess.

"What he told me is he knew something about Camille's body. I told him I didn't want to hear nothing else about it. I didn't want to know nothing else about it."

Brandi Wampler was the last person to testify that day. Wampler had babysat both Cody and Christian for a dozen hours on November 5 and into the overnight hours of November 6. She babysat for an additional six hours that morning as Heidi and Floyd continued to search for Camille. Her testimony should have made clear to all watching that young Cody Bledsoe could not have witnessed Camille's murder.

Vanderbilt asked Wampler about a phone call she had with Camille in the week before the girl's disappearance. Camille, according to Wampler, "had mentioned something about [how] she was scared to be home at night with Floyd."

"She didn't tell me why. She just mentioned that she didn't like being home alone with Floyd at night while Heidi was working and that's all…she didn't tell me why or what or anything like that."

Kurth asked no follow-up questions. Wampler walked out of the witness box and the trial's second day came to a close.

For the reporters in the gallery, the clash of brothers was the focal point, and understandably so. A photo of Tom testifying dominated the front page of the *Topeka Capital-Journal*. Under it, a headline: "Brother related confession." In her lede, Andrea Albright wrote that Kurth "appeared to rattle the prosecution's main witness." Tom, she noted, was vague in his answers and couldn't remember important details.

A *Lawrence Journal-World* headline across the top of page one was blunter: "Tom Bledsoe seeks to explain lies." Reporter Joel Mathis explained Tom's contradictions, how he claimed on the witness stand that he had previously lied to investigators, embellishing details to better sell his story to detectives.

NINE

The third day of trial in the *State of Kansas v. Floyd Scott Bledsoe* was a Wednesday, April 26, 2000. Participants, jurors, reporters and onlookers made their way to the cinderblock courtroom by 9 a.m. as they had the two days before. Judge Nafziger called his court to order and Vanderbilt called his next witness.

Erik Mitchell had wispy blonde hair and an equally blonde mustache. He was a coroner in Topeka but sometimes traveled to rural counties like Jefferson that lacked a coroner. His work in forensic pathology was so well-known in northeast Kansas that Vanderbilt and Kurth stipulated to his qualifications to save on time.

Mitchell's qualifications were hardly unimpeachable, however. Seven years earlier, he had been investigated by several state agencies in New York for removing organs from corpses without permission from families, among other ethics concerns. The district attorney in Syracuse launched a four-month investigation into Mitchell, the county's medical examiner at the time, after it was discovered a man convicted of child pornography had been given unauthorized access to the medical examiner's office and took photographs of himself with a corpse. The investigation also found employees at the morgue had taken playful photos of themselves over the body of a female suicide victim and provided a university hospital with bladders and kidneys from 150 bodies, in many cases without the consent of family members.

Years before that, Mitchell was investigated for allowing an employee to boil human bones on portable stoves in an outdoor parking lot. Three top assistants later accused him of bizarre, unethical and illegal behavior, such as allowing 100 pounds of volatile mercury to be stored in improper containers and ordering workers to dice brains and other human organs before flushing them down a toilet. One Mitchell assistant, Dr. David Rigle, told a newspaper reporter, "I feel like I'm a character in a nightmare called 'Erik Scissorhands on Elm Street' and someone devious is writing the script."

Some of Mitchell's behavior violated public health laws but the laws' vagueness made prosecution difficult, according to the Syracuse district attorney. In some cases, Mitchell's wrongdoing could not be prosecuted because statutes of limitations had expired. He was forced to resign to avoid a grand jury investigation and his top assistants were fired.

Months before he resigned, and while under investigation, Mitchell testified in the case of Hector Rivas. Rivas was charged with murder in the death of his girlfriend, Valerie Hill, in a Syracuse apartment. Mitchell originally determined Hill was killed during the last weekend in March 1993. Rivas had an airtight and corroborated alibi for the weekend; he was out of town and could not have killed Hill. During Rivas' trial, however, Mitchell revised his timeline and determined Hill could have been killed that Friday night, a time when Rivas was still in Syracuse. Rivas' attorney never noted the discrepancy and he was convicted of murder – a high-profile conviction for District Attorney William Fitzpatrick, who personally prosecuted the case and whose office was investigating Mitchell at the time.

Mitchell's revised conclusion – that Hill could have been killed before Rivas left town – was challenged by Cyril Wecht, arguably the nation's preeminent forensic scientist, who found Hill was killed after 3:30 p.m. that Saturday. Rivas maintained he was innocent and was granted a new trial by a federal court after it found Rivas' legal representation was ineffective because his lawyer never objected to Mitchell's shifting timeline. "Had the jury heard [Mitchell's] conflicting testimony," the 2nd Circuit Court of Appeals ruled, that jury would likely "lack reasonable doubt." Rivas died in jail of pancreatic cancer in 2016 before he could be retried.

Not long before he testified in the Rivas case, Mitchell testified in the murder case of Walid Daniel, who was convicted of drowning his wife, Ivet, in Liverpool, New York, in 1991. Two of Mitchell's colleagues at the medical examiner's office concluded Ivet Daniel's death was an accident, not murder, and took the unusual step of publicly accusing Mitchell of perjury for claiming under oath that Ivet was killed. Walid Daniel served 26 years in prison before being released in 2018.

When interviewed about his career in 2018, Mitchell said this about his tumultuous tenure in upstate New York: "It was obviously a while ago and I was much younger then. I was a very aggressive death investigator and there was some dispute over how I set up the office."

In Oskaloosa, Mitchell explained, in the lingo of his profession, the rigor mortis, fixed lividity and pressure pallor he found on Camille after driving to Oskaloosa overnight on November 8, 1999. He explained the autopsy he conducted, the x-rays he performed and the sexual assault kit.

There were five gunshot wounds from four gunshots. Two shots went through Camille's heart. Another went through her left breast and into her forearm. Those three were fired from the front of Camille and slightly downward. By the time they struck the girl's body, she was likely dead. That's because the first gunshot was to the back of the head and almost certainly fatal.

"Now, the gunshot to the back of the head had different entrance characteristics than the gunshots that were to the front of the body," Mitchell told the court. "The gunshots to the front of the body were not contact injuries. In other words, the gun was not in contact with the skin. These were gunshots that were delivered away from the skin."

"But the gunshot to the back of the head, which is basically at the nape of the neck or close to the nape of the neck, is a gunshot that has contact characteristics, where we see the outline of the barrel in the skin."

Cuts along Camille's back and right shoulder blade indicated she had been killed elsewhere and dragged by her feet to the brome field. The dragging would not have been enough to pull her shirt above her breasts, however. That must have occurred before she was shot, Mitchell said.

There may have been defensive injuries, indications that Camille fought her murderer before he killed her, or maybe not. There were small cuts on two fingers of her right hand and discoloration on two knuckles of her left. Mitchell's analysis was inconclusive; the injuries could have occurred during the dragging of her body.

The timing of Camille's death was also inconclusive. It must have been at least twelve hours before her body was found, likely was at least twenty-four hours before, and could have been several days before. Narrowing the time of death down further may work on television, he said, but not in reality. Also inconclusive was Mitchell's sexual assault analysis. He couldn't say whether a sexual assault had occurred. Further DNA testing, which may have shed light on that, had been halted.

Testifying next, Cathy Bledsoe, the mother of Floyd and Tom, seemed to have little to say. She explained her whereabouts during the weekend of Camille's disappearance, which shed no light. But several minutes into her testimony, she told of a conversation with Floyd. Her youngest son had called her from jail after his arrest and Tom's subsequent release.

"I didn't do it," Floyd told her.

"Well, I know Tom didn't do it," Cathy replied.

"Yes, I know Tom didn't do it, somebody else did it."

She asked her son who he thought might have committed the crime he was now behind bars for.

"Well, maybe Dad did it, then," Floyd said.

"Floyd, that's not true," Cathy told him.

To Vanderbilt and the prosecution, the relevant quote in her testimony was Floyd's second remark: that Tom didn't do it. *See, even Floyd didn't think Tom killed Camille,* Vanderbilt was saying, so who else could it have been?

Floyd sat silently as his mother testified but in his mind, he was thinking, *I didn't say that.* What he had actually told his mother that day in jail was, "Tom is not covering for me. I don't know who did it."

The Jefferson County Jail, like other jails across the country, records phone calls made and received by inmates. Yet, there is seemingly no recording of Floyd's conversation with his mother. Floyd was told there had been a glitch in the recording device. Though other calls at the jail were recorded, the one that may have shed light on a murder case was not.

"Among other people who were in the Jefferson County Jail, not a single person ever heard me say, 'I know Tom didn't do it,' or 'maybe Dad did it,'" Floyd later recalled. "Not a single person."

***

Sheriff Dunnaway explained to the court how his office treated gunfire heard by the Army colonel separately from the disappearance of Camille, whom he believed was a runaway, and the phone call he received late on the evening of November 7, 1999, telling him Tom knew where Camille was.

"I couldn't talk to Tom at that time because he was represented by an attorney, Mr. Hayes. I had Tom there and Mr. Hayes had led us to the area where we found Camille. Mr. Hayes came over to me and asked me if Tom could go home or if he was going to jail and I advised him he was going to jail."

"Couple days later, did you have a problem with the arrest of Tom?" Vanderbilt asked.

"Yes, I did."

"Were you able to show that his story wasn't panning out?"

"To me, yes."

The sheriff's moment of sudden insight and realization was, as he explained to the court, actually just basic geography. Colonel Knoebel had heard screams not far from Zule Dairy, albeit in a different direction. Floyd Bledsoe worked at Zule Dairy. This, to Dunnaway, was a revelation.

And when he met with Floyd, he became further convinced. "I spoke to Floyd at the trailer park here in the southeast of town and Floyd asked me, 'She's dead, isn't she? Do you know if she's dead?' And I said, 'I don't think she is Floyd.'"

Vanderbilt asked if Floyd's comments were "consistent with what normally happens when a fourteen-year-old girl disappears, possibly just a runaway?"

"No," the sheriff said. "I think most people put them thoughts out of their mind and still have hope that she was going to be found. I had hopes that she would be found, be all right. This to me is unusual, yes."

Kurth objected on several occasions to Vanderbilt's questioning of Dunnaway. Just before Dunnaway discussed his conversation with Floyd, Vanderbilt was told by Judge Nafziger that he couldn't ask the sheriff about Floyd's behavior. But a few questions later, he did. Nafziger said nothing and the sheriff's analysis of Floyd's question about death was heard.

Dunnaway had no physical evidence to offer the court. His office tested Floyd's burnt jeans for DNA and found none. Searches of Floyd's property came up empty. Searches of the area around Zule Dairy did too. There was no reason to believe screams the colonel heard were Camille, the sheriff said. Dunnaway couldn't say where Camille was killed. He offered no evidence linking Floyd to her disappearance.

He did, however, have plenty of evidence that Tom was guilty. Under Kurth's cross-examination, Dunnaway recalled hearing Tom tell KBI agent

George Johnson, "I killed her." A shovel near the brome field where Camille was buried had recently been used by Tom, the sheriff said.

***

Jim Woods of the Kansas Bureau of Investigation was a large, bespectacled man and experienced investigator with three decades of service to the bureau and a career in law enforcement that dated back to the Kennedy administration. He was the officer in charge, the point man for the KBI, during its investigation into Camille's murder.

The bullets that killed Camille, along with all but one of the shell casings, were found in the dirt near her body on November 14, one week after Tom led them there. While executing a search warrant on the Bledsoe property, Woods sat down on the ground and found he was sitting on shell casings.

In the courtroom, Vanderbilt made a show of the bullets and casings, hoisting up the brown paper sack that contained them for all to see. Blue and red tape showed it had been opened and resealed by forensic investigators. The prosecutor moved to admit into evidence the forensic testing of an expert, T.L. Price. But the casings and bullets, like Dunnaway's testimony, didn't link Floyd to the crime. The only conclusion was that bullets from Tom's gun killed Camille and a box of those bullets belonging to Tom were later handed over to police by Floyd Sr.

Vanderbilt turned next to the receipt from Rusty's, the outdoor store in Lawrence where Tom had bought bullets before killing Camille. The receipt had shown the purchase occurring at 4:30 p.m. that day, providing an alibi for Tom. After Tom was arrested, Woods investigated the receipt but failed to reach a conclusion in his own mind.

"Based on your investigation, did you determine that on November 5, 1999, the register that put that receipt out, the time was accurate?" Vanderbilt asked.

"The manager indicated that it was relatively accurate," Woods answered. "He could not guarantee that it was one hundred percent."

In fact, it was far from accurate. When Woods tested the register, it was one hour late, an indication that Tom actually bought the bullets at 3:30 p.m., not 4:30. But the manager at Rusty's claimed this was a recent development, not one that dated back to November 5. Woods believed him.

"Have you had any occasion or any information inconsistent with the fact that Tom Bledsoe was at Rusty's at 4:30?" Vanderbilt asked.

"No, sir," the KBI agent said.

From there, Vanderbilt could establish an alibi for his star witness. He asked if phone records showed Tom called his parents around 4:30 p.m. and Woods said they did, 4:25 p.m. to be exact. Vanderbilt asked how long it would take to drive from Rusty's to the Bledsoe property north of Oskaloosa. More than thirty minutes, the agent told him.

On cross-examination, Kurth yanked more details about the receipt out of Woods. When Woods tested the receipts himself at Rusty's, had the three cash registers revealed the correct date and time? No, only two of the registers had, Woods told him. And which cash register displayed the wrong date and time? The rear register – the one used to purchase ammunition.

"And the rear register, is that where the box of nine-millimeter ammunition was purchased at [by] Tom Bledsoe?" Kurth asked Woods.

"That's correct."

When pressed on whether Tom's receipt was accurate, the KBI's lead detective could only say that the store manager thought it probably was. Kurth asked if the store manager ever produced receipts on a prior date showing his cash registers were accurate. Woods conceded he had not. So, Tom could have left Rusty's at 3:45 p.m., not 4:45 p.m., Kurth said.

"And from 3:45 until 4:30, that would be enough time to drive from Lawrence to here in Oskaloosa?" Kurth asked Woods.

"Forty-five minutes would be adequate, I'd think, yes."

The store manager was called to the stand. Kevin Feleay told the court what he had told Woods: that he believed the time on the receipt was relatively accurate, give or take a few minutes. Feleay said he had checked a second cash register roll, known as a Z tape, to ensure Tom had purchased the ammunition around 4:30 p.m.

On cross-examination, Kurth had no problem casting doubt on that. He asked if Feleay had told Woods that all cash registers in the store were accurate prior to the investigation. Feleay admitted he had.

"And in fact they were not?" Kurth asked.

"They were not right."

Kurth had conducted his own investigation into receipts at Rusty's. On December 1, he purchased an item from the store and the receipt showed the cash register was off by twelve hours and forty-five minutes. Eight days later, on December 9, he bought another item from the store. Again, the receipt was off by more than twelve hours. A receipt from Rusty's was no basis for an alibi, he told jurors.

To speed the trial – now in its third day – along, Vanderbilt and Kurth agreed to agree on the limited DNA results, which were unremarkable. Cindy Schuler, a forensic biologist, found that a fitted sheet on Camille's bed contained the DNA of a female relative of Camille, not surprising since she lived with her sister. A single sperm was found on the sheet and an accompanying quilt, a trace amount that could not be tested. Though some DNA remained untested, that which was tested shed no light on who killed Camille.

Jim Bolinger, the interim Countryside Baptist pastor and best friend to Tom, took a seat at the witness stand to vouch for Tom's rigid religiosity, his absence of a social life and his teetotalism. When Vanderbilt asked if Tom drank beer, Bolinger said, "[I] just don't believe he'd do it" because Tom "cared about the Lord."

Vanderbilt, in response: "There's a bunch of Catholics that care about the Lord and drink, sir. And I'm not being facetious here. The point I'm trying to make is that you know a lot about Tom and there's more to it than, 'He wouldn't do it.' Did he do stuff like that?"

Again, Bolinger said Tom did not drink, adding that he also did not chase women or go to bars or get in trouble. Bolinger flatly denied knowing about a molestation allegation against Tom during a church retreat. No one had ever spoken negatively of Tom, he told the court.

Vanderbilt asked, "Do you believe that's true – that he's a good man?" Bolinger answered in a single word: "Yes."

On cross-examination, Kurth unsurprisingly recapped the voicemail messages Tom had left Bolinger, seemingly admitting to his involvement in Camille's murder. Bolinger told him that Tom had been uptight that day. Kurth ran him through a short list of Tom's behaviors – lying, watching pornography, looking at dirty magazines – that ran contradictory to church teachings.

"So, he was doing those things that you were not aware of?" the defense attorney asked and Bolinger acknowledged as much. The implication was clear: if he was committing those sins without his best friend's knowledge, what else had he been doing?

***

As Bolinger left the witness stand, jurors were escorted out of the courtroom so the attorneys and judge could have a conversation outside the presence of them, observers and the press. Vanderbilt had requested the meeting to discuss two matters, one procedural and the other crucial. He planned to call Tom Bledsoe back to the stand but wanted to wait until Mike Hayes, Tom's attorney, returned from a separate court hearing. That was the procedural matter.

"I also want to move the court to amend the complaint to file – "

Judge Nafziger cut him off. "Not going to do that. We're not going to do that in chambers…I don't want to take that step in chambers out of the presence of the press or anybody else because then they're not going to know how it came down or what happened and they should know. They're following the trial."

Vanderbilt was asking to amend the criminal complaint against Floyd to add a felony murder charge. That would give jurors the option of convicting him of felony murder – defined in Kansas law as killing another human being during the commission of an inherently dangerous felony – if jurors felt the state lacked evidence for the more serious crime of first-degree murder.

By amending the complaint, Vanderbilt was granting the jury leeway. If jurors believed Vanderbilt had proven Floyd killed Camille but not proven premeditation – required for a first-degree murder conviction – they could instead convict Floyd of the lesser murder charge. There was, however, risk in Vanderbilt's tactic. He would need to prove Camille was killed in the commission of an inherently dangerous felony – in this case, aggravated kidnapping. If he could not prove an aggravated kidnapping had occurred, his murder charge would also falter.

Nafziger turned to Kurth. "Is there going to be any objection?"

"For the record, I will, judge, but, yeah, just for the record."

Turning back to Vanderbilt, Nafziger asked what he planned to do with the other charges against Floyd – aggravated kidnapping and indecent liberties. Vanderbilt said those charges would remain.

"Well," the judge said, "while we're on the subject in here, then we'll take this back up in open court, but I haven't heard any evidence of a kidnapping yet. I'm just wondering where —"

Now it was Vanderbilt's turn to interrupt. "Kidnapping," he said, "is in keeping against the will and harm done, in the fact that she's running, screaming, 'somebody help me,' somebody's restraining her. There's evidence that she's being restrained and there's certainly evidence that she was harmed."

"Well, where is the evidence of restraint?" Nafziger asked.

"There's no evidence that was even her, judge," Kurth chimed in, referring to the woman whose screams were heard by Colonel Knoebel.

"The circumstantial evidence," Vanderbilt said, "is that Floyd said he accidentally killed her, Floyd works at the dairy, colonel heard by the dairy there was a scream, 'somebody help me, don't hurt me, somebody help me,' that was done twice. The burial site was on the Bledsoe property, she was shot and there is evidence — and one of the shots is in the back of the head so she was alive when she was being shot in the back of the head. There's evidence of defensive marks —"

The judge interrupted. "I know. So, where's the evidence of the restraint, though? That's what I want to know. I just wanted you to think about it."

"It doesn't require physical restraint," the prosecutor pleaded, "just requires preventing them from going someplace that they want to go."

"Where's proof of that? Think about it," Nafziger told him. "Anyway, we'll take that up in the presence of the jury. We'll go back out and you make your announcement, then we'll proceed."

To the jurors and reporters who were not privy to the conversation, it seemed like an unremarkable few minutes, enough time to grab a soda or quick snack. But the judge had openly doubted whether the state had evidence a kidnapping had even occurred — let alone that the defendant committed it — which cast doubt on the felony murder charge as well. Those doubts would never be heard by jurors.

***

With both sides having agreed to let Tom be recalled to the witness stand later that afternoon, Kurth moved ahead with his first witness for the defense. His name was Dan Ward, a Lawrence crime scene detective who had performed a search of Floyd and Heidi's trailer on November 14, not long after Floyd's arrest and Tom's release from jail.

Ward's testimony consisted of a quick rundown of what he had not found: blood in Floyd's car, blood in the trunk of Floyd's car, evidence of gunfire in the home. He *had* found a spot of blood in the trailer's carpet but it was not Camille's. Neither was a speck of blood on a coat in the trailer.

Karen Edmonds, co-owner of Winchester Hardware, was the second witness for the defense. She recalled Floyd's purchases on November 5 – a roll of duct tape, a sweatshirt – and their conversation. She testified that Floyd purchased the items at 4:20 p.m., the exact time when Camille was stepping off her school bus, and hung around for another ten or fifteen minutes after that, chatting. About fifteen minutes after leaving Winchester Hardware in Richard Zule's '69 Chevy, he was back at the dairy, a seemingly airtight alibi.

Jurors left for their afternoon break and Vanderbilt, this time with spectators and reporters in the room, made his motion to amend the complaint against Floyd. Nafziger remained skeptical, asking several times why Vanderbilt was changing the charges. "That's what I don't understand."

Vanderbilt declined to give a reason for his amended complaint, instead retreating to his right to do so under a Kansas Supreme Court opinion three years prior. But he had failed to give a copy of the opinion to the judge or defense attorney in advance. The judge declined to rule on the matter until he and Kurth had time to read through case law on when a prosecutor can add an alternative charge during a trial.

With that, jurors returned to the courtroom and Tom Bledsoe returned to the witness stand. Vanderbilt wanted him to explain again why he had turned himself in to police and confessed to killing Camille. Tom repeated his claim that Floyd had blackmailed him. Vanderbilt laid a verbal path for him to walk down.

"He's held that against you before, hasn't he?" Vanderbilt asked. Yes. "To get you to do what he wanted?" Yes. "You knew what he was talking about when he said that?" Yes.

"I tried to have sex with a dog," Tom told the court. There were the dirty magazines, too, he said. "I played with myself, watched some movies... dirty movies."

"Your brother has extorted things from you using exposing that information to the church and your family, hasn't he?" Vanderbilt asked. Yes, Tom agreed. "And he did it again, didn't he?" Again, yes.

With more leading questions, Vanderbilt told the court that Tom took police to Camille's body to ensure it could be moved out of the dingy brome field. Tom's guilt was in knowing where Camille was – where Floyd had left her – and not immediately telling authorities, Vanderbilt said.

"I just know that that night I wanted – I couldn't live with myself," Tom said.

"Because you killed Camille?"

"No.

"Why couldn't you live with yourself, Tom?"

"Fact that she was in that ditch and I knew where she was because Floyd told me and everyone else was wondering where she was. Floyd told me. I couldn't live with myself because Floyd – what Floyd told me."

With that, Vanderbilt was done. The state of Kansas rested its case against Floyd Scott Bledsoe. Kurth and Vanderbilt approached the bench and conferred with Nafziger outside earshot of the jurors, reporters and onlookers. The judge spoke first. "Mr. Kurth, I take it you have a motion that you want to take up?"

"We would make a motion for a judgment of acquittal in this case," Kurth said. "We believe that even in the light most favorable to the state, they have failed to show any premeditation in this case to support a first-degree murder charge, they have certainly shown no evidence toward any aggravated kidnapping or confinement, and certainly there's been no evidence of anything of a sexual nature. In fact, Sergeant Poppa testified that the evidence showed there was no sexual evidence."

It was a longshot and Nafziger, though skeptical of the evidence, quickly denied the motion. "Well, I concur, Mr. Kurth, that certainly the evidence isn't the strongest in certain instances," the judge told him. "You do have evidence of a scream which could be attributed to the victim, which would substantiate the kidnapping offense. We have the murder. Any premeditation, any time, ever so slight, is substantial to establish an element of premeditation. Plus, we have the probability that there may have been multiple shots fired and we also have the fact that her clothes were disarrayed and her breasts were exposed and from the testimony that appeared perhaps not to be accidental.

"For those reasons, the court finds that there is evidence from which a reasonable, prudent man could find an inference of guilt beyond a reasonable doubt and your motion for a directed verdict of acquittal is denied at this time."

The attorneys returned to their respective sides and Kurth called to the stand Rebecca Wheatley, an older sister of Heidi and Camille. Wheatley's home in Ottawa, fifty miles south of Oskaloosa, was one of Floyd's destinations in the frantic overnight search for Camille the night she went missing. Wheatley, like so many others, had joined Floyd and the search party during those early morning hours of November 6 to no avail, she told the court.

The last witness of the day was Annette McNary, the Oskaloosa elementary school teacher who was keeping score at a basketball tournament when Floyd showed her a flier with Camille's face on it November 6. Kurth was using his witnesses to illustrate how desperately Floyd had searched for Camille.

The day, much like the day before, granted reporters plenty to write about. Joel Mathis at the *Lawrence Journal-World* began his page one story with the testimony of Cathy Bledsoe: "In a case full of strange twists, where brother testified against brother, another came Wednesday." He replayed the supposed jailhouse conversation between Floyd and Cathy, including Floyd's suggestion that his father could have been involved.

A few paragraphs down, Mathis cut to the heart of the trial, writing that "though prosecutors summoned 28 witnesses, they produced only one whose testimony directly linked Floyd S. Bledsoe to Camille Arfmann's November slaying. That was Tom Bledsoe, Floyd's brother, the man defense lawyers say actually killed the girl." Noting that Camille had been killed with Tom's gun, Mathis wrote, "The prosecution never explained how or when Floyd S. Bledsoe might have taken, then returned, the gun."

Floyd Bledsoe, center, with his sons Cody, right, and Christian, left, in 1999. Heidi Bledsoe is seen in the background to the right.

Zetta Camille Arfmann is seen in this undated photograph. After her disappearance, the photo was provided to news outlets.

Floyd and Heidi Bledsoe sit on the porch of Floyd's parents' house north of Oskaloosa in this undated photograph.

The top half of the front page of The Oskaloosa Independent on November 11, 1999. It's the first mention of the case in the small town's weekly newspaper, six days after Camille's disappearance. Between yearbook photos of Tom Bledsoe and Camille Arfmann is a photo of the Bledsoe parents' house north of Oskaloosa.

Camille Arfmann is seen in an undated photo that was distributed after her disappearance.

Countryside Baptist Church in rural McLouth, Kansas, which the Bledsoe brothers and Camille Arfmann attended.

The front entrance to Oskaloosa High School. Camille Arfmann was a freshman at the school and excelling at the time of her disappearance and death.

It was here, on a rural stretch of Fairview Road north of Oskaloosa, that Camille Arfmann was dropped off by a school bus driver on the day of her murder.

The former Bledsoe family house at 11477 Osage Road, north of Oskaloosa. Tom Bledsoe lived here with his parents. Camille Arfmann's body was partially buried on the property.

Tom Bledsoe claimed he was driving along this rural stretch of Osage Road north of Oskaloosa when he spotted Floyd's car and flagged him down. A detective later said the odds of two brothers meeting along that road was a "one in one-thousand situation."

A light blue Fiat is seen in the parking lot of a Walmart in Bonner Springs, Kansas, in November 2015. Inside is the body of Tom Bledsoe.

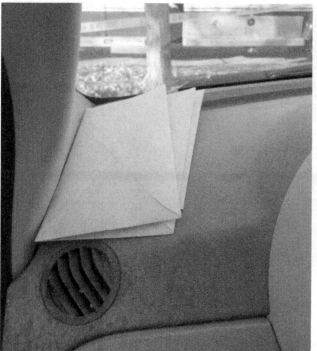

Three envelopes containing three letters were found on the dashboard of a Fiat belonging to Tom Bledsoe.

In one of his three suicide letters, Tom Bledsoe writes that he raped and killed Camille Arfmann on November 5, 1999, and alleges he was told by police and a prosecutor to lie.

Floyd Bledsoe arrives at the Jefferson County Courthouse on December 8, 2015.

Floyd Bledsoe speaks to reporters outside the Jefferson County Courthouse after his release on December 8, 2015. Immediately behind him are his legal team. From left to right: Tricia Bushnell, Jean Phillips, Elizabeth Cateforis and Alice Craig. In the back row are former interns who worked on the case, including Kaiti Smith, center left.

The front page of The Oskaloosa Independent on December 17, 2015.

Floyd Bledsoe speaks in the rotunda of the Kansas Capitol on January 28, 2016, urging lawmakers to end the death penalty.

Zetta Camille Arfmann is buried at Reformed Presbyterian Church Cemetery in Winchester, Kansas, about ten miles north of her last home at Floyd and Heidi's trailer.

TEN

The fourth and final day of the trial was April 27, 2000. It began, like every other day, at 9 a.m. Because the state had rested, it was Kurth's turn to begin. He did so by calling to the stand Kirk Vernon, the Jefferson County detective who had refused to arrest Floyd for fear he lacked probable cause.

There were no questions about the arrest of Floyd or probable cause, however. The young detective was asked whether Tommie Sue Arfmann, Camille's mother, had stopped by Zule Dairy just before midnight on the evening of November 5 and found Floyd had already left to go home. Yes, she had, Vernon told the court. And Floyd was later found at his trailer searching for Camille? "Correct."

A rancher, Fred Smelser, told the court of his interaction with Floyd on November 6. He had been driving to his home a few miles from Floyd's when the young man flagged him down along Fairview Road. "Floyd stopped me and told me that Camille was missing and 'course I was shocked. He handed me a paper with her picture on it and he said…if I saw her or had seen anything the day before…to let him know."

Smelser has not seen Camille – no one had – nor had he seen anything suspicious. The next witness for the defense had, however.

To the extent that Floyd Sr. and Cathy Bledsoe had neighbors in their rural corner of the world, Dan Courtney was one of them, living just to the south. It wasn't unusual for him to drive by the Bledsoes' house along dusty, gravelly Osage Road, as he had done the morning of November 6, the day after Camille disappeared.

"I was going over to my son's house and saw a black pickup coming… up the lane where the body was discovered." Courtney told the court it was a newer, short-bed truck, and definitely black. It was driving out of the brome field where Camille's body was. Floyd did not own a truck – he drove a green Chevy Nova – but Tom owned a black short-bed pickup truck.

The final witness for the defense and the final person to testify in the

State of Kansas v. Floyd Scott Bledsoe was Detective Randy Carreno. Few people, if any, knew more about the case and Kurth considered him key to convincing the jury to acquit. Carreno had interviewed both Floyd and Tom but Kurth wanted to know first about his interviews of Billie Summerville – the man who had once creeped out Camille – despite Summerville's undisputed alibi for the time when Camille was killed.

"She had some concerns over Billie's activities, some statements… which Billie had made to her…being of sexual content," Carreno said.

Kurth detailed those statements for the court. There was Camille's claim that Summerville had walked up to her in a towel, Camille's claim that he had told her to put on a white t-shirt so he could "wet it down and watch her." Carreno had confronted Summerville about the allegations at the time, heard his denials and told him to knock it off.

In a trial that everyone seemed to understand was about Floyd and Tom, Kurth continued to ask about Summerville. Carreno said he had known Summerville for eleven years. He knew him to be a liar, a thief and a womanizer. But there was no evidence he was a killer. Summerville had alibis for November 5 and November 6.

Vanderbilt, on cross-examination, asked, "Did you determine that Billie Summerville wasn't around when Camille disappeared?"

"That he wasn't around, that is correct."

"Did you confirm that Billie Summerville really hadn't had the opportunity to do what happened to Camille?"

"Yes, I did."

Carreno was questioned by Kurth and Vanderbilt about shoddy crime scene investigating by himself and his colleagues. A Countryside Baptist Church t-shirt, similar to the one Camille was wearing, was not removed from the brome field until November 14, about a week after she was found dead. It was set aside to be tested by the KBI for blood but that testing never occurred. When asked if he had "any idea where that t-shirt is," the detective said he did not.

Carreno's area of expertise was interrogations and he claimed to know every trick in the book. He would coddle suspects, play nice with them, hold their hand and hug them. At other times, he would lash out – screaming, yelling, hurling violent strings of profanity with his face just inches from the suspect's. When he interviewed Tom on November 24 – after he had been released and Floyd arrested – he used nearly every technique he knew.

"Stop the fucking lying!" he yelled at one point.

Tom had lied in ways that were easy for Carreno to prove. He told the detective he had moved plywood around the brome field before alerting police but later said he hadn't. He told the detective he had touched the shovel with fresh dirt on it but later said he hadn't. He told the detective Floyd had returned his gun to his truck on the night of November 5 but later said he didn't know how the gun found its way back. Then there was Tom's ever-changing timeline for the supposed roadside confession.

Kurth asked, "When he says he saw Floyd on that road, first time he told you what time it was, you called him on it, didn't you? You said, 'There's no way you could have seen him at that time because I was with Floyd.' Isn't that right?"

"I wanted to make sure that Tom had his time correct."

"And that's when his time changed, is when you called him on it? You let him know that you were with [Floyd], so it had to change, otherwise Tom's story wouldn't match up, would it?"

"Tom wasn't for sure and he wasn't trying to be exact in giving me a time in which he met his brother on the county road."

Not only did Carreno excuse Tom's first lie about when he met Floyd, he helped him come up with a second lie by telling Tom the times at which he, Carreno, was with Floyd. As the detective told the court: "I provided him with information to help him…letting him know that I was with Floyd."

Even that wasn't enough help. Tom came up with a second lie, this one also disproven by Carreno. So, he came up with a third timeline for meeting Floyd, the one he would testify to under oath at the murder trial of his brother.

This interview of Tom, unlike the interviews in which he confessed, was videotaped. The video was entered into evidence, as were Carreno's field notes. On them, he had scribbled "BS" next to many of Tom's claims.

"Does that stand for Bob Smith or Billie Summerville?" Kurth asked him.

"No, it does not."

"We know what that stands for, don't we, without having to say it?"

On cross-examination, Vanderbilt had an easy time cutting through Carreno's testimony. Sure, Carreno had accused Tom of lying, but that could just be for show, Vanderbilt said. Carreno was, after all, a master of interrogations, right? "When you would yell or accuse Tom of lying over and over, doesn't necessarily mean that he was lying, does it?" the prosecutor asked and Carreno agreed: "No, it does not."

As he had previously done, Vanderbilt homed in on Tom's emotionless nature. He asked whether yelling, "Stop the fucking lying!" had an effect on Tom. It did not, Carreno said. Didn't Tom's voice remain monotone during the interview? Yes, Carreno said. And didn't his face lack any emotion whatsoever? It did, Carreno said.

Though he was a witness for the defense, Carreno's testimony was beginning to paint Tom in a positive light. That became increasingly true when Carreno was asked about a strange interrogation on December 4, 1999.[5]

It was an interview of Floyd, who had been charged with Camille's murder. But during the interview, it was agreed that Tom would be allowed to sit in, along with his attorney, Mike Hayes. Detectives, Floyd and Tom would discuss, face-to-face, the death of Camille.

"Tom entered the room," Carreno recalled, "and the one thing that I noted quickly was that Tom got as far away from Floyd as he possibly could and put his back to the wall. The next thing that I noticed was that Floyd was – he was just staring him down, more of an intimidation-type factor, and I could tell that Tom was very, very uneasy being in that room at that time.

"The impression that I got from Tom Bledsoe was that at that point in time, he became strong. I don't know how to explain that but he – he challenged Floyd. He challenged Floyd in a way that, in my opinion, he was able to stand up for the first time in front of Floyd and tell him the truth, to state the truth."

Vanderbilt liked where this was going. He prodded, asking for more details. What had Tom said?

"That he wanted me to know the truth, he wanted everybody to know the truth, and that he wasn't going to hide the truth anymore, and I asked him what the truth was."

Another nudge from Vanderbilt: *What did Tom say next?*

---

[5] Before the trial, Judge Nafziger had ordered that Vanderbilt not be allowed "to introduce the results of the interview of KBI Agent Johnson with Floyd Bledsoe and Tom Bledsoe." Vanderbilt effectively did so anyway, through this testimony of Randy Carreno.

"The information that he gave me was that it was Floyd Bledsoe that killed Camille Arfmann."

This time, Vanderbilt gave more than a nudge. "Are you aware," he asked Carreno, "that when Tom walked out of the room, he actually said that that was the first time he had ever stood up to his brother?"

Carreno had not heard that, but it didn't matter. Jurors were hearing it. Some of the last testimony those dozen men and women heard before they deliberated was from a detective who said Tom, with a newfound strength, had told the truth: Floyd Bledsoe killed Camille Arfmann.

"It was [during] that interview with those two subjects," Carreno told the court, "that I had viewed Tom going from what I would consider to be a very weak person to a – to a strong person, person who knew the truth and wanted to make sure that it was known and wanted to make sure that – that it was known in front of his brother. He wanted his brother to hear him tell the truth."[6]

After his final witness did far more harm than good, Kurth rested his case without calling to the stand many of those at his disposal, such as Dale and Danielle Hawk, who were with Floyd on the afternoon of November 6, around the time Tom alleged the roadside meeting occurred. James Gardner had also spoken to Floyd around that time, but did not testify.

Rev. Michael Waggoner, who had watched as Tom flirted with his under-age niece, did not testify. Neither did two of Camille's best friends – Megan Koons and Tammy Dressler Arfmann – both of whom would have told the court that Camille enjoyed living with Floyd, was scared of being at the trailer alone at night, but felt safe when Floyd was there with her.

Jurors were released for a lunch break before closing statements and Judge Nafziger used the time to again consider Vanderbilt's motion to add an

---

[6] It was not the last time Carreno stretched the bounds of testimony and interrogation. The following year, Carreno repeatedly lied while interrogating murder defendant Ronald Decker, a Vietnam veteran, without reading him his Miranda rights. Carreno claimed he, too, was a Vietnam veteran who had suffered a back injury, neither of which was true. Carreno claimed to have spoken to Decker's wife, telling the defendant she "seems like a nice woman" who "really loves you." In reality, he had never met her. During Decker's trial, Carreno speculated about Decker's truthfulness, telling the court that Decker "was telling me the truth about him shooting and killing Wayne Green." Despite an order by the court to not discuss alleged desecration of the victim's body, Carreno did so anyway. Decker was convicted of first-degree murder in December of 2001.

alternative felony murder charge. Kurth objected to the change but Nafziger approved it anyway. Jurors, if they wanted to send Floyd Bledsoe away for decades, were given another mechanism for doing so.

***

In his dark suit and patterned yellow tie, Vanderbilt stood before a chalkboard on which he had written "Murder," "Oportunity," [sic] and "Motive," an apparent twist on the popular prosecutorial phrase "means, motive and opportunity." To the right of that he had written "Floyd Bledsoe." He had thirty minutes to convince twelve jurors an innocent man was guilty.

"I could stand before you going through all the testimony that's been presented and show you how Floyd Scott Bledsoe had the opportunity to kill Camille, had the opportunity to be there when the colonel heard what was going on, but I'm not going to do that because, at the same time, I could present you the same testimonies from different people showing that he couldn't."

It was not the most auspicious of beginnings. Vanderbilt was making the argument that no one knew when Floyd left Richard Zule's dairy or whether he had enough time to pick up Camille, drive to Wild Horse Road where the colonel heard the screams, and dump the body at his parents' house. He didn't have time so Vanderbilt didn't attempt an explanation.

"My point is, ladies and gentlemen, that it did happen. It did happen. Tom Bledsoe came – his heart and his head were driving him crazy – he comes to the sheriff's office. He gets Camille out of her grave. Now, how did he know that Camille was in her grave? One of two things happened, ladies and gentlemen: either he put her there or Floyd did. There you are.

"Now, I'm arguing to you that Floyd did it. Why? Opportunity and motive."

Skipping over opportunity, he turned to motive. Floyd was getting a divorce; he would be single soon. From that, Vanderbilt wove a wild tale. Floyd had driven Camille to Zule Dairy on November 5 in an attempt to convince her to marry him. He had lifted her shirt above her breasts but she broke free. In the ensuing struggle, he shot her in the back of the head. "That's a conclusion that I want you to come to," he told jurors. "You can't just come to the conclusion without facts."

Unfortunately for Vanderbilt, there were no facts to support that scenario.

Contrarily, the facts indicated it could not have occurred. Richard Zule was waiting for Floyd when he returned; he certainly would have noticed Camille in the truck. From there, Floyd went to work milking cows and never left work again until he headed home. There was no time for him to kill Camille and dispose of her body, and certainly no way for him to have done so without the Zules noticing. Rather than follow up his claim with facts, Vanderbilt turned to a defense of Tom.

Ignoring testimony that showed the Rusty's receipt was inaccurate when it read 4:30 p.m., Vanderbilt claimed it was evidence Tom was in Lawrence, not Oskaloosa, when Camille was kidnapped. Though his cell phone records showed Tom called his father from Oskaloosa, not Lawrence, around that time, Vanderbilt ignored this too. "He wouldn't have used [his cell phone] just to call from Oskaloosa. He was in Lawrence, just like he said he was." (There had been no evidence Tom only used his cell phone when out of town. To the contrary, he had used it to call Jim Bolinger from an Oskaloosa parking lot and confess.)

Then there was the jailhouse conversation between Floyd and his mother. Vanderbilt wielded it as proof that even Floyd didn't believe Tom killed Camille.

"There are two options. It wasn't Tom. Floyd tells you it wasn't Tom, Floyd tells his mom it wasn't Tom, and that was a mistake. He was comforting his mother, as his mother came up here and told you. But sticking to his guns, doesn't want to take the blame, 'Dad did it.' Dad didn't do it. Dad was with Mom.

"Why am I standing here arguing to you that Tom didn't do it? Because there's only two people that really could have done it. Tom said he did it. Tom had to get Camille out of the grave. Tom had to clear his conscience with the church," Vanderbilt said. A short time later, he added, "The physical evidence shows that Tom didn't do it."

"Floyd had the opportunity to do it. When did he do it? Can I tell you when he did it? No, I can't tell you when he did it. All right, I can't tell you when he did it. But I can tell you who was there. He wasn't alone. We know there was at least three people there: him and Camille, and he brought his son."

It had been several long days since jurors heard the testimony of Heidi Bledsoe and Rose Bolinger relaying what young Cody had told them, how he had reenacted his Aunt Millie's murder, how he had said his Uncle Tom did it and then, later, how his daddy had done it. It had also been several days since the testimony of Brandi Wampler, Cody's babysitter, made clear Cody was at her home when Camille was taken and killed. He could not have seen his Aunt Millie's murder, so Vanderbilt reached into his imagination for what came next.

"Floyd takes care of the body, gets back in the car. Cody says, 'You killed Aunt Millie.' Imagine what went through that boy's mind when Floyd Scott Bledsoe convinced his two-year-old son to say Tom did it. As soon as that powerful influence of his father was out of his presence, he was comfortable with telling the truth...two-year-old children don't use a lot of reasoning or deduction, but when he goes to Camille's grave he explains to her, because he was there, that he didn't do it. 'Aunt Millie, I didn't kill you, my dad did.'"

As if citing the words of a two-year-old child was not ignominious enough, Vanderbilt misquoted or fabricated Cody on both occasions. There was no evidence, no testimony, or even hearsay that suggested Cody told Floyd he had killed Aunt Millie. As for his graveside message to Camille, what Cody actually said, according to Heidi's testimony, was, "Aunt Mimi, I didn't shoot you. It wasn't me." He never mentioned his father.

In an attempt to preemptively cut down the defense's closing argument, Vanderbilt contended that Floyd's sleepless search for Camille, an apparent virtue, was actually evidence of his guilt. "What kind of sense does it make for a fourteen-year-old girl to be dead on a Friday night at midnight? It doesn't. Fourteen-year-old girls could be anywhere." In other words, why was Floyd trying so hard and why was he so concerned when law enforcement and his parents believed she was just another runaway? "Only Floyd during that whole time period was suggesting she was dead, she had been abducted, she was dead. Because he already knew. When did he do it? I don't know, sometime."

After that, another invention of Vanderbilt's mind, another vivid description of an event largely unsupported by evidence or testimony.

"When she was taken from 4:20 to five o'clock, at one point she was screaming for help. At one point she was standing, sitting, kneeling, laying with her breasts exposed with a gun to the back of her head. What was going on? What was she going through? How long did it take? I can't tell you that.

Even a coroner came in and said she was shot three times in the grave. Why was she shot three times in the grave? When? Somebody was very mad."

Vanderbilt told the jury that his timeline for Floyd's kidnapping and murder of Camille fits. "You can squeeze the numbers around. It's a numbers game, kind of like accounting, you can make anything work. Statistics, you can make anything work, and unfortunately, nobody's clock said the same thing at the same time in this trial."

But rather than present a timeline, he returned to Cody's words and Heidi's testimony. "Her perception – she'd raised him since he was young – Cody was there…There's only one way Cody could have been there, ladies and gentlemen. He didn't walk, he didn't crawl, he didn't ride a horse; he was with his father when Camille was killed. He was never with Tom that whole evening. He was with Floyd." With that, he asked jurors to return three guilty verdicts.

Kurth's closing statement began where the trial left off – the detrimental testimony of Detective Carreno vouching for Tom's honesty. "Keep in mind," the attorney told jurors, "that it is your determination of who is telling the truth and who isn't telling the truth, not Detective Carreno when he sat up there and he said he thought Tom was telling the truth. He doesn't know. That's your determination and no one else's."

Rather than explain there was a dearth of evidence tying Floyd to the murder and an abundance of evidence linking Tom to the murder, Kurth again pointed the finger at Billie Summerville, the man with an undisputed alibi. Grabbing a letter Camille had written to Carreno about Summerville's perverted behavior, he read it aloud. "If that doesn't send a shiver up your spine reading that, I don't know what would," Kurth said when he was done.

Then, only after five minutes of talking about Summerville, did he jump to Tom. "On that Friday, November 5th, Tom did not work, period. Did he have all the time in the world to do something or plan something? You bet he did."

Kurth said Tom purchased the ammunition that killed Camille on a cash register that was consistently forty-five minutes fast, enough time for him to drive from Lawrence to Oskaloosa and unload four bullets into the girl's head and body. Records show the phone call from Tom's cell phone to his parents' house, which went unanswered, did not occur in Lawrence, Kurth told jurors. He speculated about what that call accomplished.

"Since Mr. Vanderbilt's taken a few jumps here, let's take one. Maybe he's checking to see if anybody's home. Maybe that was his plan. He gets the answering machine so he knows nobody is home. So, then he drives to the trailer, because he knows Camille is going to be there, and he picks her up. Now, is Camille going to go with him? Well, they go to church together, it was a church night, they'd planned on going to church. In fact, apparently Tom did go to church. Were his parents around? Do they know what he did? No."

Picking up steam, Kurth turned to Tom's habitual lying. He admitted to lying to detectives during his testimony, Kurth noted. Carreno had tabulated his lies in asterisks and "BS" marks during his interrogation. If participants in the trial attempted to count Tom's lies, "We'd all run out of fingers and toes," Kurth said. It is impossible, he told jurors, to know when Tom is telling the truth and when he is not.

Vanderbilt had made Tom's blank, emotionless stares a virtue, evidence of his truth-telling. Kurth turned that on its head. "You see any emotion, anything at all from him about this girl? This girl he cared about, this girl he told Detective Carreno [he] wanted to be his first?" While Floyd searched desperately for his sister-in-law, his brother and father declined to help, Kurth told the court. "Does Tom jump up and say, 'I'm going to go help, this is somebody that I go to church with, somebody that I care about?' No."

The alleged roadside meeting where Floyd confessed to Tom was extremely improbable, Kurth said. Why would Floyd tell a brother who hated him his darkest secret?

"Tom indicated that Floyd didn't even know he bought the gun, and his parents didn't know he bought the gun, so how is Floyd – and we haven't heard this at all, ladies and gentlemen – how is Floyd supposed to even know that Tom bought this gun? Then, how is Floyd supposed to sneak off to Tom's truck, grab the gun, shoot Camille – kidnap her and shoot her – come back, bring the gun back and put it in there? And, by the way, if you recall, it's clean. There's no blood on it, there's no nothing.

"We know where Floyd was all of the time, ladies and gentlemen, and we know that Floyd was accounted for and we know that Tom had all the time and the opportunity to commit this crime."

Somewhere, in another part of the courtroom, someone flipped off the lights and Kurth turned on a projector. A timeline of events for the afternoon of November 5 appeared. At 4 p.m., Floyd went to Winchester Hardware. At

4:20 p.m., Camille walked off the bus. At 4:35 p.m., Floyd left Winchester Hardware. At roughly 4:50 p.m., he returned to Zule Dairy.

"Now, ladies and gentlemen, you're going to run off and kidnap somebody and take them back or kill them when there isn't time to do it? That's the theory the state wants you to believe. They want you to believe that between this time Floyd went and kidnapped and grabbed Camille. It is impossible, period. That's not reasonable doubt, that's all doubt, ladies and gentlemen. Couldn't happen, period.

"That's it, ladies and gentlemen. Doesn't fit. He could not have kidnapped her, gone and got the gun, killed her, and come back in any stretch of anybody's imagination at all. Impossible."

He said the word again: "Impossible." He cautioned jurors to keep their emotions in check. It was a deeply sad crime, he agreed. In fact, there aren't many crimes sadder, Kurth said. But justice must be dished out to the man who committed the crime, the person who confessed three times. That person was not his client.

"Ladies and gentlemen, this is an all or nothing case. You either believe that Floyd grabbed her and killed her or you don't, and the evidence before you says you don't and that Tom is nothing but a liar and lied to get his way out of jail, and that's exactly what he did... You should consider with caution the testimony of an informant who, for benefits from the state, testifies or produces evidence. He got a murder charge dismissed against him, ladies and gentlemen. How many people sit in jail, decide they don't like it for a week, or even a day, and say, 'I didn't really do it, somebody else did?' Quite a few. How many people does it work for? I've been doing this for about fifteen years, ladies and gentlemen. I know of one: Tom Bledsoe.

"You've got to find Floyd Bledsoe not guilty, because it just doesn't work. Thank you."

Vanderbilt had reserved several minutes of his half-hour-long closing statement for a rebuttal. In a strange twist, he used those final five minutes of the trial to introduce an entirely new theory about the murder of Camille. Rather than claim Floyd had kidnapped and killed her during the four o'clock hour, he now suggested the murder and disposal of her body occurred after 10 p.m.

"Dale Arfmann testified that at eleven o'clock, they went to the dairy and he [Floyd] wasn't there. Where was he? He was taking care of Camille," Vanderbilt told the court. Arfmann, a brother of Camille and brother-in-law to Floyd, had testified two days before that he never looked at a watch or clock but thought it was around 11 p.m. His mother, Tommie Sue Arfmann, who was with him at the time, said it was nearly midnight, not eleven o'clock.

There was a benefit to this new theory for Vanderbilt: it gave Tom an alibi. "Tom was at home asleep with the alarms and his parents while he was missing from the dairy, while Camille is gone." Detectives had discovered the Bledsoe home had noisy alarms that would have sounded if Tom left the house late that evening.

Referring to Floyd, Vanderbilt asked aloud, "Why did he tell his brother? Who knows why he told Tom he killed her. Why did he tell his mom that he knew Tom didn't do it? Why did he tell Frost that he went to the trailer? Why did he tell Orin [Turner] that he went to the trailer? He was slipping. Guilt. Why was he running around saying that, 'Oh, she's dead and here's the fliers, somebody help us find her?' Guilt."

Think, Vanderbilt said, of the goodhearted Army colonel, William Knoebel, the poor man who heard Floyd kill Camille at Zule Dairy. "The colonel, a United States Army colonel, is haunted right now because he didn't shoot two dogs to go save Camille. He knows if he'd have done it and was persistent, he might have saved her from what he did."

Those were the last words jurors heard before Judge Nafziger ended closing arguments and sent them away to deliberate. It was 2:10 p.m. Four days before, they were average rural Kansans, some slightly annoyed by their jury duty appointment. Now they were to decide whether Floyd Bledsoe spent the rest of his life in prison.

Ed Benton, the juror who became convinced of Floyd's guilt when he heard about two-year-old Cody's reenactments, said other jurors were similarly convinced. "That was the biggest swaying factor. It weighed on our minds real bad…it haunted us. We all kept going back to it."

Nearly three hours after deliberations began, Nafziger called the jury into the courtroom. "The bailiff advises me that you have been deliberating and that it's close to five o'clock. I told you I wouldn't keep you past five o'clock in the evening. Do you think it would be best to go ahead and break for the evening and come back in the morning?"

Terry Brubaker, the presiding juror, said he and the others had made progress in their deliberations but "we have a lot of issues." He recommended they break for the night. The judge obliged, sending them home, where many would think of little else but the decision before them.

Unaware of the jury's leanings, Floyd was as confident as ever in an acquittal. He wasn't the only one. A guard who walked him to and from his jail cell had some advice: "You might as well pack up your stuff, you're going home." No one who watched the trial seemed to think he would be convicted.

By the time they returned at nine o'clock the next morning, most jurors' minds were made up. Though some acknowledged the evidence wasn't definitive, it didn't take long before they had a verdict. "Everybody on that jury thought he was guilty," Benton recalled. "We didn't argue back and forth about it. We went around it several times and when we voted that was it."

At 10:06 a.m. on April 28, 2000, the dozen jurors returned to the courtroom with their three verdicts, all but two of them avoiding eye contact with the defendant as they took their seats. Brubaker handed the verdicts to a bailiff, who handed them to the court's clerk, who read them aloud.

"We, the jury, impaneled and sworn in the above-captioned case, do upon our oath find the defendant guilty of murder in the first degree."

"We, the jury, impaneled and sworn in the above-captioned case, do upon our oath find the defendant guilty of aggravated kidnapping."

"We, the jury, impaneled and sworn in the above-captioned case, do upon our oath find the defendant guilty of aggravated indecent liberties with a child."

Jurors were polled at Kurth's request. One by one, they told the judge that yes, those were their verdicts. Yes, they really did find Floyd Bledsoe guilty.

Benton, recalling the sentiment within the deliberation room, described a desire for revenge. Jurors had paid close attention to the trial and yearned to make someone pay for the brutal crime that had shocked their seemingly wholesome town. "The jury decided that the evidence wasn't overwhelming but we all decided to convict him because he was the only one we could make accountable for this poor girl's murder."

The trial had left him with a negative opinion of all male Bledsoes. None of them were angels, he said. "We knew someone in that family – one of those two boys or their father – killed that poor girl. This was our best chance to lock one of them up."

At the defense table, the man they had locked up went numb, just as he had when he was arrested. He was trapped in the amber of the moment.

To onlookers, his knees appeared to have buckled, but he couldn't feel them. The world around him had gone mad, hadn't it? Must have. His mind couldn't process what was occurring. Psychological paralysis took the place of cognition.

"It hits you pretty quick," he said years later. "First you get the numbness, then it builds and continues to build for a while."

A thought entered his mind: Where had the jurors been? Had they really been in the same courtroom – on the same planet? If so, how could they have missed so much and been fooled so grandly? A surreal trial had ended with the most surreal conclusion imaginable.

"Everything is just so crazy that you're like, 'Where are all of these people living that they can't see it?' When you sit there and you go through the trial, it's numbing. Then when you hear the jury come back with guilty verdicts, that's when you lose all feeling."

What the hell just happened, Kurth asked himself. He leaned over to Floyd and told him it wasn't over, there was still an appeals process. Then he bolted from the courtroom and sat in his pickup truck as he tried to collect his thoughts before the reporters tracked him down.

In the gallery, Heidi Bledsoe's saucer eyes and long, pale face gave her the look of Shelley Duvall in *The Shining*. As a photographer turned his lens to her, she bit down on her nails. The ensuing photograph is a stark image of a young woman, not yet old enough to drink alcohol, who has already witnessed anguish far beyond her years.

"I hope that they're right," she told a reporter. "I wasn't there. I don't know who did it, but I hope they got the right person."

Tommie Sue Arfmann, who had always held Floyd in deep suspicion, was far more pleased than her daughter, recalling for reporters the heartbreak she still felt at Camille's death, a heartbreak felt by jurors as they weighed whether to convict or acquit. In the courtroom and outside it, she wore a pin with a photo of Camille's face.

"I still wait for her to come home, but I know she's not going to. How do you justify a fourteen-year-old girl lying in her grave? There's no reason this should have happened. She was a wonderful little kid."

Tommie Sue had been convinced of Floyd's guilt from the day Camille went missing, she told reporters. When she quizzed him about his whereabouts, Floyd wouldn't look her in the eye, she said. When Floyd saw crime scene photos of Camille's body, he didn't cry, she said. "I'm just so relieved they found him guilty. I knew he was."

She remained angry at law enforcement officers for shrugging off Camille's disappearance as that of a runaway teenager and failing to search sooner. Heidi, breaking down in tears, issued a warning: "For all the kids out there who are scared, just tell somebody. Never underestimate what somebody might do."

Rosanna Erhart, Heidi and Camille's sister, did not share her mother's certainty. Floyd, she believed, was "involved after the fact" but did not commit the murder. "This took a vicious person – it was a hateful crime – and that person is still walking the streets." And who was that person? She would rather not say.

Sheriff Dunnaway was confident they locked away the right brother, telling reporters, "My true feeling is that justice has been done. We believe, very seriously, that this is the right person." He offered up one last piece of circumstantial evidence from his investigation to cap off an entirely circumstantial case: "Whenever we would go somewhere, we had information he would come behind and ask what the cops were asking. That was unusual to me." When asked pointedly why he arrested Floyd and released Tom, Dunnaway said, "There are some things I can't tell you."

Vanderbilt sounded less assured. "There's a ton of evidence out there that we don't have. Hopefully now we'll find out more, but we may never have all the answers." Both Dunnaway and Vanderbilt said they were convinced Tom had turned himself in because he feared his brother's blackmail and wanted Camille to receive a proper burial, not because he had killed the girl. Still, Vanderbilt said he was "shocked" by the guilty verdicts. "Knowing what happened and not being able to present all the evidence we could, we were worried."

The trial had remained on the front page of the *Journal-World* all week. On the day after it ended, it dominated the top half. "Murder verdict: Guilty." Front and center was Heidi's frightened face, what remained of her fingernails in her mouth. Joel Mathis' lede: "Floyd S. Bledsoe kidnapped, molested and murdered 14-year-old Camille Arfmann, jurors decided Friday."

Even as he wrote about the guilty verdicts, Mathis made clear the lack of evidence tying Floyd to the crimes. A paragraph near the end of the article noted, "Vanderbilt spent as much time at trial defending Tom Bledsoe's innocence as he did arguing Floyd Bledsoe's guilt."

After his predictions of acquittal and his shock at obtaining convictions, Vanderbilt told Mathis two seemingly contradictory sentences: "We all believed this was the right thing. It was real hard to stick to our guns and prosecute the case."

Kurth was visibly disappointed and pledged to appeal the verdicts. He told Mathis, "Floyd was ready to go home yesterday."

Jean Giles Phillips, one of the many attorneys who would later represent Floyd in his appeals, called the trial "a farce." Another one, Alice Craig, said, "The entire trial was about how it wasn't Tom."

"It was a very strange trial," Craig recalled. "When you read the transcript you wonder, how could this ever happen in our judicial system?"

Around town, skepticism of the guilty verdicts ran deep. As a reporter noted, "there are about as many opinions as to how fourteen-year-old Camille Arfmann died as there are people to ask." Across the street from the courthouse sat the Oskie Tavern, a popular watering hole, where townsfolk had spent the week whispering about the latest details over whiskey and beer.

Bartender Barbara Leger summed up what she was hearing: "That's the gist I'm getting, that it wasn't the right person or that there was more involved." There were too many discrepancies, she said. Leger, like many others at the tavern, thought there should be a new trial.

Every small town has an eccentric; some have several. Oskaloosa had, among others, Roy "Kansas" Downs, a World War II veteran and longtime civil servant who was in his mid-seventies by then. Downs styled himself a famed craps shooter, a riverboat and casino gambler of legend. He wrote a book, "Crapshooting Made Simple and Easy," and published it himself.[7] The cover featured his smiling face, topped with an orange trilby hat, his elbow leaning on a craps table. He signed it and sold it whenever possible; wherever folks would listen to his tales of Las Vegas conquests. Downs was often overheard talking about the conversations he had with jurors in the Bledsoe case, namely that a female juror told him the panel had been so outraged at

---

[7] Downs' craps advice was conservative and simple: bet on the six and the eight, which are commonly hit, while avoiding the high-paying sucker bets; quit while you're ahead, never get greedy and walk away when the dice are cold. "It is not my aim to make a living by gambling," he wrote. "Neither is it my intent to lose my living by gambling."

Camille's murder it was hellbent on punishing any defendant put forth by the prosecution.

Kurth had a professional habit of talking with jurors after a major case to learn what resonated with them and what fell flat, so he could improve as a trial attorney. The Bledsoe jury was unlike any he had ever polled. One juror said they thought Floyd was innocent but convicted him in hopes the real killer would come forward. Kurth, aghast, never talked with jurors again in his career after that.

There had been only one constant companion of Floyd during the trial, only one person who sat on the defense side day after day and joked with him during recesses to calm him. Floyd's family had all but abandoned him; some even testified against him. His estranged wife was grief-stricken and perplexed, unsure of what to think. So, Floyd's companion was a reverend forty years his senior.

Bob Penrod was a sixty-three-year-old chain-smoking minister who preached to inmates at the Jefferson County Jail. He had never met Floyd before stopping by the jail one day after his arrest. They quickly became acquaintances, then friends. Penrod took an unusual interest in the case, chatting with reporters about Floyd's innocence during breaks in the trial and volunteering to pay for a polygraph test, perhaps unaware that Floyd had already taken one.

Before the verdicts came down, Penrod never asked Floyd whether he committed murder. The young man didn't want to discuss his case; he wanted moral and religious instruction. So, that's what Penrod provided. In return, Floyd proselytized to his fellow inmates, converting at least four to Christianity in the forty days before his trial, according to the preacher.

They became so close that Floyd asked Penrod to attend the trial. The reverend agreed on one condition: Floyd must promise to remain confident it would end in acquittal. "I told Floyd, 'Let the truth come out. The truth will be what sets you free.'"

But when the verdicts were read, the truth did not come out and he was not set free. The next day, Penrod visited the Jefferson County Jail. He wanted a straight answer to the question he had never asked.

"You need to look at me and say, yes or no, did you do it?"

In response, a straight answer: "I didn't do it."

The two prayed for God's guidance. They prayed also for Tom's soul.

Penrod knew other people believed his newfound friend was a murderer who was duping the minister. The truth, Penrod believed, would become clear soon enough.

"You don't know whether you've been conned or not," Penrod told a reporter later. "The proof is in the pudding – how they live their life after the heat is off. I can't judge him. Only God knows the truth."

ELEVEN

A month later, on May 31, 2000, Tommie Sue Arfmann was shopping in Lawrence when her eyes came across a *Journal-World* headline: "Bledsoe attorney seeks review." The article said there would be a hearing that morning in Oskaloosa and John Kurth would be arguing there had been insufficient evidence to convict Floyd Bledsoe and therefore Judge Nafziger should either release him or schedule a retrial.

Tommie Sue dropped what she was doing and sped to Oskaloosa. Though Kansas law requires prosecutors to notify crime victims of all court hearings, Vanderbilt had not bothered to tell Tommie Sue about this one. "I feel kind of like it was a slap in the face," she told a reporter. "You shouldn't have to buy a paper just to find out what happened in your murdered daughter's case."

At the hearing, Kurth contended there wasn't enough evidence to convict Floyd of murder. "The theory simply doesn't add up. There wasn't sufficient time for the defendant to find the gun, use the gun and return the gun, nor was there sufficient time for the defendant to obtain custody of the victim."

Vanderbilt disagreed: "There's a lot of circumstantial evidence, but even with [Kurth's] theory of the case, we successfully proved beyond a reasonable doubt that [Floyd] committed the crime of premeditated murder."

Kurth's motion was a longshot and he knew his odds were low. Nafziger ruled the jury had "substantial and competent evidence" for all crimes. The judge said there was evidence Floyd had the time to kidnap and kill Camille.

***

After a few delays, sentencing was held on July 14, 2000. The defendant had chosen to speak in his own defense for the first time in eight months. But first, his attorney attempted another dubious maneuver.

John Kurth called to the stand Verna Walker, Floyd's first-grade teacher.

The day after Camille went missing, Walker and her niece – like many people in Oskaloosa – offered to help the Arfmann family any way they could. In her case, Walker brought Heidi some hot food and offered to take her two sons, Cody and Christian, into town and away from the frantic commotion of the search. It didn't work. "They wanted their daddy all the time they were there," Walker testified.

Next, Kurth called Richard Zule to the stand to correct a previous statement. During the trial, Zule said it would take four or four-and-a-half hours to milk his cows, as Floyd did on the day of Camille's disappearance. Actually, it would have taken an hour longer, Zule told the court now.

Then, Floyd Laverne Bledsoe, the defendant's father, stepped into the witness box. He, too, had some new information. One week after Camille's body was found, shell casings were discovered at the crime scene. The elder Floyd had heard gunshots that same morning, indicating the casings found may not have been linked to Camille's murder. Though he had told this to Detective Carreno, the information was never relayed to Kurth or mentioned during the trial.

There was one more witness to call: Catherine Bledsoe, the defendant's mother. She was annoyed about being subpoenaed to testify again and hardly the cooperative witness Kurth would have hoped for. When the defense attorney attempted to have her replay Floyd's phone call from jail, she repeatedly said she couldn't remember it. Perhaps her recollection was off when she testified at the trial, she said, or perhaps it wasn't. "I don't remember, I told you."

After the four witnesses testified, Kurth made a motion for a new trial. His reasoning: Floyd L. Bledsoe's new testimony about the gunshots and a lack of evidence that his client was guilty. "You know the jury has a tough job, judge, and this court has a difficult job in such cases, but if the jury doesn't do right, I believe it's up to the court to do right." It was another longshot and it was quickly struck down.

"The court," Nafziger said, "finds that the defendant has failed to establish by substantial competent evidence that it would be in the best interest of justice for his motion for a new trial to be granted."

With that, the two sides proceeded to sentencing. Vanderbilt recommended a life sentence for murder, a sentence of 155 months for kidnapping and an additional forty-one months for aggravated indecent liberties, all to run consecutively. "While she was alive, while she was able to perceive what was going on, he had a gun to the back of her head, her breasts exposed, and he executed her with the gun touching the back of her head. That alone is egregious enough to run the sentences consecutive."

He went on. "For public safety, a man who would commit these offenses under these circumstances should not be exposed to the public. Twenty-five years from now there is going to be another Camille Arfmann out there and he will be eligible for parole at that point. That girl, as well as all of the rest of the girls out there fourteen years of age which he may decide that he wants to take as his wife, concubine, paramour, should be protected because if they are not and they don't want to be, they can end up in a trash dump with a bullet in the back of their head and three in their chest."

Kurth, while still pleading that his client was innocent, urged Nafziger to sentence him concurrently, making Floyd eligible for parole after a quarter century. He noted that Floyd had no criminal record prior to his wrongful convictions.

Each side had one person speak on their behalf. For the defense, it would be Floyd himself. For the prosecution, it was Tommie Sue Arfmann, Camille's grieving mother. From both, passion and anger spewed out uncontrollably.

"This has been like going through hell, except here on earth," Tommie Sue told the judge. "There is no waking up from this nightmare because she's no longer there. I still look for her to come home at any minute and we know she's not going to."

She agreed with Vanderbilt's recommended sentence. "I think they should give him life. She got life. I think he should get life…I don't think he should ever walk out of that jailhouse alive. I have to live the rest of my life without my daughter and that's the hardest thing that anybody has ever had to do."

Floyd should have been ready for what came next. It was his moment to finally speak out, to decry the injustice that had stolen so much from him before it took his freedom forever. It was all too much though. There was too much to say, too much to tell those in attendance. He had sat silently for too long.

What followed was a rambling, almost incoherent monologue of more than five minutes. His chin and lower lip quivered with enmity. His knuckles rapped the defense table as he made his points. He paused several times to choke back tears.

"First off, I'd like to say I didn't do it."

"Common sense tells you if you go to the hardware store at four o'clock, arrive there at 4:15 p.m., the lady at the hardware store – who I have not even known, you know, barely at all – says, 'Yeah, he was there at 4:15 p.m. and stayed until 4:35 p.m.' Richard Zule testifies that I arrived back at the dairy at ten till five. Okay. Common sense tells you that's fifteen – fifteen [minutes]."

From there came a spattering of evidence fragments: "Colonel Knoebel testified that it was pristine," "My car has no exhaust," "Where Knoebel was was four miles west of where the dairy is," "They searched my property, nothing turned up." It was a laundry list of details that didn't add up to much. Vanderbilt had cobbled them together anyhow. Now Floyd was trying to deconstruct the narrative. The result was incoherence.

"Tom Bledsoe, my brother – why he's done this, I don't know or what he's done, I don't know. I wasn't there. All I was doing was what I thought was right. I went to work to support my family and I milked my cows. I came home, I helped to find a little girl…The person who had two hours of unaccountable time wasn't Floyd Bledsoe, it was Tom Bledsoe."

He explained how Tom's receipt from Rusty's was inaccurate. Though true, that was difficult for a judge to understand even when explained by experienced detectives. Floyd, again, was rambling. Daylight savings time, military time, cash register tapes. He had too much information in his head, too much he needed to blurt out, and almost no structure for doing so. The result, again, was incoherence.

"The problem is, they won't listen to the facts. The facts show I didn't do it. The gentleman over there that's writing on his desk," he said, motioning to Vanderbilt, "he continues to say I have two hours of unaccountable time. I want him to show where my two hours of unaccountable time is. If he can show me where my two hours is, then I'll just sit down and shut up and take this time, but he can't because I didn't do it."

Next, he turned to corruption allegations. "The sheriff's office – if they were a road, nobody would be able to drive down it because they are so crooked. There's only a few good cops left in this county." Despite his lack of a criminal record, Floyd said Detective Carreno had once attempted to frame him for a four-wheeler theft. Now he had managed to frame him for something much worse, Floyd said. "The few good officers left in this county came up and said, 'There's no way you could have done it.'"

He accosted Vanderbilt for sowing doubt about his alibi during the trial. "Sure, nobody could say exactly what time I was where, because you are talking about seven months down the road. If they could, the gentlemen over there would have said, 'Well, they're lying...it could have been a few minutes before.' I guarantee you, he couldn't have said where he was on what time and what date exactly. That's all I got."

He was done. He had spoken his piece, unburdening himself of the truth inside that had yearned to come out for those many months. Nafziger thanked him for his speech and handed down his sentence in accordance with Kansas' sentencing guidelines. For first-degree murder: life in prison. For aggravated kidnapping: 155 months. For aggravated indecent liberties with a child: forty-one months. Due to the young age of the victim, Nafziger determined the sentences would run consecutively, as Vanderbilt had hoped. With a bang of the gavel, the court was adjourned.

The sentence was not enough for Tommie Sue Arfmann, who was quick to tell reporters in the hallway, "I think he should've been fried."[8] As for his monologue on innocence, Tommie Sue said, "He's lying. You can always tell when he's lying."

Even then, with a man convicted and sentenced for the murder of Camille Arfmann, Sheriff Roy Dunnaway said, "The case is not closed. I'll put it like this: Do we know the truth, the whole truth? No, we don't. Is there someone out there who knows the whole truth? I believe that's a good possibility. It doesn't sit well with me." Vanderbilt turned the case over to the Kansas Attorney General's Office "to see if there's anything I missed." He hoped the state's attorneys could draw more suspects out.

There was someone out there who knew the whole truth. Tom Bledsoe went back to his life as a security guard, occasional hunter, and devoted

---

[8] The state of Kansas has never executed someone by electrocution and had switched to lethal injection by the time of Floyd's sentence. The state has not executed an inmate since the 1965 hangings of George York and James Latham, remorseless spree killers who murdered seven people across several states. The two were mentioned in Truman Capote's 1966 book *In Cold Blood*, which centered around Richard Hickock and Perry Smith, who had been executed by hanging the year before York and Latham.

attendee of Countryside Baptist Church. At the age of 26 he remained a member of the youth group that met at the Bolinger farm on Fridays.

One afternoon around the time of Floyd's sentencing, a reporter sat at a picnic table on the farm, talking with Jim and Rose Bolinger about Camille and the case. Tom Bledsoe and several boys piled out of a pickup. Spotting the Bolingers, Tom quickly ducked into a building without a word.

"Ever since this happened, I haven't felt at ease around Tom," Rose said. "That's the hard part. I've not only known Camille all these years, I've known Tom and Floyd all these years too. It's not just that Camille's gone –"

After stopping to wipe away a tear, she said, "It's uncertain, because no one will talk." But someone had talked. Wracked with guilt, Tom had called her husband twice the previous November, leaving two voicemail messages seeking forgiveness. He had talked a lot that night and next morning – November 7 and 8, 1999 – about the crimes he had committed. But that had largely been forgotten somehow. All that was left was Rose's unease.

***

With walls and towers of grey stone lining a grey stone building, the 120-year-old Hutchinson Correctional Facility in central Kansas looks more like an unluxurious castle than a modern prison. Inmates – even those in the prison yard – cannot see the world past the high stone walls. Those 1,800 or so prisoners range in categorization from maximum-security to low-security, their cells and freedoms adjusted accordingly.

Floyd, a maximum-security inmate, was alone in a cell. He began lifting weights and put on thirty-five pounds. His prized possessions were pictures of his family, especially his two young sons. As he showed them off to fellow inmates, he quickly learned the perils of doing so.

"That's nice," an inmate told him on the ninth day, "but if you want my advice and you want to make your time the easiest possible, look at them and then put them away. Don't sit there and stare at them because all you're going to do is wish you were there. You're going to tear yourself up."

Floyd was skeptical. *Doesn't this guy know I love my children?* "Man, that seems rough," he told him.

"Trust me. You may not believe it now coming in but a few years from now, you'll understand that it's a coping mechanism. It's learning how to function in a place you don't want to be."

Over time, Floyd would come to see the man was right. Memories of Oskaloosa and the family he left behind only worsened prison, creating mountains and valleys of emotion. What he needed was stability, a hobby to keep his mind at ease. "You are sitting there, and the days seem very long, like the time is never going to add up and start clicking along."

By his tenth day in prison, Floyd knew he needed more to do. The prison offered trade classes to teach inmates blue-collar skills but there was a catch: it wasn't available to those serving life terms or those with more than a decade before their release. The prison's logic was sound. Why train inmates who won't be released anytime soon?

On paper, Floyd Bledsoe was one of those inmates. In his mind, however, he was not. He was innocent and it was only a matter of time before people realized it. If he was going to be locked up, he would use that time to learn something new. He applied for a course on heating and cooling and a program manager went to bat for him. The selling point was, sure, he won't be released anytime soon, but he can repair the prison's heating and cooling equipment while an inmate.

"I just want to learn, in case I do get out, I'll have something to show for it," he told a board tasked with approving such applications. After a week, the board made an exception to their rigid rules and allowed Floyd in. He had a job, though life behind bars remained a bore.

"You wake up, you wash your face, you go to breakfast, you come back. If you have a job, you go to your job. Breakfast is usually between four and five in the morning, you eat lunch at 10:30, you eat supper at four o'clock. If you have a religious call out or some type of call out, that happens around six or seven o'clock, until nine. Then you go to bed, get up, and do it all over again. Five days a week you're working and two days a week – Saturday and Sunday – you have time in the yard during the day but other than that, you're stuck in your cell."

The old cells in Hutchinson were smaller than most Kansas prison cells. If inmates stood up and spread their arms to the side, many could touch the walls. In the summer, the old stones smelled of sweat.

As Chano Young, serving time for two murders, would recall of that time, "When you went to the chow hall, you couldn't just sit anywhere.

All the gangs had their own tables." Fights erupted often, seemingly out of nowhere. Cigarettes were smuggled in and sold for two dollars each. Before long, a dangerous synthetic marijuana known as K2 took the place of tobacco.

***

In Oskaloosa – and just about everywhere in America – the summer of 2000 was campaign season. Vanderbilt and Sheriff Dunnaway, fresh off their much-talked-about conviction of Floyd, were both up for re-election.

Vanderbilt, a Democrat, did not shy away from the case. Obtaining a conviction of Floyd Bledsoe had proven his talents and prosecutorial ability to the people of Jefferson County, he told reporters. The best part of his job was "putting people in prison." He added, "I've had a good experience here. It's enjoyable to work here. We've got good judges and good law enforcement."

Like many prosecutors, Vanderbilt ran a tough-on-crime campaign. "This office is no place to show mercy. That is not what I'm hired to do," he told the *Oskaloosa Independent*. "I hate the term plea bargain," said the man who had offered Floyd an unusually generous five-year plea bargain. He vowed to crack down on juvenile offenders.

Challenging him was Mike Hayes, the county attorney from 1985 through 1992, who had most recently worked as Tom Bledsoe's highly influential defense attorney. As an observer half-jokingly noted, on one side was the most powerful attorney in the county. On the other side was the county attorney.

Hayes, who defended a child murderer six months before, ran on a platform of helping children, touting his time as a family law attorney. "I don't have any of my own, but most of the kids I represent I look at as my own." The Republican ran a write-in campaign, making him a longshot against Vanderbilt, but he didn't suffer from a lack of name recognition. Plus, he was a Republican in conservative Jefferson County.

Dunnaway, also a Republican, was challenged by Democrat Gary Bledsoe Jr., a twenty-three-year-old military veteran and cousin of both Floyd and Tom. Challenging a man who had been sheriff since 1983 would not be easy for anyone. For a no-name twentysomething, it was practically impossible. Gary Jr.'s odds were worsened still when he moved to Nebraska three weeks before the election. No one in Oskaloosa could remember a Jefferson County candidate moving out of state during the campaign.[9]

Election Day was November 7 that year and the incumbents dominated. Vanderbilt trounced Hayes – 4,420 to 1,632. He told a reporter, "I thank the people who voted for me. Those who voted for Mike Hayes are clearly saying I need to make changes." If there was outrage in Oskaloosa at the prosecution of Floyd Bledsoe, it didn't show in the vote totals. Dunnaway won by an even larger margin – 6,017 votes to 1,241.

Hayes would make his return to the county attorney's office four years later, winning an uncontested election in 2004 when Vanderbilt chose not to run for reelection. Hayes lost the seat in 2008 to Caleb Stegall – later a Kansas Supreme Court justice – but before he stepped down, the county commission, in a meeting closed to the public, moved some of Stegall's budget to the county counselor's office. The county counselor was Mike Hayes' wife, Jan, and her office was Hayes & Hayes, the couple's law firm.

***

In Kansas, defendants sentenced to life in prison or the death penalty can directly appeal their conviction to the Kansas Supreme Court, bypassing the Kansas Court of Appeals, which typically handles first appeals.

Floyd's first attorney had been John Kurth. His second was Mary Curtis, a highly capable public defender who had worked on both sides of the Kansas-Missouri border and co-founded Kansas' death penalty defense unit. Between 1996 and 2006, she argued more than twenty-five cases before the high court.

"There was no evidence of Floyd Bledsoe's guilt," she wrote in a legal brief on March 23, 2001, "other than the uncorroborated, alleged admission to his brother, Tom. The circumstantial evidence is neither consistent with his guilt nor inconsistent with a reasonable theory of his innocence."

She attacked the three convictions, arguing each was unproven beyond

---

[9] Gary Bledsoe did not run for office because of Floyd and seemingly did not mention the case in interviews during the campaign. He ran on a five-point plan that included the creation of a drug task force, adding sobriety checkpoints, requiring jail inmates perform more community service and incorporating a physical fitness program within the sheriff's department "to erase the stereotype of the coffee-and-doughnut police officer," as the *Oskaloosa Independent* wrote.

a reasonable doubt and a violation of her client's due process rights. Not only had the state failed to prove Floyd committed the crimes, she said, it failed to prove two crimes had been committed *at all*. "There is no evidence the victim did not voluntarily go with her killer, or that she was confined at any point," she wrote in regard to the aggravated kidnapping charge. As for aggravated indecent liberties, "there was no evidence that the victim was alive when her shirt was pulled up, or that she was fondled or touched while she was alive...It is a mystery how the jury could have found Mr. Bledsoe guilty of any of the charges."

Curtis put the trial on trial. Admission of hearsay evidence from a two-year-old was a clear error, she said, and obviously prejudicial to her client. "If Cody witnessed the events, he would have made a powerful witness. But repetition of Cody's hearsay statements left the defense unable to cross-examine him as to whether he saw what he was describing, was told about it, or made it up out of overheard bits and pieces of the adults' conversations."

Also inadmissible, Curtis wrote, was Detective Carreno's testimony at the end of the trial that told of Tom's supposed truth-telling. Carreno had said Tom "was able to stand up for the first time in front of Floyd and tell him the truth, to state the truth." The truth, he told jurors just before they deliberated, was that Floyd killed Camille.

Kansas Supreme Court precedent bars witnesses from opining on the guilt or innocence of the defendant and narrows the scope of their testimony to matters on which they are an expert. "Police officers have an aura of special reliability and trustworthiness to the average citizen," Curtis wrote. Vanderbilt expanded that aura by "play[ing] up" Carreno's qualifications before seeking his opinion "on the credibility of the state's star witness." Because Tom's testimony "could logically be met with skepticism," it's only natural that Vanderbilt sought to bolster it. He did so, Curtis argued, through the use of inadmissible and highly prejudicial testimony.

"In this case, the prosecutor invaded the province of the jury by attempting to have...Carreno serve as a human lie detector," even after Judge Nafziger had prohibited him from doing so. She would use that term – human lie detector – twice more before she concluded. Carreno's inadmissible testimony, done in defiance of the judge, was especially troublesome because "the case hinged entirely on the jury's view of Tom's testimony...there was not sufficient evidence on any of the counts to convict Floyd Bledsoe unless the jury found Tom's testimony credible."

In a footnote to her fifty-eight-page brief, Curtis wrote, "Interestingly, the circumstantial evidence would have been more than sufficient to convict Tom of the abduction and murder of C.A., even without his confession." (In Kansas appellate courts, juvenile sexual assault victims are identified only by their initials.) With that, she urged the seven most powerful judges in Kansas to overturn Floyd's convictions and send the case back to Oskaloosa for a new trial.

In his forty-eight-page response – containing numerous typos, grammatical errors and missed punctuation – Vanderbilt wrote: "The evidence and testimony presented to the jury is sufficient for a rational factfinder to have found the defendant guilty of killing Camille Arfmann with premeditation." The supposed evidence Vanderbilt cited was either specious claims – "His son, Cody, witnessed Camille being shot and put in the ditch," "The defendant admitted to his brother, Tom Bledsoe, that he killed Camille with Tom's gun" – or disjointed details, such as the screams Knoebel (misspelled as "Knobel") heard.

Vanderbilt returned to the theory he had told during closing minutes of the trial. Floyd picked up Camille from the trailer, took her to Zule Dairy, where he "was confining her against her will," then left her there while he picked up Cody from his babysitter, shot her sometime in the overnight hours and buried her in the brome field. "The defendant simply executed Camille." It was a theory chocked full of new details that had not been mentioned, let alone proven, during the trial.

To counter Curtis' claim of insufficient evidence of a kidnapping, Vanderbilt repeated the testimony of Knoebel. "Somebody help me, please don't hurt me," were the words of someone being held against their will, he said. "Because Colonel Knoebel did not here [sic] a shot there, she had to have been moved from that location to another," he wrote, "and because Cody witnessed her being shot and he was not there until after the defendant picked him up from the babysitters [sic]...Camille was being taken or confined against her will."

To Curtis' protestation that the introduction of a two-year-old's testimony is inadmissible, Vanderbilt had a perfect retort: Kurth did it. It was John Kurth, in his cross-examination of Rose Bolinger on day one of the trial, who had first told the jury of young Cody's words. In 1993, the Kansas Supreme Court had ruled a "party who introduces hearsay evidence into the trial cannot later claim on appeal that the hearsay evidence should have been excluded."

Oral arguments before the Supreme Court in *State of Kansas v. Floyd S. Bledsoe* took place December 4, 2001. Floyd was confident, just as he was before the jury announced its verdicts, recalling how Nafziger had been skeptical of the state's evidence during the trial. "I thought, well, if one judge can see that, surely these judges can."

Curtis and Vanderbilt, each with fifteen minutes to make their case, rehashed the trial. Curtis compared it to a murder mystery, a "whodunit" with an ending that didn't fit. "This case in many ways is like one of those novels. But in this case, the state failed to solve the mystery," she told the seven justices.

Vanderbilt countered with circumstantial evidence at every turn. "The defendant had the motive and he had the opportunity. The part of the mystery that was solved was who did it and why."

Vanderbilt had two enormous points in his favor: the reluctance of Kansas appellate courts to reweigh evidence and the fact that it was Kurth, not he, who had first introduced Cody's words. When the high court issued its opinion on February 1, 2000, it was unanimous.

"The jury heard Tom's testimony," wrote Justice Fred Six. "Floyd did not testify. The case was tried and argued to the jury primarily as a contest of Tom's credibility. The jury believed Tom. That it was entitled to do. Bledsoe essentially asks us to reweigh the evidence. Our function is not to reweigh the evidence or pass on the credibility of witnesses."

The convictions were upheld, all of them. Justice Six's opinion repeated many of Vanderbilt's dubious claims: "The evidence suggests that Cody witnessed C.A. being shot and put in the ditch...Bledsoe knew Tom kept a pistol in his truck...He admitted to Tom that he killed C.A. with Tom's gun...He told Tom where the body was buried." In explaining his affirmation of the aggravated kidnapping conviction, Six repeated Vanderbilt's brief word-for-word, aside from cleaning up a few errors in Vanderbilt's verbiage and sentence structure.

Randy Carreno's testimony was deemed admissible. This was likely a surprise even to Vanderbilt, who had argued that Carreno's testimony may have been an error but was harmless. Six ruled that Carreno "was not vouching for Tom's credibility" when he repeatedly referred to Tom telling the truth. "The jury was presented with Tom's version of what happened and was left to weigh the credibility of the statements. We find no error."

It was a total and complete loss for Floyd. A dozen jurors and eight judges had now found reason to keep him locked up forever. Five years would pass before his appeal could be heard again.

***

There was a seminar on inner healing at Hutchinson Correctional one week later. Forgiveness can set you free, a lecturer told Floyd and the other men. It was an uplifting message to the man from Oskaloosa who had a lot of people to forgive – his brother, his parents, law enforcement, the county attorney. He wouldn't have to wait long to put into practice what the lecturer had preached. His parents were visiting the next day.

"My goal was to say, 'Look, I forgive you guys for everything. I forgive Tom, I forgive the state, I forgive everybody.' In my mind I thought I was the happiest person in the world because this is what I was going to use to get myself free."

In a visiting room at the prison, his parents sat at a table without a tablecloth or chairs, only a few stools. It had been eight days since his appeal was denied by the state's highest court. His mother asked, "Why are you so sad?"

Floyd, incredulous: "What?"

"Normally you're so happy."

"My direct appeal just got denied. I'm stuck in prison for the rest of my life and I'm supposed to be happy?" The forgiveness was leaving his mind.

"Well, we all know that, we read all that in the paper," Cathy Bledsoe said. "But normally you're so happy."

That was it. Forgiveness was a bust, at least for now. "I thought I could do this but I can't," he told his parents. "Don't write me, don't call me, don't come visit me. I'll let you know when I'm ready." He walked out of the visitation room mad not only at those who had raised him but he who had made him. Why had God taken away this opportunity at forgiveness, this opportunity at psychological freedom? By the time he reached his cell, tears were streaming down his face.

A guard came by to tell him there was another inner-healing seminar that day. Floyd wasn't going, he was too angry, he said. The guard responded in a curious way: by leaving the door to his cell open, in case he changed his mind.

"Well, I might as well go," Floyd told himself. "After all, they have food."

He sat in the back and heard more about forgiveness. Forgiveness, he heard, is not a weapon to be wielded. Forgiveness does not always change the offender but it sets him free. Unforgiveness is a psychological jail cell shared with those who have wronged him. He realized then that he no longer had to live with the anger, the bitterness, the resentment for what other people had done to him. "Forgiveness is not a one-time action. Forgiveness is a day-to-day activity. It's a day-to-day choice," he would say many years later.

Just two relatives had remained in contact with Floyd throughout his ordeal: his uncle Gary and aunt Jan. Other family members drifted in and out of Floyd's life, moving on when their own lives busied. But he could call his aunt and uncle, no matter what happened. They wrote letters and spoke over the phone. Floyd was upbeat ninety-nine percent of the time, but occasionally depressed by the slow churn of the legal system. Gary, who had not spoken to Floyd Sr. or Tom since 1999, sometimes considered tracking them down and striking up a conversation about the case in hopes of catching them in a confession but never did. He listened to town gossip for clues that could help Floyd but heard none.

Cindy Fullerton, Floyd's half-sister, had cut off contact after his conviction, believing him as guilty as the police and judges said he was. As time went on, she began to reconsider. She had been fed information about Floyd from his mother – that Floyd was a drug addict, for example – that she came to doubt. She began to question Floyd's guilt and what their shared mother was telling her. Before long, she believed Floyd, an innocent man, had been framed by his family. When Fullerton, who lived out of the state, visited Oskaloosa, she avoided Tom and refused to be around him alone.

"Someone who killed once can always kill again," she would say.

TWELVE

On the west side of the University of Kansas campus is Green Hall, a five-story vanilla building that houses the school of law. In one corner of one floor is the Paul E. Wilson Project for Innocence and Post-Conviction Remedies, a series of small offices overloaded with leaning piles of case work. It is staffed by three law professors and a rotating band of idealistic young law students, the sort of place that seems to run on grit and determination.

It was apparent to those at the Project for Innocence, then known as the KU Defender Project, that the Bledsoe trial was flawed. They reached out to one of the top defense attorneys in the state, Richard Ney in Wichita. Floyd had first heard the name Richard Ney one day over lunch at Hutchinson Correctional Facility. After he described his case to a fellow inmate and friend, Tom Cooley, Cooley told him, "If ten percent of what you told me is true, this man can help you."

The problem was Ney's fee: ten thousand dollars. Floyd had lost a lot of money and was earning nearly nothing; Ney's fee was not feasible. At the Project for Innocence's suggestion, Ney took the case anyway and went to work on what in Kansas is commonly called a 1507 appeal – the claim that a conviction should be reversed because the defendant's trial attorney was ineffective to the point of violating the defendant's constitutional rights.

"[Cooley] said, 'You've got to hear about this case.' I said, 'Oh, hell no,'" Ney recalls of his disbelief the first time he heard the facts. "He said, 'No, it's true.' I said, 'Well, if Floyd wants to contact me, fine.' He eventually did and we started talking about the case. I was a little skeptical that it really could be as horrific as it turned out to be but it was and more so."

There's an idiom in some of the more cynical circles of law: "When you're on trial for your life, hire either the best lawyer in town or the worst." Floyd's parents had hired the best and paid him to represent Tom. The question was whether Floyd had been appointed the worst. Sure, John Kurth had made some mistakes, but was he unconstitutionally bad at his job?

Ney believed so. On January 30, 2003, he filed a 1507 motion with the Jefferson County District Court alleging Kurth's constitutionally ineffective assistance had robbed Floyd Bledsoe of his right to a fair trial. He admitted into evidence thirteen exhibits, most of which were statements given to law enforcement by people whom Kurth did not call to testify.

"Obviously, we found that the trial attorney was unbelievably bad, just from reading the transcripts," Ney says. "We looked at the evidence, which wasn't presented or wasn't presented well. Then we filed a petition."

1507 cases make for strange bedfellows. The defense attorney must show a previous defense attorney was woefully negligent while the government defends the original defense attorney, claiming he was effective. To the layman observer, it can seem paradoxical.

***

A year after Floyd was convicted, Tim James went on trial for allegedly aiding and abetting the beating of an elderly Jefferson County man in 1999, the year Camille was killed. As in the Bledsoe case, the judge was Gary Nafziger, the prosecutor was Jim Vanderbilt and the defense attorney was John Kurth.

James' teenage stepson and a friend broke into the trailer of Judson Smith, beat him, tied him up and robbed him of money and compact discs. At a preliminary hearing, the stepson, Chris James, decided to "tell the truth," implicating his stepfather in the crime. Chris James' testimony varied wildly between the time of the crime and the preliminary hearing, then changed again between the preliminary hearing and the trial. Later, after his stepfather was tried, his story changed yet again. He would write in jailhouse letters that Tim James had no role in the crime.

Fortunately for Tim James, he had alibi witnesses. He was living with neighbors at the time of the crime and those neighbors could tell the court he was with them when the crime occurred. Unfortunately for Tim James, Kurth never called those witnesses to testify. He also didn't speak to his client's divorce attorney, who had information that could have impeached the testimony of the stepson and his friend. The jury convicted James of aiding and abetting aggravated burglary, aiding and abetting aggravated robbery, and aiding and abetting aggravated kidnapping. He was sentenced by Nafziger to 253 months in prison. His stepson and friend, who admitted to beating the victim, were sentenced to 101 months in prison after becoming star witnesses for the government.

Tim James appealed his case to the Kansas Court of Appeals. Vanderbilt, whose job duties included filing a brief in support of the convictions, never got around to doing so. On May 2, 2003, a three-judge panel reversed James' convictions, ruling that he was "prejudiced by his attorney's failure to contact witnesses, subpoena witnesses, etc." The court was also critical of Vanderbilt, noting the prosecutor "has not found it worth (his) time or effort to file a brief contesting defendant's allegations on appeal. The failure of the State to file a brief plays a significant part in our decision."

Jimmie Allen Vanderbilt's two-term tenure as county attorney was a showcase in substandard law. In his first year on the job, a man named Andrew Mavrovich was convicted. When Mavrovich appealed his sentence, Vanderbilt said he "wasn't going to waste (his) damn time responding to this crap." He also refused to write a brief in the methamphetamine case of Randy Robinson, prompting the Court of Appeals to erase Robinson's convictions in 2001.

In 2003, Vanderbilt told a judge that he sometimes declines to file briefs because he has poor oral argument and writing skills. "As a result I have always believed that my actual participation in the appellate process was insignificant."

There were other problems. While using a county-funded phone for personal use, he piled up monthly fees far exceeding his monthly allowance, then refused to reimburse the county for them. He was also slow to pay back personal expenses on the county's credit card. Two years before, he told county commissioners he was immune from their attempts to limit his spending and refused to turn in receipts, saying, "The commission cannot set my policies."[10]

The stress of the job and Vanderbilt's personal life sent him along a downward spiral. A psychologist later determined that around the time he refused

---

[10] When Vanderbilt first ran for county attorney, defeating Hayes in 1996 despite not living in Jefferson County at the time, he ran a campaign ad in the *Oskaloosa Independent*, vowing to give the position his full attention. "Jim will have NO outside law practice of any kind," the ad stated. In 2001, burdened by child support and student loan debt, he told Jefferson County commissioners that his position didn't pay enough, so he would work part-time as county attorney and part-time as a private attorney while still drawing his full salary from the county.

to prosecute Tom Bledsoe and instead prosecuted Floyd Bledsoe, Vanderbilt "was cognitively and psychologically dysfunctioning." While under investigation by the Kansas Disciplinary Administrator's Office, Vanderbilt declined to run for re-election in 2004, handing the seat to Mike Hayes. Three months after he left office, the Supreme Court suspended Vanderbilt's license for one year due to a "pattern of misconduct" that "caused actual harm" to Jefferson County.

***

It was against that backdrop that the case of Floyd Bledsoe returned to the Oskaloosa courtroom of Judge Gary Nafziger on October 22, 2004. Because Vanderbilt had turned the case over to the Kansas Attorney General's Office, the government was represented by assistant attorney general Kristafer Ailslieger.

Richard Ney, like Mary Curtis before him, put the trial on trial. His most poignant points centered on the decision by Kurth and Vanderbilt to allow the words of a two-year-old to be heard in court.

Kurth and Vanderbilt were called to testify about their pre-trial agreement. Kurth admitted on the stand that Cody Bledsoe's statements were inadmissible under the rule of evidence but he wanted jurors to hear what the young child had to say about his uncle Tom, even if it meant jurors would also hear what the boy had said about his father. "It was more beneficial to us to have the statements from the young man indicate that Tom had [killed her]."

In other words, Kurth argued, it was a strategic decision to let Heidi Bledsoe and Rose Bolinger testify about Cody's words. This was an important legal claim from Kurth. Defense attorneys are given wide latitude by Kansas courts to make strategic decisions, even if those decisions are later found to be detrimental. The burden fell on Ney to prove that Kurth's behavior was both unreasonable and prejudicial to his client's case.

He called to the stand Jean Phillips, a University of Kansas law professor and director of the KU Defender Project. Phillips had researched the use of child witnesses in Kansas cases and couldn't find a single case in the state's history in which a two-year-old was found to be a competent witness. The youngest witness she knew of was four-and-a-half years old and in that case an expert witness was called to testify about the child's competence.

Dr. Marilyn Hutchinson, a psychologist, took the stand. She had agreed to conduct research on the case pro bono and told the court what any parent could; that a two-year-old boy's "competency cannot be reliably determined," in part because a child that age is "extraordinarily suggestible." It is "almost impossible" for a two-year-old to discern truth from reality due to minimal development in the pre-frontal cortex of the brain, she said.

Ney argued that Kurth should have hired an expert like Hutchinson to inform jurors about the unreliability of a two-year-old's testimony, something Kurth, a court-appointed defender, had not even considered doing. Ney pointed to a 2002 case in which the Court of Appeals overturned the sex crime convictions of Thomas Mullins in neighboring Leavenworth County because Mullins' attorney was ineffective in failing to consider hiring an expert to testify about a child's testimony. He urged Judge Nafziger to do the same in Floyd's case.

Ney hurled nineteen other complaints about Kurth's behavior, including his failure to call certain witnesses, object to testimony that damaged his client, request the trial be moved, object to the bulletproof vest Floyd wore and interview prospective jurors further. It was no use, however. On September 28, 2005, Nafziger again sided with the state, writing that Kurth was effective, reasonable and did not prejudice Floyd's right to a defense and a fair trial.

Ney had fully expected to lose in Jefferson County. Within a week, he had filed an appeal with the Kansas Supreme Court. Within a couple months, he had written a seventy-page brief explaining why his client's convictions should be overturned. The Supreme Court agreed to hear the Bledsoe case for a second, and final, time.

***

In February of 2006, Lonnie Mast's mother died. Mast was forty years old and just eight years into a decades-long prison sentence for sex crimes. Heartbroken, he went looking for Floyd Bledsoe.

"He was at a table painting and he told me to sit down and that if I wanted to talk, I could, if I wanted to just sit and cry, I could, and that I should pay no attention to anybody else around or what they might think about me crying. I sat there and just cried and cried. My friend allowed me some time to mourn and was just so kind to me and he will never know fully what that meant to me," Mast recalled a decade later.

The two lived for several years in the same dormitory at Hutchinson, where Floyd became known for his almost saintly tranquility in a harsh and sometimes violent place.

"He always treated me and everyone around him with kindness and respect," Mast said. "Floyd was a kind of quiet guy but he was always happy and made everyone smile. There are a lot of nice guys in prison who messed up in life but Floyd was nice beyond what you would expect and I have always had the utmost respect for Floyd, for how he carried himself and conducted himself because most people, if they were in his situation, would be the complete opposite."

Due to his small stature and soft nature, Floyd faced violence. James Quinton, who was sentenced to a life sentence for sex crimes but would later have his conviction overturned, walked into a secluded part of the dorm one day to find Floyd being pinned down and assaulted. Once, inmates beat him so badly his teeth protruded through his lip.

Another time, a horse-playing inmate put Floyd in a choke hold. "We were all kind of standing around and we didn't think anything of it," Quinton recalls, "we didn't think the hold was locked in because we were all having a conversation. Then, the next thing I know, the guy lets go of Bledsoe and Bledsoe falls to the ground, passed out. Like, bumps his head and every-thing...I wouldn't say that was regular stuff but he was really kind of poked at and he handled it with such grace and dignity. I've never seen it before."

That grace and dignity disarmed fellow inmates and prison staff. Floyd was given unusual leniency for a maximum-security prison, what Quinton came to call his golden pass. "That's why they called him the Little General because he could do things that other guys really couldn't do and get away with, but he could do it in a way that he was trustworthy."

Two years before Lonnie Mast's mother passed away, Floyd was work-ing on the prison's heating and cooling system when he heard from a guard that another inmate was dying. "He doesn't have any family. Nobody. All he's going to do is sit in his cell and rot," Floyd recalls the guard saying. When Floyd asked to sit with the man, he was denied; the prison did not have a hospice program. Floyd promised himself that if such a program was ever created, he would enroll. A few months later, he spotted a flier for hospice classes. As promised, he jumped at the opportunity.

"Fortunately, 99 percent of the guys I got to sit with, I already had a previous friendship with," he recalled. Cancer sent some of his closest friends spiraling downward from perfect health to death in a year. "So, it allowed me to be able to spend the last days with some of them. Two of the guys I got to sit with, they were my work partners. They were people I hung out with for a couple years. It was my way to say that even in this situation, I'm still here, I'm still with you."

As with many religious duties, Floyd convinced a hesitant Quinton to come along. "We would go and sit for days on end over there with inmates who were dying. Floyd was one of the few men who was regularly there, could regularly be called upon."

He also volunteered in the visitation room, operating a hotdog stand or bringing visitors food and drinks, including ice cream for visiting children celebrating a birthday. The room was rife with crime among inmates. "Floyd was the one guy there who was a righteous guy," according to Quinton. "The guys working there who were doing these things, they all knew Bledsoe did not participate but all respected him enough that they knew he wasn't going to tell or let them get in any trouble. He did his thing in such a way that people really respected."

Floyd became close with Quinton's wife and son. The two inmates lived in a basement dorm with an exit to a small outdoor patio surrounded by concrete. It was directly below the door for visitors so, during a snowfall one winter, Quinton had an idea to surprise his young son. "Needless to say, out of the seventy men in the dorm, Bledsoe was the only guy who helped. He followed me in the freezing snow and we built a snowman outside so my son could look out the next day and peer down on it. I always remembered that."

It was Chano Young who had introduced Floyd to the hobby that helped him through the hardest of times – his rollercoaster appeals process, his family's near-abandonment, his inability to see Cody and Christian.

"He asked me to teach him to paint, so I did," Young recalled. "We sat together for hours. Doing the artwork and painting really eased the mind. I felt good to see his painting and I knew that I taught him something that he enjoyed."

Once an avid outdoorsman, Floyd's art centered on wildlife and rural landscapes — pheasants flying over a field, deer and bears walking across panoramic habitats. One painting was printed in a newspaper, another won an award at an art show. They became gifts, a way for Floyd to show his thanks. A painting of a frog hangs at the Project for Innocence.

Though he occasionally played cards and routinely lifted weights, painting and religion were Floyd's escapes and Mast often talked with him about both. He and other inmates came to believe Floyd's peaceful demeanor was an embodiment of his religion. As Mast put it, "He not only talked the talk, he walked the walk" of Christianity.

"I don't have one single bad thing to say about Floyd. He was and is the nicest person, who never gave up on being set free and never gave up on God," Mast said. "Floyd is a true Christian, Floyd is a true friend. Prison can turn good people into bad people, turn a positive into a negative, but Floyd never stopped believing in the Lord. Floyd served the Lord with all his heart; he loved the Lord more than anything and shared his faith when he could. I owe so much to Floyd and the friendship he gave me. He's just an all-around great person. Floyd isn't perfect and I'm sure he had bad days, as we all do, but he never let it show."

The biblical passages Floyd passed on contained hope for the future. There was Jeremiah 29:11 ("For I know the plans I have for you," declares the Lord, "plans to prosper you and not to harm you, plans to give you hope and a future") and a paraphrase of Job 12:22, "What is done in the darkness will be revealed in the light."

Floyd often spent his time helping other people, a rarity in prison life. He cooked for Young and some other guys who still recall fondly his tuna wraps and macaroni and cheese. "A lot of people liked Floyd. He just had that positive vibe."

"One thing you learn is how to make friends," Floyd recalls. "All these guys, they taught me a lot. They took me under their wing to make sure I didn't get in trouble when I first got there, didn't fall into the wrong group, get caught up in a gang or something like that."

Floyd was different than the vast majority of inmates at Hutchinson in at least one way: he didn't belong there. He was innocent and yet, that didn't matter.

"Did I ever think I was above them? No, because I was able to see the person and not what they did or what they were accused of doing. You don't sit there and talk about the case. You learn about the person and who they are. If, eventually, they tell you about it, then they tell you about it, but ninety-five percent of the time you just try to make the best of the situation. You try to forget that you're in prison, which you can never really do, but you learn how to function inside the walls."

Floyd did more than function, he befriended. His solace, grace and faith despite a hellish situation inspired inmates around him. "It's truly remarkable how someone could carry himself the way he did knowing he was innocent," Quinton recalled. "You never heard him bitch and cry and complain and whine or any of that. He just went about his business with a great attitude, was happy and would give anybody anything. He would go without if he saw somebody in need. I saw him give away his last on many occasions."

***

Under the landmark 1963 Supreme Court ruling *Brady v. Maryland*, prosecutors must hand over all exculpatory evidence to defense attorneys. Richard Ney, as he reinvestigated the trial of Floyd Bledsoe, found that did not happen in this case. Each time he filed a motion for discovery, hundreds of police reports unseen by John Kurth spilled forth. When he requested DNA, he was told there was none worth looking at. A vaginal swab had gone missing.

"That is the most egregious violation of rights that I can imagine and there should be prosecutions for withholding that evidence. There's just no excuse," Ney recalls.

Standing in front of the Kansas Supreme Court on October 25, 2006, Ney made many of the same arguments he had made to Judge Nafziger, chief among them that Kurth's behavior was constitutionally deficient and likely altered the outcome of the trial. He also added a new argument: Vanderbilt committed prosecutorial misconduct by citing hearsay evidence – Cody Bledsoe's words – while knowing it was inadmissible in a court of law. As a result, Floyd's convictions should be overturned and a new trial ordered, Ney told the seven justices.

Jared Maag, an assistant attorney general, countered by arguing Kurth's decision-making was strategic, therefore his behavior was not a violation of the defendant's constitutional rights. He said Ney failed to prove the results of the trial would be different without Kurth's missteps. As for Vanderbilt's conduct, Maag reminded the court it was the defense, not the prosecution, which first entered Cody Bledsoe's words into the trial.

As oral arguments ended, Floyd's attorney was confident. "When we finished arguments on the appeal to the Supreme Court, [Maag] came up to me and said, 'Are you going to retry this when they reverse [the convictions]?'" Ney recalled a decade later. "We were all convinced that this had been such a travesty."

One hundred days later, the Supreme Court made its decision unanimously. It was written by Justice Carol Beier, a liberal who had been student director of an innocence project while in law school at the University of Kansas and later, as a visiting professor, was the head of the project. There was reason to believe she would look favorably on Floyd's case. At first, it looked like she had.

"We ultimately conclude that Kurth's performance was constitutionally deficient," Beier wrote for the court. "His professed 'strategy' in introducing an exculpatory but nevertheless unreliable and incompetent hearsay statement of a two-year-old, which opened the door to the child's damaging hearsay statement, was objectively unreasonable.

"However, because we cannot say that the outcome would have been different had Cody's statements been excluded and Kurth's other errors not occurred, and because our confidence in the jury's verdict is not undermined, we conclude that there was no prejudice."

Ney needed to prove that Kurth's behavior was both constitutionally deficient and the reason why Floyd was convicted. The Supreme Court was telling him he had succeeded at the first and failed at the second.

Beier called Kurth's pre-trial pact with Vanderbilt "a huge mistake" and "objectively unreasonable." She questioned why he would agree to it when there was "considerable evidence pointing to Tom as the perpetrator: his gun was the murder weapon; he had purchased the bullets; he initially confessed to having killed C.A.; and he led police to the body, which was buried behind the house where he lived."

The Supreme Court chastised Kurth for failing to object to a line of questioning between Vanderbilt and Detective Troy Frost. Vanderbilt asked Frost, "When Floyd said that he had gone to the trailer that day, did you believe him?" and "When Floyd was indicating to you through your questions and his statement how he felt about her, you think he was being genuine?" Frost said yes to both, single-handedly determining fact or fiction for the jurors. Beier, in her opinion, called it "objectionable testimony that invaded the province of the jury."

The court also chastised Kurth for the bizarre moment during jury selection when he drew a comparison between Floyd's case and that of Susan Smith, the South Carolina woman who drove her car into a lake, drowning her two sons, then falsely claimed a black man had carjacked her and kidnapped her sons, setting off a nine-day search in July of 1995. Smith, like Floyd, had been on television news programs asking for the public's help. For Kurth to compare his client to a woman who drowned her two children was "clumsy" at best, Beier wrote, and "objectively unreasonable."

"We can think of many better examples he could have cited to illustrate his point that the jury must reserve judgement until it had heard both sides of the story, examples that would not have had the unfortunate parallel of Smith's televised pleas for return of her children," Beier wrote.

Turning to Vanderbilt's behavior, the court ruled that "several of the prosecutor's statements are troubling." For example, Vanderbilt said during closing arguments, "The physical evidence shows that Tom didn't do it." As Beier pointed out, that statement was unsupported and, in fact, contradicted by evidence presented during the trial. Several pieces of physical evidence – most notably the gun and the bullets – linked Tom to the murder.

Vanderbilt's theory for how the murder occurred, stated during closing arguments, was "outside the wide latitude given [to] a prosecutor in discussing the evidence," Beier wrote. She determined that Vanderbilt repeatedly made objectionable statements, which Kurth failed to object to.

After a categorical listing of the trial's many flaws, Beier wrote that Ney had not demonstrated "any one of these individual failings, or that these failings considered collectively, so undermined the fairness of his trial as to impair our confidence in its outcome."

Sure, Cody's statements were damaging to Floyd's defense, Beier wrote, but the Supreme Court did not believe it prejudiced Floyd's case. After all, jurors knew the boy was young and telling inconsistent tales. (Beier, of course, did not have the benefit of speaking to juror Ed Benton, who was immediately convinced of Floyd's guilt when he heard Cody had blamed his father.)

"On the record before us, this was a difficult case," begins her final paragraph. "Two brothers accused each other of vile crimes. There was ample evidence to support each accusation. The jury, after weighing all of its substance and the credibility of the many witnesses, was persuaded that the state prosecuted the right brother. Although, in the hands of another defense lawyer, the case may have been tried to another conclusion, 'may' is not good enough. In order to reverse, we must be convinced that, but for counsel's deficiencies, there was a reasonable probability of a different outcome. We are not so convinced. Floyd's trial, while not perfect, was fair."

A defendant facing life in prison should hire the best lawyer in town or the worst. The Supreme Court was telling Floyd he had made the mistake of being appointed someone in between. For a second time, the highest court in the state of Kansas had unanimously refused to overturn his convictions. His options were rapidly drying up.

"I was stunned that they ruled against us. I mean, just stunned," Ney recalls.

To pay for the unsuccessful appeal, Floyd had sold his land – those forty acres north of Oskaloosa where he once lived with Heidi and the boys. The land had been a gift from Ida Bledsoe, Floyd's grandmother, who gave half of her 160 acres to Floyd Sr. and split the other half between Tom and Little Floyd. At first, Floyd attempted to sell it to his parents but they refused to pay more than eighteen thousand dollars, far less than its worth, another insult to the son they had helped send to prison. With the help of Ney and his uncle Gary, Floyd put the land on the market instead and sold it for a higher price.

In what was becoming a trend, Floyd Sr. and Cathy Bledsoe did not talk to Floyd while his appeal was pending but visited when it failed. "They would talk about everything but the case," Floyd said of those meetings. "Like we were at a restaurant. It was crazy."

The land sale also covered the high cost of a DNA test but Ney and his partner on the case, Jessica Kunen, struggled to find any items worth testing and the county attorney's office wasn't helping. "They swore up and down they had no DNA," Ney recalls. He tested a t-shirt found in the ditch where Camille's body was dumped, but the results were inconclusive. "That was our one shot. We really couldn't think of anything else potentially to test."

There was something else to test: a rape kit that contained the sperm of

Camille's murderer. But Vanderbilt's office claimed no such item existed and Ney had no way of proving otherwise.

"I consider it more than a *Brady* violation," Ney says of the deception, which has frustrated him for the many years since. "Yes, I consider it a *Brady* violation but I also consider it an out-and-out lie. We were asking for evidence and that's what we were told."

Ney's office also hired an expert to reanalyze Floyd and Tom's polygraph results, which a KBI detective, George Johnson, had claimed were evidence of Floyd's deception and Tom's truthfulness. The expert discovered that not only did Tom fail the test but immediately after doing so, Tom again confessed to killing Camille. Johnson never mentioned Tom's confession.

***

In the spring of 2008, a nineteen-year-old college student walked into Hutchinson Correctional Facility, a pretty young woman surrounded by all-male medium- and maximum-security inmates, many of them murderers and rapists. She was nervous; scared even. Amanda Ingram was there to volunteer with a program called Freedom Challenge, founded a few years prior to teach Hutchinson inmates life skills through biblical principles. She signed up to do clerical work one day a week.

"You need to be careful," Paul Hughes, a Freedom Challenge co-founder, told her. "Just because inmates are friendly doesn't mean you trust them. Don't see that as an open-door invite."

Soon after she arrived, Floyd introduced himself. He was a model student, one of the first graduates of the eight-week, seven-hours-a-day Freedom Challenge program and had continued to volunteer after graduating. That first day, they talked for hours, until Ingram realized she had failed to do much work. They would talk again the next week, and again after that.

To better help inmates, Ingram decided on a policy of blissful ignorance; she refused to learn what each inmate had been convicted of. Floyd was challenging that policy. He never talked about his case but she was curious. *He hasn't done anything too bad, he is too nice*, she thought. So, she peeked. The state of Kansas operates a public database of inmates, complete with their criminal histories and disciplinary records. For Floyd, it listed murder, aggravated kidnapping and aggravated indecent liberties with a child. She was shocked. That short, kind guy with a warm demeanor was a convicted child molester and child murderer.

The internet had much more to say about Floyd Bledsoe though. She scanned through stories of his trial, stories of Camille's disappearance, stories of the appeals. Even to the untrained mind, there were flaws. Surprise at his criminal history turned to surprise at his convictions. In March, she wrote on a card that she supported him and handed it to her newfound friend. That simple gesture would remain a memory of his for a decade.

Among the inmates in Freedom Challenge, Floyd's nickname, the Little General, was said with joking affection. He was no-nonsense, direct and to the point, unafraid of being blunt. He was, for a prisoner, unusually pious and willing to remind inmates of right and wrong. He had character. He did not bend his beliefs. With that came respect. As one fellow inmate put it, "I respect those who respect themselves." As Hughes said, "He knew who he was and he was okay with the truth." Few in Hutchinson could say the same.

Floyd and Ingram grew closer, so close that Floyd began discussing his case with her. It was platonic, sure, but it was closer than most friendships forged behind bars. They shared a faith, a belief that God would see them through. Floyd told her that God had, after all, made him a promise as he laid in his jail cell on Christmas Eve 1999. The star in the sky said one day this would all be over.

THIRTEEN

With his appeals in state court exhausted, Floyd was left with a longshot federal case. Richard Ney was no longer representing him, leaving it in the hands of the Defender Project at the University of Kansas. On March 13, 2007, two attorneys at the project, Elizabeth Cateforis and Alice White, filed the opening salvo in *Floyd S. Bledsoe v. Louis Bruce and Paul Morrison.*

Morrison was a longtime prosecutor who had been elected the state's attorney general the prior November and taken office just two months before. Bruce was the warden at Hutchinson Correctional Facility. Cateforis and White had filed a writ of habeas corpus, claiming Floyd was being held unlawfully due to his innocence.

Not unlike Ney before them, Floyd's latest attorneys alleged both ineffective counsel by John Kurth and prosecutorial misconduct by Jim Vanderbilt. The litany of claims supporting their first allegation was lengthy. As in prior appeals, the admission of two-year-old Cody's memories was at the top of the list.

"Trial counsel's performance was constitutionally deficient under the Sixth Amendment to the United States Constitution and rendered the Petitioner's trial fundamentally unfair, requiring reversal of Petitioner's convictions," wrote Cateforis and White.

The government also had a new attorney. Jared Maag, who had opposed Ney in Floyd's earlier appeal, was now the deputy solicitor general and wrote a forty-six-page response to Cateforis and White the following April. By then, there was a new attorney general in Topeka after Morrison was brought down by an office sex scandal less than a year into the job. Maag's boss was now Attorney General Stephen Six, the son of Kansas Supreme Court Justice Fred Six, who had written the opinion denying Floyd's first appeal.

As Floyd found, state appellate courts are hesitant to reverse lower court judges and juries. Federal courts are similarly hesitant to reverse state courts.

Floyd's case had been denied by the Kansas Supreme Court twice. His odds in federal court were not high.

Maag attacked the importance of Kurth's mistakes. There was no denying that John Kurth failed to represent Floyd adequately – the Supreme Court had already reached that conclusion. But Maag, like government attorneys before him, would claim those failures did not alter the course of the trial.

"Because Cody's statements were nothing more than the inconsistent statements of a two-year-old offered through testimony of third parties," Maag wrote in April of 2008, "it is unlikely that they had a significant effect on the jury's determination of Tom's credibility." This was patently false, though Maag had no way of knowing it. The words and behaviors of Cody Bledsoe had convinced jurors that Floyd's son watched as his father molested and murdered Camille Arfmann.

Maag leaned heavily on the Supreme Court's opinion, and understandably so. The high court had found clear deficiencies in Kurth's actions but refused to overturn Floyd's convictions. Maag was requesting a federal judge in Topeka, Richard Rogers, do the same.

Nearly bald, his head largely pockmarked, Rogers had been a federal judge since the Ford administration and had seen a lot of law. He had been a B-24 bombardier over Italy and Eastern Europe during the Second World War, an attorney for thirty years and a judge for just as long. He had been mayor of Manhattan in central Kansas, a county attorney, a city commissioner, a professor, a certified massage therapist, a Kansas House member, a state senator and president of the Kansas Senate.

He had reopened the *Brown v. Board* school segregation case and sentenced notorious Aryan Brotherhood murderer Thomas Silverstein to Leavenworth, where a special cell was created for him. He favored probation in unusually high numbers of cases, including virtually all white-collar cases, a preference that was called into question after an embezzler backed by former Arkansas Gov. Orville Faubus was released on probation and immediately resumed his thievery. It was Rogers who released former Kansas Lt. Gov. David Owen after he was convicted of accepting $100,000 from a person seeking a state betting license.

He called young attorneys into his chambers during tense jury deliberations and regaled them with war stories and bad jokes ("What do you get from a cow with short legs? Dragon milk."). He treated law clerks like his children and kept them around indefinitely, unlike most federal judges. When one made the mistake of telling the judge he would wear jeans and tennis shoes on a flight to Denver, Rogers lectured that a lawyer should always overdress and never underdress. The clerk arrived at the airport in an impeccable suit and top hat.

***

As Rogers was considering the case, KBI detectives were sent to Hutchinson Correctional Facility to find evidence against Floyd. In police work, the lowest hanging fruit on the evidence tree is a jailhouse confession or, at the very least, an inmate willing to claim he heard a confession.

"Did he ever say he's guilty?" a detective asked Freedom Challenge co-founder Don Starnes. "No, he's always maintained he was innocent," came the response. Not even the inmates annoyed by Floyd's piousness and Little General style would claim he was guilty. As one told the KBI, "I don't even like the man but I won't say anything bad about him." They asked Freedom Challenge volunteers about his behavior and his work ethic, both of which were lauded. They asked prison staff about his disciplinary record, which was flawless. In Hutchinson, the detectives struck out.

On June 23, 2008, a prison guard in Hutchinson approached Floyd. "Hey, I think something's happened on your case," she told him. Richard Ney had called the prison, asking to speak to Floyd. Then Alice White called, also wanting to speak to her client. "It's not uncommon for one attorney to call, but when two attorneys call from two different offices, I think it's a major thing," the guard told him.

It was, in fact, a major thing. The eighty-four-year-old judge had done what so many other judges would not do. He had seen what the other judges, and justices, had not seen. "The court finds that petitioner was denied his constitutional right to the effective assistance of counsel. The state court's conclusion to the contrary represents an unreasonable application of clearly established federal law," Rogers wrote.

Rogers delved into his disagreements with the Supreme Court's ruling. The high court had determined, "Although, in the hands of another defense lawyer, the case may have been tried to another conclusion, *may* is not good enough." Rogers' response: "It is unclear why *may* is not good enough."

"If by 'may have been tried to another conclusion' the Kansas Supreme Court meant that there was a reasonable probability of a different outcome, then *may* is good enough," he wrote.

In spotting Kurth's failures, Rogers went further than the Supreme Court. He said the court had incorrectly "brushed aside" Kurth's refusal to object to Vanderbilt's fictitious closing argument and was "objectively unreasonable" when it ignored Cathy Bledsoe's testimony in which she said Tom didn't kill Camille. By allowing Cathy Bledsoe's testimony to be heard by jurors, Kurth allowed Tom's credibility to be bolstered. In a case where one of the two brothers committed the crime, Kurth allowed jurors to hear that Tom did not. Rogers, unlike the Supreme Court, would not let him off the hook for it. Where the Supreme Court had found four deficiencies in Kurth's performance, Rogers found five.

The kicker came on the forty eighth page of the fifty-two-page ruling. It was what Floyd and his tally of attorneys had waited eight years to hear. It was the culmination of an appeals process that had twice taken them from the Jefferson County Courthouse to the Kansas Supreme Court and now to federal court.

"But for the mistakes of [Floyd's] trial counsel, the prosecutor could not have referred to Cody's alleged eyewitness statement or Mom's judgment that Tom Bledsoe did not commit the crime and, inferentially, was a credible witness. Without this evidence and without any physical evidence pointing to petitioner, the case against petitioner would largely boil down to Tom's claim that petitioner confessed to him. In the absence of the previously described errors of counsel and Cathy Bledsoe's 'Tom didn't do it' testimony, there is a reasonable probability that a jury would not believe Tom's testimony and find that petitioner was not guilty," Rogers wrote.

It was a mammoth decision clothed in the necessary legal language. The octogenarian judge had not only found deep flaws in the case, he believed they warranted a retrial. Maag vowed to appeal the ruling to the Tenth Circuit Court in Denver but that was another matter for another day.

After Alice White explained all of this to Floyd over the phone, the inmate had a question: "If they reversed my conviction, do I get out?" It was a matter not yet decided. Maag filed a motion to stay the ruling until the Tenth Circuit could decide, telling Rogers, "there is a strong possibility that the Tenth Circuit will reverse this court's decision."

Floyd, Maag wrote, "was convicted of murdering and molesting his 14-year-old niece." (A factual mistake; Camille was his sister-in-law, not a niece.) He went on: "That the State has a vested interest in keeping murderers incarcerated is undeniable. Here this concern is heightened by the fact that petitioner's brother, Tom Bledsoe, was his primary accuser. The State and public have a strong interest in avoiding a confrontation between the two brothers."

White fired back. "There is no probability that the Tenth Circuit will reverse the decision of this court," she told Rogers. As for Floyd, "He has been, and continues to be, incarcerated for a crime that he did not commit and has stable housing and employment as a dairy farmer in Hutchinson, ensuring he is not a flight risk."

Judge Rogers made his decision on August 13, 2008, fifty-one days after his initial ruling. "Upon the court's study of this matter, the court believes that petitioner is not a significant threat to flee and that bond conditions can be established to reduce that threat further. The court is also convinced that petitioner is not a danger to the community or to his brother."

After nearly nine years in prison, Floyd was free – under certain conditions. He must remain employed, not travel more than seventy-five miles outside Hutchinson, not contact anyone involved in his case – including his parents and ex-wife – and not possess alcohol or a gun. None of those conditions concerned Floyd. He was free.

"His goal is to start anew," White told reporters.

At Hutchinson, fellow inmates celebrated. The man they believed was innocent, the man who had harbored a saintly peacefulness throughout it all, was finally getting out. His connections through Freedom Challenge and reputation as a hard worker led to many job offers on the outside. He longed to be a dairy farmer again.

"I was having a good time," Floyd recalled. God had, after all, made him a promise as he laid in his jail cell on Christmas Eve 1999. The star in the sky said one day this would all be over.

A reporter called John Kurth to ask for his opinion. Kurth had always believed his client was innocent but was again forced to confront his conduct during the trial. "I don't think the state proved its case, but I didn't think (the guilty verdict) was my doing," he told the *Lawrence Journal-World*. "We got a bad verdict."

Floyd found work in Hutchinson at Miller Dairy, operated by fourth-generation dairy farmers Orville and Mary Jane Miller. He was one of a half-dozen employees milking 180 cows. The dairy adopted the tag line "Where happy cows live" after incorporating scraps from a nearby chocolate factory into their feed. Orville and Floyd became close friends and Orville, like many folks who befriended Floyd, came to believe he was innocent. "He's the kind of guy I want as a neighbor. He's got a heart for people."

Floyd took off work each Monday to drive to Wichita and help former inmates rejoin society. He talked of establishing a halfway house. In Hutchinson, he remained in contact with James Quinton's wife and son, this time without the barrier of prison rules. He took Quinton's son fishing for the first time one Super Bowl Sunday.

As Floyd returned to reality, the attorneys geared up for yet another appeal. The Oskaloosa case had been heard twice there, three times in Topeka, and would now be considered in Colorado before the Tenth Circuit. Two of the three judges hearing the case – Deanell Reece Tacha and Mary Beck Briscoe – were Kansas natives and graduates of the University of Kansas, just twenty miles south of Oskaloosa.

"I thought, either this is really going to help us or really going to hurt us," Alice White recalled. "It turns out, it hurt us."

Under a 1996 federal law – the Antiterrorism and Effective Death Penalty Act – introduced by Kansas Sen. Bob Dole in response to the 1993 World Trade Center bombing and 1995 Oklahoma City bombing, federal judges are severely limited in their ability to release convicted inmates, as Rogers did with Floyd. The law requires federal courts to assume juries and judges correctly interpreted the facts in every case. As a result, the burden fell on Floyd and his attorney – not the government – to prove to the Tenth Circuit by clear and convincing evidence that the Kansas Supreme Court had erred.

On June 26, 2009, the highest court across six states handed down its opinion in the case that had come to be known as *Bledsoe v. Bruce.* The legal rollercoaster was dipping again.

Even before the judges reached their legal conclusion, the opinion contained an obvious factual error. The judges contradictorily wrote that Camille "was killed on Friday, November 5, 1999" and "The evidence suggests that Cody witnessed [Camille] being shot and put in the ditch" and "At 12:45 a.m. [Floyd] picked up his son Cody from the babysitter." It is impossible for Cody to have witnessed the November 5 murder of Camille when he wasn't picked up from a babysitter until 12:45 a.m. on November 6.

The Supreme Court had found four deficiencies in Kurth's trial conduct but determined they did not alter the jury's decision. Judge Rogers had found five deficiencies and determined they did alter the jury's decision. The Tenth Circuit sided with the Supreme Court.

"We agree that, considering all of the evidence and noting that the jury had the opportunity to hear Tom's testimony and judge his credibility, there is not a reasonable probability that but for [Kurth]'s errors the result of the proceeding would have been different," wrote Judge Briscoe.

Briscoe may have given jurors too much credit. After carefully detailing Vanderbilt's misstatements and outright fictions during his closing argument, the judge claimed they "were not enough to take the jury's eyes off the ball" because jurors had been told by Judge Nafziger that closing statements are not evidence. Briscoe's conclusion assumed jurors could identify Vanderbilt's mistruths as he stated them, and ignore them accordingly.

Briscoe criticized Judge Rogers for failing to give deference to the state court rulings and defended Kurth's use of the bizarre Susan Smith analogy, claiming "the point…was the value of waiting to hear both sides of the story." With that, the Tenth Circuit reversed the ruling of Rogers and reinstated Floyd's life sentence.

"We're pretty devastated," White told a reporter.

That day, June 26, 2009, was a sweltering Friday. In Lawrence, she paced the University of Kansas campus, dreading the phone call she had to make.

Floyd was at a Burger King in Hutchinson, just sitting down to a meal. As he heard of the court's ruling, the numbness returned – that same numbness that had accompanied the guilty verdicts and the life sentence. "I lost my appetite. I walked around trying to figure it all out. Once again, it's like that sinking feeling. Everything just continues to build and build and build." At some point, he picked himself up and turned himself in to the authorities. He had been a free man for just nine months.

"When they sent him back to prison, you could really see it in his eyes," Chano Young, the inmate and painting partner, recalled. He returned to D3, his old cell block in Hutchinson. "When he got sent back he wanted to ease his mind so he got paints and brushes and canvas from me and painted some dolphins. It was nice. I know when they brought him back he was sad."

White asked the Tenth Circuit to reconsider. It refused. She then asked the U.S. Supreme Court to hear the case. It refused. The federal appeals process had reached its end. Without new evidence, Floyd would spend the rest of his life in prison. Not long after he painted dolphins with Chano Young, he was transferred to Lansing Correctional Facility, the state's oldest and largest prison.

"We are pleased," the attorney general's office told reporters, "that the Tenth Circuit Court of Appeals upheld the jury's guilty verdict."

Back in Oskaloosa, Sheriff Dunnaway had retired, leaving former Undersheriff Jeff Herrig in charge. "I think it's wonderful," Herrig said of Floyd's return to prison. "It's a good deal all around for Jefferson County... We knew that he was involved one way or another. There could've been someone else involved."

Floyd's return to prison devastated the employees of Miller Farm, the Hutchinson dairy operation where he worked after Judge Rogers' decision. Orville Miller called it "a pretty rough afternoon."

Jim Bolinger, the lay minister at Countryside Baptist Church, said the case was history. "It's all passed. I just kind of blacked it out of my mind."

Bolinger was interviewed by Shaun Hittle, an eager young journalist fresh out of grad school at KU. There is an aura around the Bledsoe case that grabs the attention of lawyers and reporters who get near it, a gravitational pull that draws them in. Hittle, with all the conviction of a young man ready to change the world, wanted to free Floyd. He went beyond the assignments he was given by editors. It's how he became the only journalist to make contact with Tom Bledsoe after the trial.

Outside a dilapidated home in rural Jefferson County – a washer and dryer on the lawn outside – Hittle found Tom mowing. Nearly deaf and with a lawnmower roaring under him, Tom was oblivious as Hittle waved his arms at the short, stocky man. Finally, he looked over and noticed the unexpected visitor. When Hittle introduced himself, Tom dropped everything.

"No comment, no comment," he said as he stormed off toward the house.

After the murder, Tom lived a quiet life in rural McLouth, just east of Oskaloosa. His house was less than two miles and just one left turn from Countryside Baptist Church. He had never moved out of Jefferson County and never would. With the exception of a misdemeanor criminal damage to property charge in 2012 – he pleaded no contest – there would be no further legal issues.

Online, Tom used variations of the same username: huntertom, an allusion to his favorite hobby. In June of 2007, huntertom33, a likely reference to his age at the time, began posting to the discussion board website MyLot. Beside innocuous questions about the virtues of working from home and dating were two unsettling posts. One was titled "Rape" followed by ten exclamation points and a brief passage: "discuss it here, let's all learn how to prevent it and deal with it." MyLot allows users to choose tags for each post. In this case, Tom's tags were: Brother, Dad, Help, Life, Mom, Sex, Sister, Strongwill and Wanted. The next day, huntertom33 wrote a post titled "duct tape, what have you used it for…." with the tags Car, Dad, Help, Mom, Romance, Sis, Tape. Neither of the posts garnered a response from his fellow MyLot users.

Hittle also stopped by Tom and Floyd's childhood home, the house on Osage Road where Camille's body was left. Floyd Sr. and Cathy had moved to Florida in 2005 but a man who purchased the home from them opened the door and offered Hittle a soda. He not only knew about the case and the murder at his house, he was fascinated by it. As he and Hittle drank Coke, they discussed the case, the resident knowing as much as the reporter at times. He also showed Hittle something the former homeowners had left behind: a stack of Floyd's letters from prison. His parents had not bothered to take them when they left Oskaloosa.

Hittle's investigating eventually led him to Floyd who, despite his predicament, was as gracious as ever that a reporter had taken interest in his case. Floyd hand-painted all of his Christmas cards and Hittle received one that December. One day, at the prison in Lansing, Hittle asked him why he didn't run away during his time between appeals. Floyd had an answer immediately: "Because I know I'm going to get out one day for good."

Following their usual pattern, Floyd Sr. and Cathy Bledsoe did not visit their son in prison while the case was pending before Judge Rogers but reconnected soon after his U.S. Supreme Court appeal failed. Before visiting Oskaloosa one holiday weekend in 2012, they wrote Floyd to tell him they would like to see him. Floyd sent his uncle Gary a note with the dates and time they could visit the prison. Gary, who had not spoken to his brother and sister-in-law since 2000, passed the message along to Cathy. She took it, said, "Okay," but didn't visit Floyd that weekend or any time after. Neither did her husband.

Some years they mailed birthday cards, some years they did not. One of those birthday cards would help solve the murder of Camille Arfmann.

FOURTEEN

On June 3, 2011, the Kansas Supreme Court indefinitely suspended the law license of Jim Vanderbilt. The year before, he had been arrested for failing to attend a court hearing at which his wife claimed he owed sixty thousand dollars in child support. Because he was in jail, he didn't appear in court on behalf of three clients and never notified his clients or judges of his predicament. He was also found to have driven to a court hearing on a driver's license that had been suspended months before. An investigator determined Vanderbilt knowingly "violated his duty to the legal system, legal profession, and public."

The Supreme Court agreed, unanimously writing, "It is therefore ordered that Jimmie A. Vanderbilt be indefinitely suspended from the practice of law in the state of Kansas." It had been a long fall for the former two-term county attorney. His law office in Lawrence had closed years ago; he had been working out of law libraries and his car in the waning years of his career.

Elsewhere in Lawrence, the Project for Innocence was weighing how to overturn Vanderbilt's largest failure. They would need to prove Floyd Bledsoe is innocent, an incredibly tall order. At their disposal were limited funds, a handful of eager young law students and an unending belief that Floyd did not kill Camille.

Kaiti Smith was a second-year law student with a sharp mind and an unusual undergraduate degree for an aspiring lawyer: a bachelor's in forensic science. "I knew a lot about DNA, so I thought I could help." On her first day at the Project, attorneys were discussing their exhaustion of legal remedies in Floyd's case. She was fascinated by what appeared so plainly to be a wrongful conviction. So, she took the case, in addition to those she was assigned.

For four years, Project for Innocence director Jean Phillips had been lecturing law students about the Bledsoe case, calling it a classic example of injustice. It was the Project's cornerstone case and Smith set out to solve it, poring through boxes of court transcripts, notes and evidence. She chased random leads and spoke with Kansas Bureau of Investigation agents. When she met Floyd in Lansing, her passion for the case was further heightened. The maximum-security inmate bought her a Sprite with his commissary money. He was the kindest person she had ever met and certainly not a killer, she thought. Her one-bedroom apartment became her office, with notes and documents attached to the walls, Hollywood's image of an obsessed investigator or conspiracy theorist. When she couldn't sleep, she would wake up, flip on a light and work the case. With her husband stationed overseas in the warzones of Afghanistan, the Bledsoe case was Smith's distraction, a constant companion. She spent many nights alone in her apartment, thinking of poor, innocent Camille and the murderer who was still living freely just twenty-five miles to the north.

After a year and a half, Smith had a theory: Floyd Laverne Bledsoe, the father of her client, had been involved. "I remember emailing Jean and asking if we could meet. I told her, 'You're going to think I'm crazy.'" Actually, Phillips considered the theory plausible.

The centerpiece of Smith's theory was a document that had been collecting dust for a dozen-plus years, hidden in plain sight. It had been available to each of Floyd's attorneys and yet none had mentioned it in a courtroom. It might as well have been written in a foreign language only Smith could speak.

When DNA analysts reach conclusions, they hand over to attorneys not only those synopses but also bench notes – the scientist's jottings. In Floyd's case, the DNA analysis was inconclusive. However, the bench notes – which few attorneys bother to read because they are largely indecipherable to laymen – held further information. There was a DNA match for an unknown person who wasn't Camille, Floyd Jr. or Tom. The DNA was distinct, but similar, to the DNA profiles of both Floyd and Tom. In other words, it belonged to a relative of the two.

From there, a theory began to take shape. Smith believed Tom was not intelligent enough to mastermind a murder, dispose of a body and frame his brother. The only people who vouched for Tom's alibi the night of the murder were his parents and members of Countryside Baptist Church. He had no relatives at the church retreat that night, so Smith focused on the parents. By protecting Tom, was his father also protecting himself?

It was just a theory. With Floyd's appeals spent, the Project for Innocence would need to prove Floyd did not kill Camille. It was a longshot, longer than any of the longshot appeals had been. Floyd's last chance at freedom rested in the hands of a young law student.

There had been, from the start of the case, a consensus that Camille was killed in one location and dragged to the brome field ditch where she was haphazardly buried. There were cuts along her back pointing to this. If the person who dragged her to the ditch had lifted from under her arms, those cuts would likely not have occurred. Therefore, Smith reasoned, a DNA test on Camille's socks could uncover who pulled her into the ditch by her ankles.

As Phillips recalled, "She came to me and said, 'Touch DNA. We're going with touch DNA to see if we can get something off of her clothing.'"

Touch DNA, so named because it analyzes skin cells that remain after someone touches a body or object, has existed since the mid-aughts but came into vogue around 2008, the year it was used to exonerate the parents of JonBenét Ramsey in the Colorado girl's infamous murder. It replaced DNA techniques of the 1980s and 1990s that required blood and semen. The trick is guessing where on the victim's body or clothing the assailant's skin cells reside.

They would need a judge's order granting new DNA testing. Smith had unlikely allies in the Jefferson County attorney's office, who met with her on weekends to discuss her request for testing. They told her the county attorney's office wouldn't fight a motion for testing but warned that her odds were long. She was told the people of Oskaloosa did not want to revisit such a dark period in their town's history, nor would a judge want to dredge up the possibility that he presided over an injustice. Any motion would be heard by Judge Gary Nafziger, the judge in Floyd's original trial, who was up for retention that fall.

On June 20, 2012, the Project for Innocence filed a motion in Jefferson County District Court seeking permission to test DNA evidence in the case. As promised, Jefferson County Attorney Jason Belveal, the fifth county attorney there in eight years, did not contest the motion. On June 25, Smith wrote on Twitter, "DNA Motion filed! Keep your fingers crossed for Floyd!"

Under Kansas law, a court can order DNA testing after a conviction if the judge believes DNA "may produce noncumulative, exculpatory evidence" relevant to the defendant's claim of wrongful conviction. Project for Innocence attorneys told Nafziger that would occur in this case. They noted the decision by Sheriff Dunnaway, Vanderbilt and KBI special agent Jim Woods to cancel DNA testing in December of 1999.

"The State failed to submit crucial pieces of evidence for testing, which [Floyd] argues would have proven his innocence by implicating another perpetrator and corroborating his own version of events," wrote Elizabeth Cateforis. "Further, because of technological advances, there are now newer testing methods which are proven to produce more probative and accurate results."

The attorneys told the judge of scientific advances over the past dozen years and listed the items they hoped to test. In addition to the jeans and socks Camille died in were two articles of clothing that had previously been tested: a dark blue jacket taken from Camille's room that was stained with blood and found in 2000 to contain the DNA of several people; and a black Countryside Baptist Church t-shirt tossed in the ditch next to Camille's body. Richard Ney had ordered tests on the t-shirt in 2003. Analysts found male DNA but could not determine who it belonged to. Floyd's attorneys were hopeful they now could.

"There is no evidence which implicates Floyd Bledsoe and none of the previously tested forensic evidence conclusively established guilt," they wrote. "The jury had no forensic or physical evidence to rely upon in reaching their verdict. The testing that was previously conducted has been greatly improved upon and more probative and reliable results which will exonerate [Floyd] are extremely likely to be produced by testing with modern technology."

In Oskaloosa, the motion was granted by Judge Nafziger and the Project for Innocence team went to work gathering objects to send off for testing.

Because Tom and Floyd had both been suspects in Camille's murder, their DNA was on file. That wasn't the case, however, for the elder Floyd. Floyd Sr. and Cathy Bledsoe had moved from Florida to Texas. To find out where they lived, Kaiti Smith asked the younger Floyd, who had occasionally received birthday cards and letters from his parents.

"I said, 'I have a letter so I'll just send the whole thing to you,'" Floyd recalled. "She was like, 'Well, I don't need the whole thing, just the address.' I said, 'Nah, I'm done with it anyway. Either I send it to you or I throw it in the trash.' So, I sent the whole thing to her."

When mail arrives at Kansas prisons, it's opened with a slit across the top of the envelope and scanned for contraband. As a result, the portion of the envelope that is licked by the sender is never touched, leaving the saliva intact. Floyd's father had licked two of the manila envelopes he sent Floyd – one with a letter inside and another with a Hallmark card, a blue jay on the front. The Project for Innocence now had the DNA of a man it believed participated in the disappearance of Camille Arfmann.

***

On the morning of February 24, 1986, Sherri Rasmussen was beaten and shot to death in her Los Angeles home. For more than two decades, the case remained unsolved until DNA from a bite mark pointed to Stephanie Lazarus, an LAPD detective, who was convicted in 2012.

Six months earlier, on August 12, 1985, the body of sixteen-year-old Tracey Wooden had been found in a downtown Denver alley. She had been sexually assaulted and strangled. It took thirty years for DNA evidence to match Daniel Fellovetr, a convicted rapist.

Paul Layton Keesling's thirty-six-year career of crime, for which he earned the moniker "Dinnertime Bandit" by targeting Southern California homes between 5 p.m. and 7 p.m., ended in 2007 when he left skin cells on a Newport Beach closet. For stealing millions of dollars, he was sentenced to forty-five years in prison.

Each of the three cases was solved with the assistance of DNA analysts in a clinically white research park in Richmond, Calif., just across the bay from San Francisco, home to the nonprofit Serological Research Institute and its small staff of scientists.

It was a SERI analysis that helped free the West Memphis Three, teenagers sentenced to life for killing three boys as part of a satanic ritual. It was a SERI analysis that freed Michael Hanline, thirty-six years after he was wrongfully convicted of murder in California. In 2010, a SERI analysis not only freed a man wrongfully accused of killing two Virginia girls but also pointed to a convicted killer.

In the spring of 2013, Kaiti Smith contacted Tom Fedor at SERI about the Bledsoes. They would speak often in those months about the case and what was needed to determine whether Smith's theory about Floyd Sr. was accurate.

"After we had talked with one of their technicians, they said, 'Send us the rape kit because we can do better testing now than we could then,'" Phillips recalled, referring to the original tests conducted by the Kansas Bureau of Investigation in 1999. The KBI lab in 1999 required the presence of a sperm cell to prove sexual assault. When it failed to find one, the result was inconclusive. SERI, in 2013, did not need a sperm cell to test for male DNA.

A swab of the sexual assault kit had been preserved since 1999 at a Missouri lab, Genetic Technologies, but it was incomplete. Half of the swab had been clipped and removed. When the Project for Innocence searched for it, they ran into one dead end after another. The sheriff's department couldn't find it; neither could the KBI. So they split the remaining swab into two to preserve half, sending just one-fourth of the original swab to SERI.

To help the attorneys determine which clothes to test for touch DNA, SERI's analysts studied the case. Their conclusion was the same as Smith's: analyze Camille's socks and the bottom of her pant legs, assuming the person who dragged her to the ditch grabbed one of those two items of clothing, if not both. A lab technician scraped the back of each pant leg separately, along with the front of each pant leg, to determine whether more of the DNA was on the back of the pants or front of the pants. The same was done with both socks.

By the summer of 2013, as it was moving ahead toward testing, the Project for Innocence needed a replacement for the irreplaceable Kaiti Smith, who graduated that May and had already stayed at the project for a year longer than the typical tenure. Her final year had been dedicated solely to the Bledsoe case.

They also needed money to pay for the tests, which were estimated to cost fifty thousand dollars. (That was later negotiated down to fifteen thousand.) They would find it forty miles east, in Kansas City, by partnering with the Midwest Innocence Project. Smith was replaced by two more law students, Peter Conley and Emily Barclay, who would spend the next two years shepherding evidence from Kansas to California and filing motions. Eight items were sent by Conley on April 30, 2014. Nine items were sent by the KBI on November 7 of that year. On May 13, 2015, Barclay sent two items to SERI. On July 1, the KBI sent two more.

A SERI analyst, Casseday Baker, went to work analyzing both of Camille's size six-and-a-half shoes, the right one stained with blood above the upper toe; both of her socks; the Faded Glory blue jeans she was wearing; her blood-stained bra; her panties and the sexual assault kit. Swabs were taken from both of Camille's wrists, her mouth, and below her waist. The adhesive on Floyd Sr.'s envelopes was carefully removed and processed through a series of chemical solutions until only amylase enzymes – those found in saliva – remained.

The fronts and backs of the socks and pant legs were scraped and swabbed; debris freed was placed into separate tubes. The debris was analyzed through a Nobel Prize-winning process known as polymerase chain reaction, in which the samples are repeatedly exposed to heat and cold, causing them to react and DNA to emerge. That DNA then becomes a template as the process is repeated and the targeted DNA is magnified.

Back in Kansas, the Project for Innocence remained in contact with Floyd.

"He would call at least once a week, sometimes more, to get updates," Conley recalled. "You don't want to break his heart but he was always hopeful; his faith is really strong. I wanted to be as confident as he was that DNA testing would overturn his conviction, but I wasn't always certain that he would be released."

In Richard Ney, his former attorney, Floyd would confide his frustration at the glacial pace of DNA testing and legal motions. *Why is this not going faster? What's going on?* Ney tried to ease his mind but the aggressive and outspoken Wichita attorney believed Floyd's attorneys were moving slower than necessary.

Preliminary results hinted at good news for Floyd, but no one wanted to get his hopes up. Barclay and the former Alice White – now Alice Craig – visited Floyd in Lansing on a spring day in 2014 to pass along their tentative optimism. "Everybody was incredibly excited but really cautious," Barclay recalled. "Nobody wanted to say this is, for sure, going to seal the deal."

Floyd's case had been a fifteen-year rollercoaster, full of dips and dives that surprised everyone involved. To predict the next twist would be an exercise in futility and false hope. No one at the Project for Innocence wanted the disappointment of another failed appeal. There would not be another opportunity. Their state appeals had been exhausted; their federal appeals had been exhausted. Everything hinged on the findings of forensic serologist Casseday Baker.

"This was a last-ditch effort for us," Phillips said. "We thought, either this is going to work or we're not going to be able to help Floyd. To us, that seemed like an intolerable solution because we really, truly, believe he did not do this."

"Honestly," Elizabeth Cateforis said, "I don't think we knew what results we were looking for. We knew what results we hoped for but not necessarily what was going to be there."

One concern was the brome field where Camille's body was dropped. Because it had been used as a trash dump by the Bledsoe family, the place where they tossed discarded food and toiletries, there undoubtedly was a lot of DNA within it. Would SERI's results be credible? By pulling DNA directly off Camille's clothes, Baker felt confident that yes, they would.

Baker's thirteen-page report – the culmination of years of work by attorneys, interns and SERI experts – was sent to the Project for Innocence on September 2, 2015. The client's name was listed as Kaiti Smith, who had left the Project more than two years ago, a sign of both the glacial pace of DNA testing and Smith's indelible mark on the case. The report seemed written for Smith, too, with its dense scientific explanations of DNA analysis processes. The results, however, were clear to any layman.

"DNA recovered from the vaginal swab's sperm fraction is a mixture of at least three people, including a discernable major female contributor and at least one male contributor," Baker wrote. "Zetta Arfmann is included as the major contributor to the mixture, which, given the intimate nature of the sample, is not an unexpected result…Thomas Edward Bledsoe is included as a possible minor contributor to the mixture. The chance a randomly selected, unrelated person would be similarly included as a possible minor contributor is about one in 300. Floyd Scott Bledsoe and Floyd Laverne Bledsoe are each excluded as possible contributors to the mixture."

Nearly sixteen years after the rape and murder of Camille, DNA evidence, for the first time, indicated Tom Bledsoe, not his brother, committed the crime. Floyd Scott Bledsoe – Floyd Jr. – had been excluded entirely; he could not have possibly contributed to the sperm found inside the victim. One-in-300 was not the ratio the Project for Innocence had hoped for in proving Tom had raped Camille, but it was still a strong indicator. Other conclusions in the Baker report would prove more absolute.

"DNA recovered from the back of the left sock is a mixture of at least two contributors, including a discernible major male contributor. Floyd Laverne Bledsoe has the same DNA profile as the major contributor. The chance a randomly selected unrelated person would have the same DNA profile is about one in twenty sextillion."

Twenty sextillion is twenty followed by twenty-one zeros, an astronomical number. By comparison, about 108 billion people have ever existed. The number twenty sextillion is 185 times larger than the human population throughout all of Earth's history.

At the prison in Lansing, Floyd struggled to grasp the DNA results, though not for mathematical reasons. They were a positive development for his case and for his future. But they were also unsettling. "I figured it would come back with Tom's DNA. Now, how much of it, or whether there would be enough, we didn't know. I always hoped there would be enough quantity there for them to be able to figure it out but that was no one hundred percent thing.

"When Alice came up and told me about Dad, that's when it took me by shock. I was actually numb walking back to my cell because I didn't know what to think or how to process that. That was something I never expected. It's like you're trying to wrap your head around somebody that unexpectedly dies. It's that same shock. I guess our minds are made to try to make that connection as a coping mechanism but I never could."

**

A month and a half after the DNA results arrived, on October 20, 2015, a legal document landed on the desk of County Attorney Jason Belveal. A round Republican man with a sometimes bearded, boyish face and short brown hair combed to the right, Belveal had been a defense attorney before being chosen in 2011 to replace County Attorney Caleb Stegall. Stegall became chief counsel to Governor Sam Brownback, then a Kansas Court of Appeals judge, then a Kansas Supreme Court justice.

The motion before Belveal came from Alice Craig. At the top, in bold-face font, it read "MOTION TO VACATE JUDGMENT AND DISCHARGE PETITIONER FROM CUSTODY."

"The results of extensive DNA analysis establish that the State's assertions at trial are false. Tom Bledsoe's DNA is consistent with the semen found on the vaginal swab taken from C.A.," Craig wrote, using Camille's initials. "The DNA of Tom's father was found on C.A.'s socks in a location that is consistent with dragging C.A. to the burial site, which was conveniently located on the property where Tom and his father live.

"Because the DNA results directly contradict the State's theory of the case, they are favorable, material, and create a reasonable probability of a different outcome…and the interests of justice require that Floyd's conviction be vacated, and he be discharged from custody."

Craig reiterated, for what seemed to be the umpteenth time, the list of evidence against Tom: his repeated confessions to his Sunday school teacher and police; his ownership and sole possession of the murder weapon and bullets; his access to and familiarity with the brome field where the body was hastily buried. "These facts make the inclusion of his DNA statistically more significant than 1 in 300 random people off the street. Viewed in the totality of the record, the testing results completely negate both Tom's and [his] father's veracity and reveal that Tom, his father, and his mother lied about material facts under oath at trial."

Craig recapped the tortuously long appeals process and how much of the evidence once used against Floyd had since been deemed inadmissible: hearsay statements, law enforcement officers vouching for Tom's credibility, Jim Vanderbilt's patently false theory during closing arguments. The Kansas Supreme Court had deemed the case a close call. Craig was arguing the case was no longer close, it was clear. "The State's entire theory of its case against Floyd, tenuous at the outset, weakened further by the Kansas Supreme Court ruling in Floyd's 1507 appeal, has collapsed."

Belveal and Jefferson County police didn't see it that way. Sure, the DNA results had shown Tom was involved, but the police and prosecutor didn't believe they exonerated Floyd or even proved his trial had been deeply flawed.

The case would return to the Oskaloosa courtroom where it began, that of Judge Gary Nafziger, his hair now wispy white on the sides with a swoosh of gray on top. Floyd's attorneys had made their final move – a last-ditch DNA test and a motion to vacate his convictions. If they failed, their client would spend the rest of his days behind bars. If they succeeded, an innocent man would finally be freed. What Belveal and Nafziger would do, no one could say for sure.

***

Two days later, a reporter found a hard-to-come-by parking spot by the KU Law School, walked the three flights of stairs to the Project for Innocence and sat in Craig's office, along with Jean Phillips and Elizabeth Cateforis.

On the phone was Tricia Bushnell, the top attorney at the Midwest Innocence Project, a shrewd and intellectually intimidating figure packed into the small, athletic frame of a frequent runner.

In that room was a cautious optimism that is common among allies of Floyd, like weathered Oskaloosa farmers who expect a bumper crop but have seen nature's wrath in prior years. The test results were a positive development, no doubt, but were they enough?

"It didn't come out as strongly as we had hoped – one in three hundred," Craig said.

"Yeah," Phillips retorted, "but not one in three hundred people confessed and had possession of the murder weapon and owned the murder weapon." She turned toward the reporter. "So, that changes the statistics in our opinion."

They were a team, had been for years. Jean was at the top, the director of the program. It had been her who gave the go-ahead to Kaiti Smith. Alice was on the front lines, the trial attorney; it would be her standing in Judge Nafziger's courtroom if a hearing was held. Elizabeth was a former appellate defender and capital punishment expert. There was professional respect among them and, even beyond that, foxhole friendships.

"It depends on whether the court's going to require us to put on evidence," Craig said. "At this point, it would be the county attorney and us making their case to the court and whatever position the county attorney takes. If there's an evidentiary hearing then it would be us putting on the expert from SERI, putting on other evidence that we think is important."

"I don't know at this point what Judge Nafziger is going to require," Phillips said. "I don't know if the prosecution is going to oppose the motion. I don't know what their position is at this point. I think it depends what the county attorney decides to do and…whether Judge Nafziger wants to have an evidentiary hearing or if he's, you know, comfortable ruling on what he's got before him. We'll just have to wait and see what he does."

Bushnell's soft voice spoke up through a loudspeaker on Craig's desk. "Right now, we're trying very hard to fix those mistakes, but we can't predict what anyone else will do."

The oddity of the Bledsoe trial, as those four knew well enough, was that it was a dual proceeding. The prosecution argued the defense of Tom Bledsoe and the guilt of Floyd Bledsoe; the defense argued the opposite. To undo the injustice of that trial, the Project for Innocence felt it must reverse both prongs of the two-pronged charade. They would not only argue their client was innocent, as they had countless times, but that his brother was the murderer.

Phillips explained: "If we had come back with DNA evidence that said Floyd's DNA is not there, the court would say, 'That doesn't mean he didn't kill her. It just means you couldn't find Floyd's DNA.' But when we find someone else's DNA and the DNA we do find fits with the way the prosecution set this case up – that you should believe Tom – we now have the ability to say, 'No, you shouldn't believe Tom' and that completely flips the prosecution's case. So, if we have to show reasonable probability of a different outcome, there's the reasonable probability of a different outcome."

"We're looking for justice," Bushnell said through the phone. "We don't get to control what the prosecution is going to do but when courts are deciding whether to review the case, they want to know what happened, not just that your client didn't do it. They want to know what really happened and we know that here."

Police and prosecutors had opposed Floyd every step of that way; there was no use in assuming that had changed. The team sitting around the table on that October day had taken the case nine years before. Twelve interns had spent their days – and sometimes their nights – on the case. They would take nothing for granted.

"We often say, 'We *believe* our client is innocent.' Floyd is innocent," Cateforis said. "There's no *belief* about it. He just is innocent and I don't think a day goes by that we don't think about this case."

Nafziger set a hearing date for December 8, 2015. The only large courtroom in the county was reserved. Buzz returned to Oskaloosa's red brick courthouse square and the Bledsoe case returned to the front page of the *Oskaloosa Independent*. There was talk of it at Rose's Café and on the bar stools in town. But as the two sides prepared for one final hearing to decide the fate of Floyd Bledsoe, events outside their control would change everything.

FIFTEEN

Michael Partnoy was blowing leaves at a suburban Kansas City Walmart when he first saw what he believed to be a mannequin. It was the early afternoon of November 9, 2015, and the thirty-four-year-old groundskeeper was staring inside a powder blue Fiat 500 sitting crookedly in the northwest corner of the parking lot, far from other cars.

As he peered into the tiny two-door, Partnoy saw a man, not a mannequin, with a plastic bag tied tightly over his head. The man was not breathing and Partnoy, as he later told police, "freaked out." After alerting a Walmart employee about the discovery, the two called the Bonner Springs Police Department.

The dispatcher's call to officers that day included few details about the report of a dead body. It had been found in the Walmart parking lot, she said, and the man "has a bag tied around his head. There is some kind of a tank hooked up to the bag."

Jeff Weissman was the first officer on the scene. He confirmed the man in the driver's seat was dead. In the passenger seat sat the culprit: a helium canister designed for inflating balloons. Another helium tank was in the back, along with plastic bags, a notepad, pens and envelopes. Strewn across the floorboard was a twelve-pack of Natural Light and empty Folgers can.

"The body appeared to have been there for a few days as the skin was purple and yellow," a detective, Daniel Farr, wrote in his report.

Weissman grabbed the man's wallet and found a driver's license. The deceased was Thomas Edward Bledsoe, who had gone missing from his rural northeast Kansas home eight days before. A missing person report stated Tom had "been acting strange the last couple of days" before his disappearance. On his phone, he had read The Peaceful Pill, an online guide to various methods of suicide. His body was found nearly sixteen years to the day after that early morning of November 8, 1999, when he led police to Camille's body, turned over the murder weapon, was arrested and confessed.

At 11:10 p.m. on November 1, Tom had walked into the Walmart, bought the items later found in his car, drove the car to a corner of the parking lot and committed suicide by a method known as an exit bag. A hose ran from a pink Balloon Time canister and into the bag around his head. His body had been there for more than a week by the time Partnoy stumbled upon it.

The morbidly public suicide of Tom Bledsoe, a deeply depressed man, could have faded into obscurity. Instead, it attracted detectives from several counties west of Bonner Springs and garnered months of attention by the press, due not to what he did with the helium tank and oven bags but with the other items he bought.

Farr was the first person to notice the three sealed envelopes on the driver's side of the Fiat dashboard. He opened them as Weissman took photos, unknowingly unsealing sixteen-year-old secrets. Riddled with misspellings and grammatical nescience but scrawled in a clear calligraphy, the first letter was addressed "to my mom and dad floyed and cathy bledsoe."

Dear mom and dad.
I am sorry I have cosed all this pain.
Floyd is innocent. The C.A. made my lye and keep my mouth shut.
Please don't Be upset with me.
Please tell Floyd I am sorry.
Love,
Tom.

The second letter was addressed to his wife, Mary Shaver.

Dear Mary.
I am sorry. I really love you, but I cannot go on. It's tearing me up inside. I now the Lord will take care OF you hope you can Forgive me. IF not that's Fine I don't think god will Forgive me For what I have done.
Best wishes to you and your kids.

Sorry,
Tom B.

P.S. Please cremate me. It's the cheapest way.

The third, and most descriptive, was addressed "to whomever cares" and "whome this values." In it, Tom described the events of November 5, 1999.

I sent a innocent man to prison. The Jefferson county police and county attorney Jim Vanderbilt made me do it.

I was told by Vanderbilt to keep my mouth shut.

Now I am going to set thing right.

I killed Camille Arfmann on Nov. 5, 1999.

I had sex with her and I killed her.

On Nov. 5 1999 I stopped by my Brothers house around 4:30 to 5 p.m. and Camille was there. We talked a little and the[n] went to my parents house and she helped me do something. Sorry my mind is blank on what we did, then we talked and then the conversation got moved to sex and she told me she's had sex before with whome I don't know. Then she asked me and I said no, then it happed so Fast I don't Remember much. We had sex on my parrents Bed, that's how my Fathers DNA got on her clothes. Afterwards we were leaving and I asked her Not to tell, that's when I Found out she was 14, and I freaked out so I drove up to the ditch where the Family dump trash and Tried to convice her Not to tell. Everything was happening so Fast I couldn't think.

I went to the truck and got my 9m gun that was behind my seat and pushed her to the ground to try to scare her, but it Faild when the gun went OFF behind her head. It was accident I didn't mean to kill her.

I as well might go ahead and say it. I Raped and murdered a 14 year girl.

I tried telling the truth but No one would listen. I was told to keep my mouth shut. It tore me up doing it.

I would ask for Forgiveness, But I Know None will come, Not even From God.

Floyd S. Bledsoe is innocent man.

Thomas E. Bledsoe is the guilty one.

And here is the proofe. The crime seinee is Less than 20 yards From the grave site where I berried her.

Tom then drew a crude map of the place where he buried Camille beneath a mound of trash on his parents' property. A note on the map said detectives could find an empty nine-millimeter shell no more than twenty yards from the ditch where the body was dumped. The letter ended with a final apology:

"All that I can say is sorry to all and I seek Forgiveness, But I don't deserve any, Not Even From God."

It had been two weeks since the DNA findings were made public. The website history on Tom's cell phone, found among a few crinkled dollar bills in the car where he died, showed he read newspaper articles about the DNA report and Camille's murder soon before his death.

If Tom Bledsoe's suicide notes are to be believed, he felt an overwhelmingly amount of guilt and grief in the final minutes before he died. But, as his cell phone history shows, he also knew of recent developments that could lead to his arrest, prosecution and imprisonment. His narrative of how the murder of Camille unfolded is implausible, if not impossible, and DNA experts both in law enforcement and outside of it reject his explanation of how his father's DNA landed on Camille's socks. Even as Tom was confessing, he was holding back; even as he was admitting to a coverup, he was continuing to conceal.

Back in Oskaloosa, the suicide was front-page news: "One-time accused murderer found dead in Bonner Springs." In the *Independent*, Rick Nichols began, "Whatever Tom Bledsoe may have known about Zetta Camille Arfmann's death 16 years ago that he failed to tell the Jefferson County Sheriff's Office will go to the grave with him, if it hasn't already." A few paragraphs later, Nichols told readers he had asked the sheriff's office whether Tom left behind a suicide note but didn't receive a response.

Outside Kansas, Floyd and Tom's half-sister, Cindy Fullerton, received word of the suicide and met it with a shrug. She had told family members for months that Tom would never go to prison, just as he had refused to in November of 1999. She had half-expected him to commit suicide and was unsurprised when he did.

Gary Bledsoe, the uncle and former police officer who had considered contacting Tom over the years in search of evidence to free Floyd, heard of his nephew's suicide through news reports. He called Alice Craig in hopes of learning more and scoured the internet for information and an obituary. The former Jefferson County undersheriff found a silver lining in the location of Tom's demise: it wasn't in Jefferson County.

"If Tom would have committed suicide in this county, I have doubts whether those suicide notes would have even survived."

***

Jason Belveal, the county attorney, was at the sheriff's office that afternoon for a meeting to determine whether to reopen an investigation into Camille's murder. Detectives were digging through a box of old files and maps when Ramon Gonzalez, a special investigator, received a call from Bonner Springs. Jefferson County detectives had been looking for Tom, but not to arrest him. Despite the DNA evidence against him, they wanted only to ask him a few questions.

As Gonzalez stepped out of the meeting to take the call from Bonner Springs, he was expecting to learn Tom had been pulled over. He planned to ask police there to pass along a message to Tom: the Jefferson County sheriff's office would like to have a conversation with you, please call. Instead, Tom was dead. Before officers could remove his body from the Fiat, Gonzalez drove from Jefferson County, where he was a small-town police chief and state legislator, to see the letters with his own eyes.

Quivery and coy with a wit drier than west Kansas dirt, Gonzalez had been tasked with objectively reviewing the sixteen-year-old case. He was chosen because he had no ties to the original investigation. The man who hired him was Kirk Vernon, now the chief of detectives for the Jefferson County Sheriff's Department. It was Vernon who, as a young detective in 1999, refused to sign an arrest warrant for Floyd because he believed police lacked probable cause.

It was not Gonzalez's job to exonerate Floyd and he didn't set out to do so. He had spent decades in Jefferson County law enforcement; decades around the detectives and officers who helped convict Floyd. Tasked with reinvestigating the case, he set out to find evidence that would keep Floyd behind bars. He read through the trial transcript five times. "When I first started the investigation, that was my whole purpose, in my mind. I wanted to find something solid that would implicate Floyd Bledsoe in the murder."

Gonzalez arrived on the scene and found the Fiat's driver side door open. Tom's left hand was hanging out; old bandages were wrapped around the wrist. Before he went missing, he had arrived at his home one night and told his wife he attempted to slit his wrist but failed to cut deep enough. Four months before, he had attempted to hang himself.

What stood out to Gonzalez in the three suicide notes was the mention of

187

a shell casing and the specificity of Tom's diagram. After Tom led police to Camille's body in 1999, four bullets had been found but only three casings. Could this be the missing one? In his reinvestigation of the case, Gonzalez realized the Bledsoe family property – where a girl was found murdered and a suspect arrested – had unexplainably not been searched. "Here you have a guy that says, 'Here's where I killed her.' So that was a lead that I felt that we needed to follow."

Eight days later, Vernon and Gonzalez joined two of the Arfmann case's original investigators, Robert Poppa and Troy Frost, at the brome field where Camille's body was discovered. The trash ditch had since been cleaned, returning it to a field of native grasses. They marked the site where Poppa and Frost believed they removed the girl's body sixteen years prior, marked the edges of the ditch and then began combing the ground with a metal detector. Within ten minutes, they found a nine-millimeter shell casing buried about an inch underground. Tom had told them they would find the casing less than twenty yards from the burial site. They found it eight yards away.

On November 18, Vernon obtained a DNA sample from Floyd Sr. and sent it to a KBI lab for testing. There it was determined that the sample SERI tested – the one lifted from the birthday card envelopes – was in fact DNA from the elder Floyd. It was further validation of the jolting DNA results that strongly indicate Floyd Sr. helped dispose of Camille's body.

That same week, detectives handed over the suicide notes to Alice Craig. "They were pretty clear with us from pretty early on about what happened and what the facts were but they waited to give us the specifics, just so they could follow up on their investigation."

Tom was buried on November 21, 2015, sixteen years and eight days after his victim was. A small memorial service was held not at Countryside Baptist but at a church southeast of Oskaloosa. His parents traveled from south Texas to bury him. Gary Bledsoe Sr., his uncle, did not attend. An online guest book was signed by only one person, an in-law sending prayers to his family.

As the December 8 hearing date neared, Vernon and Gonzalez continued their reinvestigation. Despite their intended goal of finding evidence of Floyd's guilt, they instead stumbled upon massive flaws in the original investigation and further evidence of Tom's guilt. They were unearthing secrets their own law enforcement agency had missed or ignored for sixteen years.

December 8 was a Tuesday, a warmer than usual one in Oskaloosa. The high of fifty-four degrees was nearly a record and came late in the day, as the Jefferson County Courthouse began to swell with people. A walk-through metal detector was arranged outside the large courtroom where Floyd's hearing was scheduled. As it became apparent that searching everyone would clog the halls, the metal detector was turned off. The result was a zoo-like atmosphere. Though cell phones were to be turned off and electronics banned, those rules were rapidly ignored as onlookers carried cameras and phones into the courtroom without objection. A bored child played video games before the hearing.

Floyd's supporters packed both sides of the courtroom. Gary Bledsoe was there, confident his nephew would be released. John Kurth stood near the back of the room; he had come to see "a wrong righted," he said. Paul Hughes, the Freedom Challenge co-founder, hung around. Many of the interns who had worked on the case, including Kaiti Smith, returned to Oskaloosa to watch the culmination of their work. They packed the rows immediately behind the defense table. Tricia Bushnell milled about, shaking hands and introducing people to one another. Only Camille's mother, Tommie Sue Arfmann, sitting one row behind newspaper reporters and two rows behind the prosecution, seemed unenthused by the proceedings.

Wearing oversized blue jeans, a long-sleeve white shirt underneath his light blue prison polo and bright orange prison shoes, Floyd left Lansing Correctional Facility and rode the thirty rural miles between there and the courthouse. Shackles tied his feet and handcuffs were around his wrists. Jailer Kendra Kennedy with the Jefferson County Sheriff's Department, considerably larger than Floyd, parked in a sallyport and led the prisoner inside as a *Topeka Capital-Journal* photographer clicked his camera.

When the attorneys had taken their positions – Jean Phillips, Alice Craig and Elizabeth Cateforis on the defense side, County Attorney Jason Belveal on the government's side – Nafziger entered, took a seat and quieted his unusually noisy courtroom. The *State of Kansas vs. Floyd S. Bledsoe* was back in session.

Craig told the judge that since October 20, when she filed her original motion, further exculpatory evidence had emerged from the suicide of Tom

Bledsoe and the sheriff's department's investigation. If there was no objection, she planned to present that evidence. This would be the first opportunity Floyd's supporters had to determine whose side Belveal was on. The big man rose from his dark wooden chair.

"Judge, we've reviewed all the DNA analysis. We reviewed the additional exculpatory evidence. In fact, our office provided that to counsel.

"We believe that the DNA results are favorable and the State is prepared to ask that your honor enter orders that serve the best interest of justice. We believe that those would include vacating and setting aside the judgment and granting a new trial in regard to Floyd Bledsoe." As he sat, the dozens of Floyd supporters sighed in relief. The same office that had wrongfully charged and prosecuted him would no longer act as a barrier to justice.

"Thank you," Judge Nafziger said. Then, motioning to Craig: "You may proceed. Call your first witness."

"At this time," she said, "I'd like to call Detective Kirk Vernon to the stand."

Vernon is a large man with light brown hair in a crewcut and small glasses on a round face. He made his way to the court reporter, was sworn in, and sat in a witness chair to the right of the judge, just as he had during the Bledsoe trial fifteen years before. Under questioning from Craig, he spent several minutes recapping the murder of Camille, his role in the original investigation and that investigation's twists and turns. He explained, for the first time under oath, how the polygraph results of Tom and Floyd were misconstrued and why he didn't sign his name in the usual manner on Floyd's arrest report.

"I had concerns at that point in time that we had reached a level of probable cause concerning Floyd Scott –"

"You mean that you were concerned you didn't have that level –"

"That is correct."

Craig verbally walked Vernon, and the court, through the DNA results. The detective had received them in September, before they were made public. Craig asked whether Floyd Sr.'s DNA could have been transmitted to Camille's socks through casual touching or transference; in other words, whether Tom's defense of his father was plausible.

"The way it was explained to me by both the head biologist from the KBI and another scientist from another crime lab, they both used the same phrase, being that it was possible but highly unlikely," Vernon told the court.

Vernon said there was no evidence Tom called anyone before killing himself. When the detective mentioned three letters were found inside Tom's car, whispers and hushed conversations broke out in the crowded gallery. "Did he say letters?" someone asked from three rows back. "Like suicide notes?" Police had never told the public that Tom left behind letters, let alone that they had relevance to the case against his brother.

One by one, the letters and their accompanying envelopes were entered into evidence by Craig with no objection from Belveal. Placing the letters before Vernon, she asked the detective to read each of them aloud to the best of his ability, considering Tom's misspellings and grammatical mishaps. As he did, reporters scribbled furiously onto notepads and typed quickly on their phones. Spectators stared at each other in wide-eyed amazement. Here was the truth they had all believed, laid out by the man they had all believed was the killer. What this meant for Floyd had not yet set in. For now, the audience was only awestruck.

"In that note," Craig said after Vernon had read the third letter, "he specifically exonerates Floyd Scott Bledsoe, is that correct?"

"That is correct."

"And he indicates he is solely responsible for Camille's death?"

"That is correct."

"Does the timing provided by Tom Bledsoe in the note match the evidence of when Camille disappeared?"

"Yes, it does."

Vernon recalled how he and three other detectives found the shell casing mentioned in Tom's third suicide note, pausing in his testimony to note the failure of detectives in 1999 to search the Bledsoe property. Because the shell casing had been found only three weeks before, forensic evidence had not yet linked it to Tom or the murder.

"When you compare," Craig asked, "the information provided by Tom Bledsoe in the suicide note to the timeline of Camille's disappearance, does it fit? Does it match?"

"From the time his last known whereabouts are to where he reappears, it absolutely can fit within, you know, his explanation of what happened within that window."

"Do you have to make any jumps or inferences to make it fit?"

"No."

Craig's final question was both obvious and ultimate: "Does your current investigation undermine your confidence in the original conviction of Floyd Scott Bledsoe?" Vernon's answer was an adamant "Yes." Belveal stood to say he would not cross-examine the witness and Vernon was excused by the judge. He was replaced by the second and final witness, Ramon Gonzalez.

Gonzalez stepped slowly and deliberately to the witness stand, his 71 years of age evident in his walk but not in his mind. He was sworn in, took his seat and introduced himself to the court.

Gonzalez had found a glaring flaw in the original investigation, one that seemed so obvious yet somehow escaped detectives in 1999 and 2000. On December 3, he had interviewed Cathy Bledsoe, the brothers' mother. It was around the same time that he interviewed the former Heidi Bledsoe (she had since remarried). He had questions about Tom's hearing impairment.

"So, then I asked [Cathy] how far Tom would be from you to be able to hear you clearly," Gonzalez told the court. "She stated that he was good at reading lips. So, as long as he was facing you, he could kind of communicate with you, but if he turned his back on you and walked away three feet, you would have to either yell a little louder or tap him to get his attention." Heidi had told Gonzalez and a KBI agent the same thing.

"In my review of the case, the part that struck me during the core testimony was that he stated – this was one of his many stories – that when he talked to Floyd, he had his hand over his head and was mumbling something about 'I' or 'we' or 'they.'"

In his search for evidence to implicate Floyd, Gonzalez had come across one of the more baffling aspects of the original investigation: the decision by detectives to believe Tom's unbelievable tale about a meeting alongside Osage Road. How could a man who struggled to hear inside a quiet courtroom be believed when he claimed to hear Floyd confess over the sound of two puttering vehicles while Floyd's head was buried in his arm? Especially when Tom had repeatedly admitted to lying and changing his stories?

"I had quite a few concerns. Every time the story changed, it was more to fit what happened at the crime scene rather than having Floyd be at the scene," Gonzalez said. He called the odds of two brothers crossing a backcountry Jefferson County road like that "a one in one-thousand situation."

Asked by Craig whether he had found any evidence linking Floyd Bledsoe to the murder of Camille Arfmann, Gonzalez dryly responded, "Not at this time. I'm still looking." Reporters scribbled each of those seven words and whispered among themselves ("They're still investigating!") when in fact, it was an example of Gonzalez's dry humor. Delivered in the same tone he delivered the rest of his testimony, few noticed.

As she moved toward her finale, Craig pressed Gonzalez for more details on flaws in the original investigation. "Does the lack of investigation during the original investigation concern you?" Gonzalez said it wasn't a lack of investigating; officers acted on what information they had at the time. "My concern, again, was we have a guy confessing multiple times and I don't know why we didn't search his room, his house, and the surrounding area. We did that with Floyd's residence and surrounding area. But, again, I don't see it as a lack. Maybe a lack of direction by somebody to say, 'Hey, we need to do this.'" Gonzalez, like Vernon, said his confidence in the conviction of Floyd had been undermined. Craig rested her case.

"Very well," Judge Nafziger said, turning to Belveal. "Are you going to present any evidence?"

"I'm not, judge. I don't have any rebuttal evidence."

The forces that, sixteen years ago, had lined up in opposition to Floyd – the Jefferson County Sheriff's Department, the Kansas Bureau of Investigation, the Jefferson County Attorney's Office – were now in his corner. Only one barrier remained, and he was the most important. What would Nafziger do?

"Not only do we have a confession," Craig told the judge during closing arguments, "but we have a confession with confirmatory evidence. That is evidence that clearly exculpates Floyd Scott Bledsoe and indicates his actual innocence and we're asking, at this time, to take all of this into consideration by the court, vacate his convictions and do one of two things.

"Our request would be that the convictions be vacated, and he be released from custody, but at the very least, vacate his convictions and leave it up to the county attorney as to whether or not additional investigation should occur and a new trial should be ordered."

Belveal rose and repeated his belief that Floyd's convictions should be overturned in the interest of justice. "I believe that the appropriate thing to do would be to order a new trial for the defendant, leaving it up to the state to determine whether or not there's enough evidence to proceed against him again." He agreed with Vernon and Gonzalez that the jury's verdict had been undermined by the wave of new evidence.

As Belveal sat down, spectators inched forward in their wooden pews. A decision was near, they knew. But Nafziger would disappoint them, at least temporarily, by calling a fifteen-minute recess. "I need to look at the DNA exhibit. I haven't seen that." There were deep sighs. Nafziger rose, walked to his left and stepped into his private chambers. For a few seconds, everyone remained quiet but the stillness was not to last. Seemingly at once, questions and comments spilled forth. Reporters talked among themselves about the shocking testimony, comparing notes to ensure they heard correctly. Floyd's supporters felt the onrush of that most common of emotions, cautious optimism. Floyd, upbeat, talked with his attorneys.

When Nafziger returned, the room went silent, in part due to judicial reverence but largely because no one wanted to miss a word. Some, like John Kurth, had waited a decade and a half to hear a court declare Floyd not guilty. Others had been children when he was convicted but devoted a segment of their adult life to the case. For Floyd, it was the last opportunity to leave a courtroom a free man rather than one doomed to life in a cage.

"After considering the testimony and evidence, including exhibits one through five presented at this hearing, and considering the arguments advanced by counsel, the court finds that a reasonable probability exists that the newly discovered evidence would result in a different outcome at trial," Nafziger said. "Therefore...I find that it serves the interest of justice that defendant be granted a new trial. I'm going to set this matter for tomorrow afternoon, Wednesday the 9th, at 2:30 so we can address the issue of counsel, bond, and, if necessary, a trial setting."

But before Nafziger could adjourn, another fifteen-minute recess was called, this time at the request of the attorneys. Nafziger stepped out of the courtroom and it came to life again. Questions abounded. Tricia Bushnell told reporters that Floyd's attorneys were pushing for his immediate release. Whispers spread, then louder voices. It had been a victory, though a partial one. Now the push was on for total victory, total justice.

"Be seated, please," Nafziger said as spectators scrambled back to their seats one last time. The judge looked to his right, at Belveal. "I'm advised, counsel, that you wish to address the court."

The lumbering county attorney stood for a final time. "Judge, following your ruling to overturn the conviction and order a new trial of Mr. Bledsoe, the state would ask that the court dismiss *State of Kansas versus Floyd S. Bledsoe*. I would ask that you do that without prejudice."

"Is there objection?"

Craig nearly blurted out her answer. "No, your honor! Not at all."

"Very well. The state's motion to dismiss without prejudice to refiling is granted. Defendant is to be released."

According to an official transcript, Craig and Belveal then thanked the judge, as is customary. No one in the gallery heard that, however. Cheering had erupted after those five words so many had waited so long to hear: "Defendant is to be released." Behavior indecorous for a court of law emanated from every row, even from the young lawyers in the crowd. Several people wept openly. Floyd hugged his attorneys as hard as he's ever hugged anyone.

Asked about that moment a couple years later, he said, "I remember sitting in that chair and just taking a deep breath and saying, 'Is this really over? Did this really happen?'" God had fulfilled the promise he made as Floyd laid in his jail cell on Christmas Eve 1999. The star in the sky had said that one day this would all be over, and now it was.

People lunged over the bar that separates attorneys from laymen, reaching out to hug a man freed after sixteen long years. Kendra Kennedy, the imposing jailer who had escorted Floyd into the courthouse, took his shackles off with a smile. A television cameraman began questioning Floyd. In doing so, the cameraman, who had been ordered by Nafziger to provide video for all news outlets present, unplugged a rival television station's live feed before conducting his impromptu interview with a man who had little to say, his words caught somewhere deep down his throat. Photos were snapped from every direction.

As the joyous crowd slowly made its way out of the courtroom, Floyd was ushered into a courthouse conference room for some privacy and a change of clothes. Reporters waited in the hallway and nagged the court clerk for copies of Tom's suicide letters to no avail. Elsewhere, Nafziger and Belveal made their decisions official with some paperwork. The moment was so unusual that on the custody slip – the judge's order to a prison to release an inmate – there was no box for Nafziger to check that explained what he had just done. So, he drew a small box with his pen, wrote "conviction overturned by court," checked his own hand-drawn box and signed below it.

Only Tommie Sue Arfmann was unhappy. She scowled throughout the proceeding and verbally sparred with celebratory spectators afterward. She no longer believed Floyd guilty of murdering her daughter – as she had once believed so passionately – but thought he should remain behind bars for failing to protect her daughter from Tom. No one near her agreed but she remained stubborn in her objections. One person noted that if Floyd had received the death penalty, as she had hoped he would all those years ago, then he would have died an innocent man before seeing freedom.

Outside the courthouse, a line of television cameras awaited, an unusual sight in downtown Oskaloosa. When he walked out, around 4:30 p.m., Floyd wore blue jeans and a checkered flannel shirt, an outfit befitting a harmless dairy farmer. His full legal team, past and present, stood around him in a large half-circle. Kaiti Smith, considerably taller than the rest, could be seen in the back. Floyd paused at the top of the steps for his first breaths of freedom, stuck his hands in his jean pockets and made his way to ten reporters blocking the sidewalk.

"What are you going to do now? What is the first thing you want to do?" Floyd began to answer. "I want to go…" before hitting a mental block and saying, "I don't know." The crowd laughed, Floyd laughed, reporters laughed. "It's all barely sinking in…it's been a long time. I just want to take everything slow and take it all in."

Another reporter asked, "What do you plan to do now?" Floyd's response: "Going back to milking cows. Something peaceful and quiet for a while."

Next question: "Are you staying in the area?" Next answer: "I haven't decided on that yet. I just try to take it one day at a time."

When an *Associated Press* reporter asked about Floyd's opinion of his brother, Phillips rubbed his back and whispered in his ear. Before he could answer, Bushnell said, "It's been a very emotional day. I think Floyd is here and he's happy to answer questions but I think he's going to need some time to process the things that are going on."

"I'm ready to move behind the last sixteen and into the next fifty, sixty, seventy years. I can't do anything about the past. All I can do is change the future," Floyd said.

The final question was, "I have to imagine there is something you're dying to eat." Floyd laughed, as did many behind him. "That's what everybody keeps asking me. I still haven't figured that out." Eventually he came up with an answer: "A really good steak. That's one thing you don't get in prison."

When Detective Vernon stepped out of the courthouse door and walked past the crowd, Craig said, "My star witness!" and gave him a hug. Rick Nichols with the *Oskaloosa Independent* asked him what's next for the investigation. "We've got stuff we've got to follow up on now," he told the reporter, still holding the bright orange prison slippers Floyd had worn to the hearing but since traded in for tennis shoes.

Floyd did have that steak, along with champagne, at a local pub. The manager threw in a free dessert – it's not every day you give an exoneree his first meal as a free man.

For the first time since the trial a decade and a half prior, Floyd's face and case returned to the front page of eastern Kansas newspapers. In the *Independent*, the headline was "Case against Floyd Bledsoe is dismissed" alongside a photo of Floyd soon after his handcuffs were removed. To the left was a sub-headline: "Free at last, free at last!"

That night, Lonnie Mast heard about Floyd's release on TV. His former cellblock buddy, the unusually calm man who seemed like he had done no harm and could do no harm, was now free. The next morning, he told Chano Young over breakfast.

"I told Floyd that he has something that a lot of people in the free world don't understand," Young said. "He sees life differently now. He has had those years to think and I know over the years there might have been a time or two when he probably wondered to himself if he would get out of prison. It's a hard feeling not knowing if you are ever going to have that chance to be free."

There was at least one place where the people were unconvinced Floyd was innocent: the Jefferson County sheriff's office. "I think there were a few people who, in their own minds, were still convinced that Floyd was involved," Belveal recalls. "Not necessarily that he was the primary person behind the kidnap and the homicide but there were people who still thought he was probably involved."

***

Floyd was free to navigate a world more technologically advanced than the one he left in 2009 and far more technologically advanced than the one he left in 1999. Smart phones were an enigma at first. Job applications were now filed online, not in person. At a Burger King, he stood at the digital soda machine before him, saw a button on the touch screen for ice and pressed it. Then he turned to the employee and asked, "Now, where's the soda machine?" She calmly explained to the confused customer that he was standing in front of it.

He found people were far more impersonal, that fewer people spoke in person, that too many spent their time staring at a phone. He rediscovered the beauty of Kansas, a state he had come to take for granted. He looked out over Clinton Lake south of Lawrence and found charm. He drove through the rolling Flint Hills and found more. "The worst day out here is better than the best day in there," he said on a blue-sky day in Wichita, wearing a t-shirt that read "I Love My Country…It's My Government I Can't Stand!" and staring skyward. "It doesn't get any better than this."

Newspapers and television stations across the state – and beyond – reported on his release, making the dairy farmer from Oskaloosa a minor celebrity. At a Walmart, someone said, "Hey, Floyd, I just want to say congratulations." He heard the same at a hotel in Lawrence and while eating pizza with his uncle Gary. At a Denny's restaurant, another man stopped by his table to congratulate him. In each case, Floyd wondered if he knew, or should know, the person before him. There had been a sixteen-year gap in friendships. People had aged, their children had grown up, some had moved on or passed away.

The Midwest Innocence Project helped him return to life outside of a cage. He had to find his birth certificate, then apply for a driver's license, then open a bank account. He needed a medical exam and a dental screening. He was given a cell phone the day after his release, though texting skills would require time to acquire. Loans were difficult to obtain, due to the 16-year gap in his credit history. At job interviews, the same gap raised the same questions.

Six days after his release, a reporter returned to the Project for Innocence and the roundtable of attorneys he had visited with before the hearing. Whereas that first meeting had been forward-looking, entirely focused on the DNA results and the upcoming hearing, the second meeting was retrospective, centered around the actions of others that had brought about the injustice those four attorneys had just righted. There were questions about Tom's suicide notes. Could his version of events – the consensual sex, the bewilderment upon learning Camille's age, the accidental gunshot – be accurate? And could Floyd Sr.'s DNA really have found its way onto Camille's socks without his participation in the crime or coverup?

Jean Phillips, never one to mince words, spoke first. "We think that [version of events] is a lie and trying to exclude his dad is a lie." The others agreed. A SERI analyst and KBI biologist had discussed Tom's claim and found it highly unlikely. The extreme ratio – one in twenty sextillion – signified Floyd Sr's DNA had transferred to the socks at a high rate only associated with direct touching and friction. If the DNA had come from Camille's presence on the parents' bed, why was Cathy Bledsoe's DNA not on the victim's clothes? Alice Craig spoke next. "There's just no reason for his DNA to be anywhere on her and certainly not as a major contributor."

Tom had portrayed his suicide notes as a *mea culpa*, a last act of honesty after a lifetime of lies. But the mistruths within them discolored that claim. If he would lie even in his confessionary last words, what else in the suicide notes could be believed? Craig had a theory: "He spent sixteen years justifying what happened. There must be a lot of that left over."

In the months since the DNA results had been made public, speculation had mounted in Oskaloosa over whether the elder Floyd would be charged with disposing of Camille's body and covering up her murder. It was a question the Project for Innocence attorneys had considered as well. "There isn't enough evidence," Phillips said. "I think without Tom and because Tom excluded his dad's participation, it would be hard." There were doubts about whether the county attorney wanted to prolong legal proceedings that had shone a negative light on Jefferson County. "With all the problems," Craig said, "I don't think they will prosecute unless they get a huge public outcry."

There was speculation too about Floyd's next move. Would he return to Oskaloosa? The consensus answer was no. "That's because there are still some people who believe he did it or had some role," Elizabeth Cateforis said.

The largest question, the one no one at the table and few outside of it could answer definitively, was *how did this happen?* Craig had asked Kirk Vernon and Jefferson County detective Troy Frost that same question. "I don't think they know, which is troubling. Investigators look back on it and they're mortified." The voices of skeptical detectives, like Vernon, were ignored as the investigation turned, in mid-November of 1999, to Floyd. Polygraph answers were distorted and then became the basis for that twist in the investigation. "They said Floyd failed and Tom passed so we're done," Tricia Bushnell said, "we don't need to look at Tom anymore and they just disregarded all the rest of the facts from there on out to make it about Floyd." Tom's influential defense attorney, Mike Hayes, was blamed. So, too, was John Kurth, Floyd's trial attorney, for his failure to object to inadmissible testimony. "You can't let the testimony of a two-year-old come in," Phillips said, shaking her head.

Later that month, Vernon told *The Associated Press* that the Jefferson County Sheriff's Department was formally reopening the Arfmann case, despite the death of its leading suspect. "We are open to all possibilities that he may have had assistance." The KBI said it would assist in the investigation. Like the sheriff's department, the KBI had begun reexamining the case after SERI's DNA results were revealed in September. Asked about the younger Floyd, Vernon said, "At this point in time, there is no reason to believe that he is involved." To the dismay of some, the chief of detectives said the investigation would be narrow in scope and would not include any actions by Jim Vanderbilt or former Sheriff Dunnaway. "At this time, there's no information or suggestion of any wrongdoing by the former prosecutor or sheriff."

A few weeks later, Belveal went further, saying Vanderbilt, Dunnaway and KBI special agent Jim Woods made mistakes with DNA and polygraph results but those mistakes were unintentional. "It's just kind of, unfortunately, one of those things," he told a reporter. "Mistakes just got compounded, but I think they were honest mistakes. I don't think anybody did anything sinister."

Dunnaway, in his only public comments about the case after Floyd's release, told the *Lawrence Journal-World* that he couldn't explain why he had ordered DNA testing to stop in December of 1999. Dunnaway's signature was on the stop order, along with his department's letterhead. "I can't even see me signing anything like that. There's no way I would have stopped DNA testing. I like the truth, and whatever the truth is, get it out there and get it going."

Mark Malick, a senior special agent with the KBI, said his bureau was reopening the case to look "for any additional investigative leads" or evidence but would not draw conclusions about conduct in the original investigation. After Malick said the KBI would issue a report, Belveal predicted the report, which had not even begun to be written, would say, "Here is what happened, here is where the wheels came off. In the future, we would suggest that these sort of things be handled differently. I doubt very seriously if they will say there was something sinister going on, and therefore we should look at some type of prosecution, you know, something internal."

In the end, the KBI report said nothing because no report was ever written. The bureau's top lawyer says Malick likely misspoke or "was misunderstood or his comments were taken out of context or…circumstances changed after he spoke." The bureau's many mistakes – its failure to secure the crime scene, its misreading or mistruths about the polygraph results, its decision to trust a serial liar and Camille's murderer – have never been acknowledged by the state's premier law enforcement agency.

As the Project for Innocence attorneys expected, Belveal was doubtful he could secure a conviction of Floyd Sr. and showed little interest in trying. "The DNA on the socks, it's a match for Floyd Sr., with apparent utter certainty. But I don't think we can say any more than that with any degree of certainty. We can all speculate as to what the explanation is, but can you prove it beyond a reasonable doubt is obviously the question." There is no statute of limitations for murder but a lesser charge could carry limitations. On the other hand, if Floyd Sr. concealed his involvement, a statute of limitations could be nullified.

***

Another detail deftly predicted by Floyd's attorneys was where he would settle down after leaving prison. Around Oskaloosa, he is a minor celebrity, attracting gawks at restaurants and stores. Some there, including a few in the sheriff's department, still believe he is an accomplice to murder. For that reason and others, Floyd settled three hours away, in Hutchinson, as he had during his brief release in 2008 and 2009.

Raising a young son and slogging through a divorce two states away in Illinois, Amanda Ingram, the former Freedom's Challenge intern who befriended Floyd in prison, got word he was free. They reconnected in Hutchinson a few months later, in February 2016. Faith remained a powerful bond and they caught up in a hurry. Floyd would stop by for dinner and play with her young son, Blake, who learned to wait by the window for him to arrive late in the afternoon. Floyd helped her through the divorce, she helped him get reacquainted with the free world. He complimented her cooking like no ever had; it was drastically better than prison fare. Before long, they were dating. Eight months later, they were married.

SIXTEEN

It was sometime after 7 p.m. on April 19, 2016, when he walked to a ballroom stage at the Marriott Hotel in downtown Kansas City. His head inched just above the lectern; his mouth was well below the microphone. As he started to speak, the crowd began to applaud. A few people stood as they clapped, then more, then the entire room.

Floyd stopped speaking and looked out over the crowd, his eyes watering. For about thirty seconds, he just watched, emotionally moved, as a room of nine hundred people cheered. When he began again to deliver the night's invocation, his voice was shaky.

"Our Lord, thank you for this night. We thank you for the privilege it is to come together in one room to become those lights shining in the darkness, those lights that shine and bring forth justice where justice is very, very needed. Lord, you help us and you set the standard of what forgiveness truly is. Lord, we ask you go help us forgive those who have wronged us as you have forgiven us for what we've done."

The event was an annual fundraiser for the Midwest Innocence Project. It would include a moment when Floyd, standing alongside Dennis Fritz and other wrongfully convicted men, held a piece of paper in his hands with his prison number on it and, to more cheers from the crowd, ripped the paper in half.

"Lord, I thank you for the people in this room. I thank you for their hearts and their willingness to step out and step in and step out of their mold, to walk on water and perform those things that you've said you do, that you want them to do. We thank you and we praise you. In Jesus's name, amen."

Jason Belveal and Kirk Vernon attended. Belveal purchased a painting of Floyd's at the benefit auction and hung it in the county attorney's office, where it remained during the rest of his tenure in elected office.

After his release, Floyd accepted nearly every speaking gig that came his way and there were a lot of offers. He had a hard time saying no, doing so only when it conflicted with his attempts at rejoining the work force.

At Iola High School in southeast Kansas, he was asked by student reporter Allie Utley of The Messenger high school newspaper whether he harbored resentment of Tom. He answered indirectly. "There's times where I ask myself, 'Could I have done things differently to change his life, to help him from making the actions that he did later on?' Could I have been a better brother? Sure. Is it my responsibility? No. But it is, in essence, because in every life no person is alone. Every person we touch touches other lives and it's got that ripple effect. And for some people, we only get one opportunity to change their life. So, is it going to be for the better or for the worse?"

Many of his speaking appearances were at the Kansas Capitol in Topeka, a two-and-a-half-hour drive from his home in Hutchinson. The state was considering what, if anything, needed to change in the wake of Floyd's wrongful conviction. The first piece of legislation was introduced by Rep. Ramon Gonzalez, a Jefferson County Republican. The same Ramon Gonzalez who, as a special investigator, had reopened the Arfmann murder case and found no evidence of Floyd's guilt. The same Ramon Gonzalez who testified on December 8, 2015, the day Floyd was released.

Gonzalez's bill would have allowed defendants wrongfully convicted of state crimes to sue for compensation within two years of their release. Compensation would be doled out using a formula in the bill. "A claimant entitled to damages...shall be awarded damages in the amount of the federal minimum wage multiplied by 2,080 for each year the claimant was incarcerated," it stated. 2,080 is the number of hours a full-time, forty-hour-per-week employee works in one year.

Floyd would have been eligible for $235,248 under the bill, an amount many of his supporters considered a paltry sum considering all he had lost. Still, the bill was a beginning. It was the first acknowledgement by a member of state government that Kansas owed something to a man it had taken so much from.

"I will let each member think about how they would function financially if they had to face a similar wrong conviction," Gonzalez told fellow members of the House Judiciary Committee on February 15, 2016. Floyd told legislators to "go inside a cell and imagine your life there. Think about being one of the people you see locked up, and then wonder what it would be like to know you have done none of the things you have been accused of."

"The missing years can never come back. I will never get that time back or the relationships or career that could have been built during that time. As this committee considers HB 2611, I hope it will also consider – how much is that loss worth?" he told them.

The bill had the support of the Innocence Project, Midwest Innocence Project and Floyd's former attorneys at the University of Kansas. Many set aside misgivings about the relatively small amount of compensation or other perceived flaws in the bill to thank Gonzalez for starting a dialogue at the Capitol. The bill never came up for a vote and died in committee.

Gonzalez also introduced legislation requiring law enforcement agencies to videotape interrogations of murder defendants in the state. Some interrogations of the Bledsoe brothers were not recorded, including those in which Tom confessed to killing Camille.

An early draft of the bill contained no punishments for law enforcement agencies or recourse for defendants if an interrogation is not recorded. It drew initial opposition from the Innocence Project. When Gonzalez added a provision requiring judges to tell jurors that police had defied state law by not recording, the Innocence Project endorsed the bill.

A hearing on the recording bill was also in mid-February 2016, this time before the House Committee on Corrections and Juvenile Justice. Gonzalez, a police chief and lifelong cop, told the committee that "videotaping of these cases validates the integrity and credibility of law enforcement in the interrogation process." Floyd, speaking of his brother's confessions, said, "If we would have had the recordings, there would have been no doubt. The cameras don't lie."

Lining up in opposition were the Kansas Bureau of Investigation, prosecutors and several law enforcement groups — the Kansas Association of Chiefs of Police, Kansas Sheriffs' Association and Kansas Peace Officers Association. Many agreed with the need for recorded interrogations but argued a legislative mandate was imprudent. Though the bill was written by a career cop, some argued it was anti-law enforcement.

Charles Branson, the district attorney in Douglas County, just south of Oskaloosa, claimed recorded interrogations would not have changed the outcome in Floyd's case. "This bill would do nothing to substantiate the rights of the defendant," he said. "It would do nothing to increase those rights, but it would increase the cost and burden on law enforcement and the court system itself." Innocence groups instead claimed recordings would ultimately save counties money by somewhat protecting them from punitive civil lawsuits stemming from exonerations.

The bill, facing staunch opposition from police and prosecutors, never came up for a vote and died in committee. The so-called Bledsoe bills were oh-for-two.

Floyd also became a champion of repealing the state's death penalty statute, an endeavor considered trivial by some since Kansas hasn't put anyone to death since 1965. Fifty-one days after his release from Lansing Correctional Facility, he stood at a microphone in the Capitol Rotunda and said, "We must stop the death penalty today. Tomorrow it might be too late for one person."

Floyd said his experience proved the fallibility of Kansas courts. "The death penalty is unjust. Please stop it." He endorsed a bill banning the practice, which was co-sponsored by ten Republicans and six Democrats. Its author was Rep. Steven Becker, a Republican and retired judge, who said he, too, had seen flaws in the criminal justice system and called the reasonable doubt standard for proof paradoxical to the death penalty. "How can we impose the absolute certainty of death when we don't require the absolute certainty of guilt?" Rep. Jerry Henry, a Democrat, made the Christian case for repeal: "Jesus Christ, our lord and savior, was himself a victim of capital punishment."

***

The following February, Bledsoe bills returned to the Kansas Legislature and Floyd returned to the Capitol to push for them. He was without his House ally this time; Rep. Gonzalez had declined to run for re-election in 2016.

A compensation bill was instead introduced in the Senate by David Haley, a Kansas City Democrat and veteran lawmaker. His father, George Haley, had been a college classmate of Martin Luther King Jr. and an attorney on the *Brown v. Board* school integration case. His uncle was Pulitzer Prize winner Alex Haley, author of "Roots" and "The Autobiography of Malcolm X."

Senate Bill 125 was far more robust than Gonzalez's effort the previous year. Exonerees would be eligible for $80,000 for each year in prison and a bulk sum of one million dollars if they were on death row, along with a repayment of attorney fees. Floyd would be eligible for $1,248,000 under the Haley bill, along with about $200,000 in attorney fees. To the dismay of the Innocence Project, the legislation would not apply to defendants who pleaded guilty to a crime they didn't commit.

"The day I was released from prison," Floyd told the Senate Judiciary Committee, "I had nothing but the clothing that the law school provided for me. I had no money and no place to live. Before I went to prison, my grand-mother had left me land to start my own farm. The land and my livestock had to be sold. As you can imagine, this entire ordeal tore my family apart, so I could not rely on them for assistance. When I applied for jobs, employers were nervous to hire someone who had been incarcerated, despite the fact that I was innocent."

Due to a strange quirk in state law, Floyd was given less upon his release from prison than an actual murderer would have been given. Inmates leaving Kansas prisons are offered a hundred dollars, job training and mentorship programs. The wrongfully convicted receive none of that and societal mores make matters worse. When he applied for a car loan, the interest rate was twenty-four percent due to his lack of a credit history. When he applied for a job, the background check showed he was still in prison for murder.

"There are so many things that I lost because of my wrongful convic-tion," Floyd told senators. "I lost the opportunity to watch my sons grow up. I lost my property and my career. I lost my freedom. Senate Bill 125 would ensure that other Kansans like me receive the financial compensation they need to get back on their feet and recover from the nightmare of a wrongful conviction. I hope you will support this bill."

A conservative lawmaker, Sen. Mary Pilcher-Cook, had a question. Would it be possible for con artists to take advantage of the bill by allow-ing themselves to be wrongfully convicted, serving time in prison and then presenting evidence they had previously withheld in order to win a payout from the state? Floyd's response: "With all due respect, no one in their right mind would do that."

Though no one testified in opposition to the bill, the state's years-long budget crunch was an elephant in the room. Any legislation that carried a price tag was seen as suspect. The committee took no action on the bill and it stalled there.

Floyd and innocence advocates fared better on the less costly issue of recorded interrogations. Unlike the Gonzalez bill the year before, which required videotaped interrogations, Senate Bill 92 allowed for audio recordings as an alternative. That eliminated the objections of the same law enforcement groups that had opposed the Gonzalez bill.

Ed Klumpp, a lobbyist for police chiefs, officers and sheriffs, told the Senate Judiciary Committee, "We think this is a good bill and addresses our concerns." Sen. Steve Fitzgerald, a conservative Republican, backed recorded interrogations, saying, "The cost of technology is going down and this is becoming just routine and mundane."

Haley asked Michelle Feldman, a lobbyist for the Innocence Project, whether the bill was watered down by only requiring interrogations in cases of murder and felony sex crimes. Feldman said the bill was similar to laws in twenty-one states that require recorded interrogations. Once officers become accustomed to recording interrogations for serious crimes, they will instinctively do so for less serious crimes, she told the senator.

The Judiciary Committee passed the bill the next day and the full Senate considered it two weeks later, on February 21, 2017. After rejecting an amendment from Haley that would have required videotaped interrogations in all cases, the Senate passed the bill unanimously, 40-0. It then passed the House by a vote of 115 to 9. That May, Gov. Sam Brownback signed the bill, the first change in Kansas law to emanate from the Bledsoe case.

The next year, Floyd had company at the Kansas Capitol as he again pushed for wrongful conviction compensation. Two other former Lansing inmates, Lamonte McIntyre and Richard Jones, had been exonerated in the two years after Floyd but not before spending twenty-three years and sixteen years, respectively, in prison. The three men – all coincidentally forty-one years old – made a formidable triumvirate. With the state's budget woes in the past and the need for compensation as evident as ever, the Kansas House and Senate unanimously passed a bill providing $65,000 for each year wrongfully spent in prison, along with access to social services – legislation hailed by innocence activists as a gold standard for the nation.

Gov. Jeff Colyer, who took over for Brownback after his ascension to a State Department post, signed the bill at a modest church, Mount Zion

Church of God in Christ, in Kansas City, Kansas, on May 15, 2018. "A great injustice was done to these three gentlemen," he said of Floyd, McIntyre and Jones. "These three men showed compassion, they showed courage and they showed concern for other Kansans. These men stood up, and as Kansans, they were wise and gracious." He told those in attendance – family members of the exonerees, activists and politicians – that the three men emerged from prison unconsumed by anger. "It would have turned us to madness. What I want to say to Lamonte McIntyre, to Floyd Bledsoe, to Richard Jones: We apologize to you, we love you and we will make it right."

After Colyer signed the bill, the three exonerees drove to the prison in Lansing where they once lived, only to discover their former building had since been torn down. They took a photo outside the prison's barbed-wire-topped walls, the other two men towering over Floyd, and posed with copies of the signed legislation. Jones remarked: "It finally felt like some justice was served today."

In the year after that remark, five men filed for wrongful conviction compensation in Kansas – the trio at the bill signing, along with two men who had served less than two years in prison. Floyd at first filed his application for innocence – a 264-page account of his wrongful conviction – in Jefferson County District Court but it was moved to a Topeka court and settled in May of 2019 for just over $1 million, along with a tuition waiver for 130 college credit hours and counseling assistance. He was also given what the state calls a Certificate of Innocence.

***

One midsummer Saturday night in 1981, twenty-two-year-old Army corporal Eddie Lowery hopped in his car and went to buy cigarettes in Riley, Kansas, a town of less than a thousand people a hundred miles west of Oskaloosa. On his way back, he was in a minor accident, hitting a parked car on the side of the road. Lowery was questioned by Riley police – not about the traffic accident, but about the rape of an elderly woman is nearby Ogden that night.

Lowery told them the truth, that he had no knowledge of the rape and certainly wasn't involved. A polygraph test said otherwise. The ensuing interrogation dragged on for eight hours without food. When the young corporal requested a lawyer, police denied him one. To escape the mental exhaustion of a seemingly endless interrogation, he confessed to a crime he did not commit. With the confession, which was not recorded, as the state's only credible evidence against Lowery, he was convicted and sentenced to eleven years to life in prison.

After a decade in Lansing, Lowery was released on parole in 1991 but forced to register as a sex offender. On a journey to clear his name, the Innocence Project and a local attorney found a rape kit from the case, tested it for DNA and exonerated their client in 2003. Another man, Daniel Brewer, was convicted of the crime in 2012.

Among Floyd's supporters, the Lowery case was much discussed, not because the cases were similar – there are far more differences than similarities – but because of how it ended. After his exoneration, Lowery won a $7.5 million settlement from Riley County, or about two thousand dollars for every day he wrongfully spent in a cage. Within days of Floyd's release, rumors of a similar lawsuit were whispered about.

On May 10, 2016, it happened. Sitting next to Exoneration Project attorney Russell Ainsworth at a press conference, Floyd told those in attendance that "today is the day we start a journey to find the truth, to find out why things went the way they did." His twenty-six-page federal lawsuit named Jefferson County as a defendant, along with eleven people: Roy Dunnaway, the former sheriff; Jim Vanderbilt, the former county attorney; Jefferson County deputies Randy Carreno, Troy Frost, Orin Turner and Robert Poppa; KBI detectives George Johnson, Jim Woods and Terry Morgan; Jeff Herrig, the current sheriff; and Mike Hayes, Tom Bledsoe's former defense attorney.

"It wasn't a decision that was easy to make," Floyd said of the decision to sue. "But ultimately, accountability has to happen. People cannot just randomly pick and choose what they want and who they want to blame. And for that very reason we are here today."

The lawsuit was blunt, to-the-point and unfailingly accusatory. "Despite knowledge of Tom's guilt, the defendants framed Floyd for the murder," it alleged on just the second page. "As the centerpiece of their scheme, the defendants fabricated, orchestrated and staged a false recantation by Tom that implicated Floyd. In the weeks that followed, the defendants continued to fabricate and shape Tom's story to fit facts emerging from the criminal investigation and silenced Tom when he repeatedly tried to come clean."

For sixteen years, those who believed Floyd to be innocent had faced a cynical but inevitable question: was he investigated, tried and convicted due to incompetence or corruption? The lawsuit was alleging, for the first time in a court of law, the latter. Tom's absurd claim that Floyd confessed on the side of the Osage Road was a police scheme, it claimed. The officers' inexplicable lack of recordings, police reports or notes of any kind from their interviews of Tom – interviews in which he confessed to murder – were proof that evidence was "concealed and suppressed," it claimed. And the detectives' decision to not search Tom's bedroom or truck, even as he was confessing to murder, was proof of a conspiracy, it claimed.

"Sixteen years later, we have not been provided any police reports documenting Tom's initial statements and confessions to the police, which is extremely suspicious," Ainsworth said at the press conference. "When you have a case where someone is confessing to murder, Homicide 101 tells you to write down the confessions. Had Floyd had the initial confession documented and provided to him, he would have known that Tom was providing facts that could only have been known by the true killer."

The conspiracy theory went like this: On November 7, 1999, when Tom and Mike Hayes met officers at the sheriff's office before taking them to Camille's body, Tom revealed intimate details about the murder that proved he had committed it. A few days later, Hayes and Vanderbilt met with several officers to devise a plan for framing Floyd whereby Tom would recant his confession and claim to have met Floyd on the side of Osage Road at a time when the officers believed Floyd was without an alibi. KBI agent George Johnson then distorted the results of the polygraph tests and instructed Tom to continue lying. Vanderbilt went along with the injustice because he was indebted to Hayes, who had helped Vanderbilt avoid exposure for misappropriating county funds.

The lawsuit relied, in part, on Tom's own words from the suicide notes: "The Jefferson County police and Jim Vanderbilt made me do it" and "I was told by Vanderbilt to keep my mouth shut" and "I tried telling the truth but no one would listen." Of course, relying on the words of a serial liar – even the dying words – is an exercise in risked credibility. Other evidence of the alleged conspiracy was filed under seal, placing it outside the scrutiny of the public.

The lawsuit put forth a new theory for why Camille was killed, different from that suggested by Tom in his suicide notes. In his confession to police in the early morning hours after he led them to Camille's body, Tom told officers he attempted to have sex with Camille in his truck, she laughed at the idea and he then shot her in the head, according to the lawsuit.

The defendants denied that in a forty-three-page response filed two months later and adamantly denied taking party in a conspiracy to frame Floyd for a murder they knew Tom committed. The Jefferson County officers had "performed their jobs with integrity," their attorney wrote, and the lawsuit contained "speculation and conspiracy theories in lieu of factual allegations."

For more than a year after the lawsuit was filed, it lingered idly as attorneys filed motions to delay, motions to quash, motions to continue. The case would occasionally go months without an update. On August 4, 2017, District Judge Daniel Crabtree made the first significant ruling in the lawsuit, denying attempts by Hayes, Vanderbilt and the KBI defendants – Morgan, Woods and Johnson – to have their names removed.

Crabtree's decision to keep Hayes on the lawsuit pleasantly surprised Floyd. Hayes had claimed that since he was not working on behalf of the government – not a "state actor," in legal parlance – he could not be sued as such. Crabtree disagreed, ruling that the lawsuit alleged Hayes had conspired with state actors in the conspiracy to frame Floyd and therefore acted as a state actor himself. He, too, could be sued by Floyd, the judge determined.

Vanderbilt had claimed immunity for the opposite reason – because he was a government employee, in this case a county attorney. Prosecutors are granted absolute immunity from lawsuits for their actions as an officer of the court. Floyd's lawsuit, however, went beyond that, alleging wrongdoing by Vanderbilt before a jury was convened, in this case when deciding to release Tom and charge Floyd with Camille's murder. Crabtree determined Vanderbilt was not acting simply as a courtroom prosecutor "when he allegedly conspired with other defendants to pin Camille's murder on plaintiff. Mr. Vanderbilt thus is not entitled to absolute immunity for this alleged conduct." Vanderbilt appealed Crabtree's ruling to the Tenth Circuit Court in Denver, where arguments were heard in November of 2018.

"'I sent an innocent man to prison. The Jefferson County police and Jim Vanderbilt made me do it. I was told by Vanderbilt to keep my mouth shut.' Those are Tom Bledsoe's words, made in his suicide note," Ainsworth told the Tenth Circuit. "...Those were Jim Vanderbilt's actions that sent

Floyd Bledsoe on a 16-year nightmare of incarceration for a crime he did not commit."

Vanderbilt's attorney, Patric Linden, argued his client had absolute immunity and therefore could not be sued. "A prosecutor must be free to make decisions on what evidence to present at a criminal trial," he told a three-judge panel. But the judges were skeptical that Vanderbilt was acting as a prosecutor when he allegedly framed Floyd. Like Crabtree, they believed he was acting as an investigator at that time and therefore was not immune. "The allegations in this complaint are about participation in the detectives' investigation," said Judge Carolyn B. McHugh.

Vanderbilt's appeal stopped progress on informal talks between Floyd, his legal team, and the defendants, who had begun searching for a settlement, until the Tenth Circuit issued its opinion in August of 2019. A three-judge panel ruled 3-0 against Vanderbilt, finding he "does not enjoy absolute immunity…for allegedly fabricating evidence against" Floyd.

Yet still the case dragged on. In October 2019, months after Floyd had received a Certificate of Innocence from the state of Kansas, an attorney for Jefferson County was still arguing Floyd may have killed Camille. "The only explanation" for the officers' decision to ignore Tom's repeated confessions, "is an honest belief that Floyd – not Tom – was the culprit," attorney David E. Rogers told a federal court. "If any of the defendants made the wrong choice [and it has not been established that they did], that is a matter of good-faith mistake or, at worst, negligence – not malice."

In December 2020, the county's attorneys went farther, telling a federal judge that "Floyd has not been exonerated and, based upon information and belief, the State of Kansas and/or federal authorities may still be able to file criminal charges against Floyd for the murder of Camille Arfmann."

***

Standing before the U.S. Supreme Court on April 19, 2005, Ohio State Solicitor Douglas Cole told the justices: "One of the old saws of American law is, it's better one guilty person should go free than that one innocent person should be punished." The murder of Camille Arfmann is a dual legal tragedy because both occurred. The man who killed her and confessed to doing so went free as the man who had searched sleeplessly for her was punished, betrayed by his family and sentenced to die behind bars.

Floyd Bledsoe was one of 157 people in the United States to be exonerated in 2015 – a single-year record. Each case was different, each with its own villains: racist cops or corrupt prosecutors or bumbling defense attorneys or lazy judges. In some cases, the people in power were honest and so were their mistakes; in other cases, they were not.

For sixteen years between November 5, 1999, and December 8, 2015, the biggest question in the Camille Arfmann case was, who kidnapped and killed her? That question has since been answered. Now, the question on the lips of those who have followed the Arfmann case – the lawyers, the journalists, the activists – is, why was Floyd investigated, charged and convicted?

The great shortcoming of this book is that it leaves that question unanswered. The few people who hold the answers are either dead or unwilling to discuss the case. Floyd doesn't know and neither do his attorneys, though several are willing to wager a guess. The journalists don't know, though several have certainly speculated over coffee and cocktails. The activists don't know either and are rightly more interested in preventing the next wrongful conviction.

During jury selection, defense attorney John Kurth told jurors that the question of Floyd Bledsoe's guilt ultimately rested with them. "If you come back and say the sky is purple, we have to look outside and say, 'Sure is.'" Terry Brubaker, the first juror chosen, once told this reporter by way of avoiding his questions, "All I am going to say is that we made a decision on what was presented to us." What was presented to jurors were falsehoods: that Floyd Bledsoe was guilty, that Tom Bledsoe was innocent, that the sky is purple.

Let blame fall then on those who said the sky is purple. On the since disbarred prosecutor, Jim Vanderbilt, who told jurors exactly that. On the detectives who ignored evidence the sky is blue or gray and insisted, beyond reason, that it must be purple. On the KBI agents who should have been more talented, more objective and better shielded from local biases than the Jefferson County detectives but who watched and participated in the purple sky scheme. On the judge who saw no evidence of a purple sky but let the court proceed anyway.

For in the end, be it through incompetence or corruption, the man who killed Camille – that sweet, shy girl who wanted to be a police officer herself – spent not a day in prison and never will.

"I want answers, you know," Floyd told the *Lawrence Journal-World* at the end of 2020. "And I may never get them."

***

Zetta Camille Arfmann is buried at Reformed Presbyterian Church Cemetery in Winchester, Kansas, about ten miles north of her last home at Floyd's trailer and nine miles northeast of where she was murdered. Her gravestone reads:

Daughter
Zetta Camille
Arfmann
Mar. 4   Nov. 5
1985   1999

On the backside is an inscription – "WE LOVE YOU MILLY!" – along with an engraved photo of Camille, laying on her side in a plaid shirt and an effortless pose. Big bangs cover her forehead and pale dimples bulge from both sides of her mouth, which is open in a warm smile.

EPILOGUE

Floyd and Amanda Bledsoe were married in the fall of 2016 and she was pregnant early the next year. They welcomed their first child, Bryce, in December of 2017 and Brynlee Alice Jean Bledsoe soon after that. Her two middle namesakes are Alice Craig and Jean Phillips. The couple and their children live in a modest home in Hutchinson, not far from the prison where Floyd still volunteers, and have some land outside of town with cows and chickens. Paintings of wildlife by Floyd and Chano Young hang on the walls.

The legacy of Floyd Scott Bledsoe may well go beyond the legislation he has helped usher into creation. On that day in December of 2015 when he was released from so many years of wrongful incarceration, when the world would not blame him for a period of self-indulgence, he thought still of another man. To the familiar faces who offered to help, he told them a name: Trevor Corbett. Floyd had known him in Lansing prison and grew convinced he was innocent of murdering his ex-wife in Hutchinson, a crime he is serving a life sentence for. At Floyd's urging, his former lawyers at the KU Project for Innocence and Midwest Innocence Project took the case and were granted permission from a judge to perform new DNA testing in May of 2018.

Sheriff Roy Dunnaway retired in 2008 and died in 2017. Rick Nichols, writing in the *Oskaloosa Independent*, remembered him this way: "I was in former Sheriff Roy Dunnaway's presence on only one occasion that I'm aware of, but judging from the number of people and especially law enforcement officers who turned out for his funeral last week in Perry, he was a much-admired lawman and was well respected by his colleagues, not only here in Jefferson County but elsewhere in Kansas, too. For 39 years, he put his life on the line every day of the week in serving others and that's quite commendable to be sure. That said, Dunnaway's legacy stands to be tarnished if the Bledsoe case ultimately results in a trial and he and other officers are found to have been guilty of framing the plaintiff for the murder of Camille Arfmann 18 years ago. In short, then, MUCH is at stake as this case slowly works its way toward some sort of a disposition or resolution."

Jeff Herrig, the undersheriff during the Bledsoe case, became sheriff following Dunnaway's retirement. Herrig won re-election in 2016, in part because his opponent was facing criminal charges and a federal lawsuit at the time. Herrig was also facing a federal lawsuit during the campaign – Floyd's. He won re-election again in 2020.

Mike Hayes, Tom's former defense attorney, left Kansas for Colorado. John Kurth, Floyd's former defense attorney, is still practicing law in Atchison, Kansas. He has never forgotten the Bledsoe case and keeps a diagram of the crime scene on one wall of his office. "That one bothered me more than others," he once said. "Most guilty verdicts I can walk out and say, 'Okay, if the jury says the sky's orange today, I guess the sky's orange' but that one just bothered me, especially after talking with the jury. It's like, what the heck?"

Several of the detectives who worked Floyd's case were later promoted. Randy Carreno, the lead detective, became a captain and was awarded the Kansas Sheriffs' Association's deputy of the year award in 2014. Kirk Vernon was promoted to captain of detectives. Robert Poppa was promoted to a lieutenant and Troy Frost remains a detective. Orin Turner retired in 2002 and died in 2013.

Jason Belveal lost re-election in 2016, a fact he attributes to the political acumen of his opponent and not his decision to side with Floyd. "In fact, I think public support was really behind what we did," he said. Belveal returned to private practice and took Floyd's painting with him. It now hangs in his law office.

Kaiti Smith became a public defender in Kentucky and hopes one day to run an innocence clinic like the one at the University of Kansas. She told her alma mater in 2016: "I hope that I have the opportunity to influence another big case someday, but you know what? I would be happy with this as my one big, good deed in life." She continues to analyze DNA bench notes in her own cases.

Peter Conley and Emily Barclay both became public defenders in eastern Kansas after graduating from KU Law School and the Project for Innocence. Richard Ney is still a defense attorney in Wichita.

Judge Gary Nafziger, who presided over Floyd's trial in 2000 and ordered him to be released in 2015, retired in 2021. Richard Rogers, the federal judge who released Floyd in 2008, died at a Topeka care center in 2016. J. Thomas Marten, the chief federal judge in Kansas, remembered him as "an exquisite human being and a hero to a whole lot of people, including me."

Erik Mitchell, the medical examiner, left Kansas after a quarter century in 2018 and became the chief medical examiner in Fond du Lac, Wisconsin. The county executive who hired Mitchell told a local reporter at the time that he was aware of Mitchell's troubles in New York and had no concerns: "He came with glowing recommendations and his 25 years of work in Kansas speaks for itself."

Shaun Hittle left journalism to become a private investigator, specializing in innocence cases. He now lives in Oklahoma.

All of the reporters who covered Camille's disappearance or Floyd's original trial have since retired from journalism or moved on to other reporting positions with the exception of Tim Hrenchir, who covered early details in the case for the *Topeka Capital-Journal*. He remains at the *Capital-Journal* as a local government reporter.

ACKNOWLEDGEMENTS

A reporter is only as good as his sources. For all the people who refused to be interviewed for this book, there were far more who donated their own time to tell me a story, several stories, or a dozen stories. In that vein, thank you to Floyd Bledsoe for enduring my calls and questions at all hours and for opening up about times good and bad – but mostly bad – in life.

Thank you also to the many sources who cannot be named – those who passed along confidential documents or crucial information anonymously. This book would not have been as thorough without you.

Thank you to my former editors at the *Topeka Capital-Journal* for improving and publishing "Four Shots in Oskie," a three-part series about the Bledsoe case, in January 2016. That series was the catalyst for my fascination with the case and a basis for this book.

An unsung hero is Deanna Warner, the court reporter at Jefferson County District Court. Thanks go to her for detailed transcripts and kind words of encouragement. Likewise, thank you to the Kansas Supreme Court's law librarians for their diligent assistance.

Alice Craig, Jean Phillips, Elizabeth Cateforis and everyone at the Paul E. Wilson Project for Innocence and Post-Conviction Remedies at the University of Kansas deserve tremendous thanks for answering my unending questions, providing invaluable documentation and, most importantly, for working tirelessly on behalf of Floyd to right a wrong. Similarly, thank you to Tricia Bushnell and her crew at the Midwest Innocence Project for their work on the case and assistance with this book.

Thank you to the talented Kansas journalists who wrote about Camille's disappearance, Floyd's trial and every event that followed, providing the first draft of history that is invaluable to any nonfiction author. They include Joe Miller of *The Pitch*; Andrea Albright and Tim Hrenchir of the *Topeka Capital-Journal*; Erwin Seba, Donna Bergmann, Joel Mathis, Shaun Hittle and Karen Dillon of the *Lawrence Journal-World*; Jolie Kearns of the *Oska-*

loosa Independent and many, many more. Thanks to the photojournalists who covered the case, namely Chris Neal of the *Capital-Journal*, who also took photos for this book.

Similarly, the archives of several newspapers were of tremendous assistance. Thanks especially to Rick Nichols, who not only covered the case's later stages but compiled much of the *Oskaloosa Independent* archives and allowed me to scour through them, all while offering me a warm cup of coffee.

Thank you to those who took time to read early drafts of this book, improving it as you did, especially Rick, Andy Marso and Katie Moore. Thanks also to the people of Oskaloosa who corrected me when I got something wrong about their town.

Thanks to the many fine folks at Mission Point Press: Doug, Tanya, Bob, Noah, Heather, Tricia, Hart, Leah, and all the others. I couldn't have done it without you.

Thanks most of all to my favorite journalist: my wife, Megan. She endured countless hours of conversation about the case, traveled with me as I researched, edited early drafts, and encouraged me at every turn. She is the best wife a man, and a reporter, could ask for.

ABOUT THE AUTHOR

Justin Wingerter is a reporter for *The Denver Post*. He was born in Granite City, Ill., graduated from Southern Illinois University with a degree in journalism, and went to work writing about government and politics. He lives in Denver with his wife, Megan, who is also a writer.

Made in the USA
Monee, IL
05 June 2021